Xabi Alonso

82 Passing, Positional Possession, Games, Patterns, and Attacking Practices Direct from Bayer Leverkusen Training Sessions

+ Tactical Analysis

Published by

Xabi Alonso

82 Passing, Positional Possession, Games, Patterns, and Attacking Practices Direct from Bayer Leverkusen Training Sessions

+ Tactical Analysis

First published August 2024 by SoccerTutor.com
info@soccertutor.com | www.SoccerTutor.com

UK: 0208 1234 007 | **US:** (305) 767 4443 | **ROTW:** +44 208 1234 007
ISBN: 978-1-910491-73-7

Copyright: SoccerTutor.com Limited © 2024. All Rights Reserved.

All rights reserved. No part of this publication may be reproduced, stored in a retrieval system, or transmitted in any form or by any means, electronic, mechanical, photocopy, recording or otherwise, without prior written permission of the copyright owner. Nor can it be circulated in any form of binding or cover other than that in which it is published and without similar condition including this condition being imposed on a subsequent purchaser.

Edited by
Alex Fitzgerald - SoccerTutor.com

Diagrams
Diagram designs by SoccerTutor.com. All the diagrams in this book have been created using SoccerTutor.com Tactics Manager Software available from www.SoccerTutor.com

Note: While every effort has been made to ensure the technical accuracy of the content of this book, neither the author nor publishers can accept any responsibility for any injury or loss sustained as a result of the use of this material.

CONTENTS

Xabi Alonso's Incredible Success at Bayer Leverkusen 8
Coach Profile: Xabi Alonso...9
Xabi Alonso's Trophies and Records at Bayer Leverkusen...11
Bayer Leverkusen's Historic Undefeated Bundesliga Triumph...13
Bayer Leverkusen's Historic 51 Match Unbeaten Run 15
Key Aspects of Bayer Leverkusen's Record Breaking Unbeaten Run 16
Key Aspects of Xabi Alonso's Success at Bayer Leverkusen...18

Xabi Alonso's Bayer Leverkusen: Tactical Philosophy..........19
Xabi Alonso's Bayer Leverkusen: 3-4-2-1 Formation 21
Xabi Alonso's Bayer Leverkusen: Key Attacking Tactics..22
Relational Play and Positional Play: A Big Influence on Xabi Alonso's Style 23
Xabi Alonso's Tactical Philosophy and Style of Play..24

Diagram Key..26
Xabi Alonso's Coaching Style During Bayer Leverkusen Training Sessions 27

Warm Ups..28
1. Dribble, Pass, and Switch Positions Activation Warm Up.......................................29
2. Dribble, One-Two, and Lay-off to Switch Positions Activation Warm Up 30
3. Speed Work, Dynamic Movements, and Quick Return Passing Warm Up............................31
4. Technical Pass, Receive and Dribble Speed and Agility Warm Up 32
5. Technical One-Two, Move to Receive, and Dribble Speed and Agility Warm Up...................33
6. Technical Skill Variations to Pass, Volley, and Dribble Speed and Agility Warm Up 34
7. Pass and Receive, One-Two, and Run With the Ball Warm Up Circuit 35
8. One Touch Passing Triangle with Coordination Exercise 36
9. Passing Triangle with Coordination Exercise and Directional First Touch.....................37
10. One Touch Passing Triangle with Coordination Exercise and Give & Go with Defensive Pressure..38
11. Dynamic Speed, Agility, and Movement Passing Warm Up Circuit..............................39
12. Speed, Agility and Quickness (SAQ) Circuit...40
13. Speed, Agility and Quickness (SAQ) Circuit With a Ball 41
Variation: Adjusted Floor and Upright Pole Exercises 42
14. Technical Pass, Volley, and Heading Warm Up Conditioning Circuit 43

Contents

Passing Combinations 45

1. Timing of Movement and Support Play Passing Combination. 47
2. Timing of Movement and Support Play Passing Combination with Defensive Pressure (Variation 1) 48
3. Timing of Movement and Support Play Passing Combination with Defensive Pressure (Variation 2) 49
4. Pass and Move with Central Player Support and Combination Play 50
5. One-Two, Give & Go, and Directional First Touch Diamond Passing Circuit with Defensive Pressure 51
6. One-Two, Give & Goes, and Switch of Play Diamond Passing Circuit with Defensive Pressure ... 52
7. Two Ball Passing Circuit with Central Link Players and Defensive Pressure (Variation 1) 53
8. Two Ball Passing Circuit with Central Link Players and Defensive Pressure (Variation 2) 54
9. End to End Passing Combinations and Support Play to Break the Lines (Variation 1) 55
10. End to End Passing Combinations and Support Play to Break the Lines (Variation 2) 56

Xabi Alonso's Bayer Leverkusen: Build Up Play Tactics 57

Xabi Alonso's Bayer Leverkusen 3-4-2-1 Formation with Wing Backs 59
Xabi Alonso's Bayer Leverkusen 3-2-5 Build Up Play Shape 60
Xabi Alonso's Bayer Leverkusen 2-3-5 Build Up Play Shape (Variation) 63
Xabi Alonso's Bayer Leverkusen 4-2-4 Build Up Play Shape 64
Creating Overload on Right Side of Pitch and then Switching Play 66
Xabi Alonso's Bayer Leverkusen 4-2-4 Build Up Play Shape from Goal Kicks 67

Positional Build Up Play Combinations 68

1. Build Up and Breaking Midfield Line End to End Combination Circuit (Variation 1) 69
2. Build Up and Breaking Midfield Line End to End Combination Circuit (Variation 2) 70
3. Build Up Combinations, Through Pass to Break Midfield Line, and Dribble Passing Circuit 71
4. Build Up Play Combinations and Breaking Midfield Line (Through Pass) Circuit 72
5. Build Up Combinations, Switch Play, and Give & Go to Break Midfield Line Passing Circuit 73
6. Build Up and Break Midfield Line Passing Circuit with Pressing Variations (1) 74
7. Build Up and Break Midfield Line Passing Circuit with Pressing Variations (2) 75
8. Positional Build Up/Combinations Through Blocked Lanes Passing Circuit (Variation 1) 76
9. Positional Build Up/Combinations Through Blocked Lanes Passing Circuit (Variation 2) 77
10. Positional Build Up/Combinations Through Blocked Lanes Passing Circuit (Variation 3) 78
11. Positional Build Up/Combinations Through Blocked Lanes Passing Circuit (Variation 4) 79
12. Positional Build Up/Combinations Through Blocked Lanes Passing Circuit (Variation 5) 80
13. Positional Build Up/Combinations Through Blocked Lanes Passing Circuit (Variation 6) 81
14. Positional Build Up/Combinations Through Blocked Lanes Passing Circuit (Variation 7) 82

Contents

Xabi Alonso's Bayer Leverkusen: Possession and Midfield Control Tactics 83

Xabi Alonso's Bayer Leverkusen 3-2-5 Possession Phase Shape 85
The Tempo and Rhythm of Bayer Leverkusen's Possession Play 86
Xabi Alonso's Bayer Leverkusen Midfield Control (3-2-5) 87
Body Shape and Spatial Awareness in Bayer Leverkusen's Possession (3-2-5) 88
Creating Overload on Right Side of Pitch and then Switching Play (4-2-4) 90
Xabi Alonso's Bayer Leverkusen Progression from Possession to Attack 91

Positional Possession Games 92

1. Pass Through Central Gate 4v4 (+3) Positional Possession Game 94
2. Build Up in 3-2 Shape and Progress Play Through Centre 5v5 (+3) Positional Possession Game . 95
3. Three Team High Speed of Play End to End 4v4 (+4) Positional Possession Game 96
4. Support Play in the Centre End to End 5v5 (+3) Positional Possession Game 97
4.1. Alonso's Positional Coaching During Practice Setup 98
4.2. Alonso's Coaching Points for Support Play Movements 99
4.3. Alonso's Coaching Points for Wide Players 100
5. Open Up and Spread Out to Maximise Space and Play Through Pressure 7v7 (+3) Positional Possession Game 101
6. Build Up with Different Positional Structures 8v8 (+4) Possession Game 102
7. 8v8 (+5) Positional Possession Game with Jokers in Plus (+) Shape 103
8. Progress Play with 3-5 (from 2-3-5) Attacking Shape 8v8 (+6) Positional Possession Game 104
9. Build Up in 2-3 Shape and Play Through the Lines 6v6 (+6) Positional Possession Game 105
10. Build Up in 3-2 Shape and Play Through the Lines 8v8 (+4) Positional Possession Game 106
10.1. Xabi Alonso Coaching Points for Opening Up Wide 107
10.2. Xabi Alonso Coaching Points for Decision Making 108
10.3. Xabi Alonso Coaching Points for Quickly Breaking Lines 109
11. Build Up in 4-2 Shape and Play Through the Lines 8v8 (+6) Positional Possession Game 110
Xabi Alonso's Coaching During Positional Possession Games 111

Xabi Alonso's Bayer Leverkusen: Attacking in the Final Third Tactics 112

Attacking Through the Centre 113
The Wing Backs as Key Attacking Players 114
Tactical and Positional Fluidity in Attack: Left Wing Back Grimaldo 115
Right Wing Back Frimpong Used as a "High Flying Winger" 117
Bayer Leverkusen's Overloading Final Zone of Pitch to Finish Attacks 118

Contents

Attacking Positional Patterns of Play 119

Xabi Alonso's Bayer Leverkusen 3-4-2-1 Formation. 121
Positional Patterns Training Setup with 3-1-5 Shape (from 3-2-5) 122
1. Draw in Press to Play Out, Switch, and Attacking Midfielder's Through Pass to Wing Back from the Half Space 123
2. Centre Back Runs Out with Ball, Switch, and Through Pass to Wing Back for Cross with Supporting Runs into Box 124
3. Support to Play Out, Switch, Through Pass to Wing Back, and Cut Back for Attacking Midfielder's Run into Box 125
4. Switch to Play Out, Switch Again, Attacking Midfielder's Through Pass to Wing Back, and Supporting Runs into Box 126
5. Short Passing Build Up, Play Out, Forward's Support Play, and Attacking Midfielder's Third Man Run in Behind 127
6. Short Passing Build Up Play in Centre, Play Out, and Attack with Right Wing Back Moving Inside to Dribble into Box 128
7. Long Aerial Switch of Play to Left Wing Back, Attacking Midfielder's Third Man Run in Behind, Cut Back, and Finish 129
8. Long Aerial Switch of Play to Right Wing Back, Attacking Midfielder's Third Man Run in Behind, Cross, and Finish 130
Positional Patterns Training Setup with 2-5 Shape (from 3-2-5) 131
1. Long Aerial Switch of Play to Left Wing Back, Defensive Midfielder's Supporting Run, Through Pass, and Cut Back 132
2. Diagonal Pass to Attacking Midfielder, Give & Go with Centre Forward to Receive in the Box, and Shoot 133
3. Diagonal Pass to Attacking Midfielder, Centre Forward Drops Off to Receive, and Shoot from Distance 134
4. Forward Pass to Centre Forward with Back to Goal, Lay-off, Deep Third Man Run, and Shot from Distance 135
5. Defensive Midfielder's Deep Through Pass in Behind and into Box for the Run of the Centre Forward 136

Attacking Positional Patterns of Play + 2nd Ball Finishing 137

Xabi Alonso's Positional Patterns + 2nd Ball Finishing Training Setup. 138
1. Switch Play Combinations, Wide Through Pass for Cut Back Finish + 2nd Ball Finish for Deep Run 139
2. Switch Play Combinations, Give & Go in Behind for Cut Back Finish + 2nd Ball Shot from Distance 140
3. Long Switch of Play, Give & Go in Behind for Cut Back Finish + 2nd Ball Shot from Distance ... 141
4. Long Aerial Switch of Play, Through Pass, Cut Back Finish + 2nd Ball Shot from Distance 142

Contents

Attacking and Finishing 143
1. Long Aerial Cross-Field Pass to Wide Player and Cross for Players Finishing in the Box vs Defender + GK 144
2. Crossing and Finishing with Different Types of Delivery Team Scoring Competition 145
3. Build Up, Attacking Combination on the Flank, Crossing and Finishing + 2nd Ball Transition Play 146

Positional Training Games 147
1. High Tempo Three Team 4v4 (+GKs) "Winner Stays On" Small Sided Game 149
2. Build Up Play vs Compact Middle Zone Pressing 6v7 (+GKs) Transition Game 150
3. Combination Play from Defence to Attack Zonal 8v8 (+1) +GKs Conditioned Game. 151
4. Build Up Play and Playing in Behind to Score 9v9 (+1) 6-Goal Game with Offside Rule 152
5. Combination Play from Defence to Attack 9v9 (+GKs) Conditioned Zonal Game + 2nd Ball Transition 153
6. Build Up and Creating Opportunities to Score 9v9 (+2) 6-Goal Game with Changing Conditions 154
7. Build Up and Creating Opportunities to Score 9v9 (+1) +GKs Game with Changing Conditions 155

Attacking Set Plays 156
1. Coordinated Timing and Movement of Runs into Box and Finishing from Out-swinging Corners 157
2. Coordinated Timing and Movement of Runs into Box and Finishing from Free Kicks Near Byline 158
3. Coordinated Timing and Movement of Runs into Box and Finishing from Free Kicks (Level with Penalty Spot) 159
4. Coordinated Timing and Movement of Runs into Box and Finishing from Free Kicks (Level with Edge of Box) 160
5. Coordinated Timing and Movement of Runs into Box and Finishing from In-swinging Free Kick 161
6. Receiving a Throw-in Under Pressure, Turn and Cross + Timing and Movement of Runs into Box and Finishing 162

Xabi Alonso's Incredible Success at Bayer Leverkusen

Xabi Alonso's Incredible Success at Bayer Leverkusen

Coach Profile: Xabi Alonso

Coaching Career

- **Bayer Leverkusen** (2022 →)
- **Real Sociedad B** (2019 - 2022)

Playing Career

- **Bayern Munich** (2014 - 2017)
- **Real Madrid** (2009 - 2014)
- **Liverpool** (2004 - 2009)
- **Real Sociedad** (2000 - 2004)
- **Real Sociedad B** (1999 - 2000)

Managing Bayer Leverkusen

Xabi Alonso took charge of Bayer Leverkusen in October 2022 with the club struggling in 17th in the league table. From there, he transformed the team with a dynamic and fluid playing style. The 2023-24 season saw a remarkable **51-match unbeaten run across all competitions**, showcasing high level tactics, quality, and consistency. They won the **DFB-Pokal German Cup in consecutive years (2023 & 2024)** and the **Bundesliga title in 2023-24**, ending Bayern Munich's 11-year dominance.

Managing Real Sociedad B

Xabi Alonso started his managerial career with Real Sociedad B in 2019, significantly improving the team with a focus on possession and high pressing. They were **promoted to the Segunda División for the first time in 60 years** (2020-21).

Playing for World's Biggest Clubs

Xabi Alonso had an exceptional playing career as a central midfielder known for his passing, vision, and tactical intelligence. He played for **Real Sociedad, Liverpool, Real Madrid,** and **Bayern Munich**, winning the following trophies:

- 2 x **UEFA Champions League**
- 3 x **Bundesliga**
- 1 x **La Liga**
- 1 x **FA Cup**, 1 x **DFB-Pokal** (German Cup)

Success with Spain on World Stage

Xabi Alonso earned **114 caps for Spain** and played a key role in their golden era, winning the **UEFA European Championships twice (2008 & 2012)**, and the **FIFA World Cup (2010)**.

Coaching and Leadership

"A great leader inspires his team not just through words, but through actions. As a coach, you must lead by example and earn the respect of your players through your dedication and vision."

Xabi Alonso

Xabi Alonso's Incredible Success at Bayer Leverkusen

Xabi Alonso's Trophies and Records at Bayer Leverkusen

2022-2023

DFB-Pokal (German Cup)

2023-2024

Bundesliga (German League)

+

DFB-Pokal (German Cup)

Transformation, Unbeaten Run, and Domestic Success

When Xabi Alonso took over as Bayer Leverkusen's manager in October 2022, the team was in 17th place in the league. By the end of the 2022/23 season, they had climbed to sixth and won the DFB-Pokal German Cup. From there, their trajectory has been nothing but upward.

In 2023-2024, **Bayer Leverkusen achieved a remarkable 51-match unbeaten run across all competitions**, showcasing high level tactics, quality, teamwork, and consistency. Alonso's approach focuses on possession, midfield control, attacking wing backs, high pressing, and quick transitions.

They **won the Bundesliga title, completing an unthinkable feat of going the entire season unbeaten whilst setting club records of 90 points, 89 goals, and 24 goals conceded**. They also clinched **consecutive DFB-Pokal victories (2023 & 2024)**.

European Competitions

Alonso guided Leverkusen to the **UEFA Europa League semi-finals in 2022-2023 and the final in 2023-2024**. Although they were defeated in the final, their performances underscored Alonso's tactical intelligence and the team's growing stature on the European stage.

Player and Team Development

Xabi Alonso successfully integrated young talents like **Florian Wirtz** and **Jeremie Frimpong**, who became pivotal to the team's success. His focus on youth development and tactical innovation has set a solid foundation for the club's future.

Xabi Alonso - Elite Manager

By season's end in May 2024, **Alonso has cemented his status as an elite manager**, combining tactical expertise with game insight, making Leverkusen a formidable force in domestic and European football.

Xabi Alonso's Incredible Success at Bayer Leverkusen

Bayer Leverkusen's Historic Undefeated Bundesliga Triumph

Bayer Leverkusen's First Ever League Title

In the 2023-24 season, **Bayer Leverkusen clinched their first Bundesliga title in their history**. From their 34 matches played, they gained **90 points (club record)**. They finished 17 points above VfB Stuttgart and 18 points ahead of Bayern Munich, winning the title with 5 matches left, and setting **new club records of 89 goals scored and just 24 goals conceded**.

Unbeaten Season and Attempts for a Treble

Alonso's team not only won the Bundesliga, but did so **unbeaten (28 wins, 6 draws in 34 games played)**. Bayer Leverkusen also went an incredible 51 games across all competitions without losing, setting a new German record (details on page 15). Their dominance spanned the Bundesliga, UEFA Europa League, and DFB-Pokal (German Cup), positioning themselves for a potential treble, only falling short in the Europa League final versus a strong Atalanta team.

Xabi Alonso's Impact to Break Bayern Munich's Dominance

Xabi Alonso became Bayer Leverkusen's Head Coach in October 2022 and Bayern Munich had dominated the Bundesliga for many years. Alonso aimed to break Bayern's dominance with a mix of young talents and experienced players. His management and Leverkusen's strategic approach gave them a fighting chance to challenge Bayern, though it required near-perfect execution throughout the season. This is what they achieved, and **Leverkusen ended Bayern Munich's 11 year reign as Bundesliga champions**, becoming the first team to do so since Borussia Dortmund won the league in 2012 under Jürgen Klopp. Xabi Alonso's leadership and tactical knowledge, coupled with strategic signings, played a significant role in overcoming their reputation as the nearly team in German football.

Key Players and Performances

Bayer Leverkusen's 2023-2024 season was marked by star performances from key players. **Attacking midfielder Florian Wirtz**, **the Bundesliga Player of the Season**, **contributed 11 goals and 11 assists**, earning 3 Player of the Month awards.

The **left wing back Alejandro Grimaldo excelled with 10 goals and 13 assists**, proving vital in both defence and attack. The **right wing back Jeremie Frimpong added speed and dynamism with 9 goals and 7 assists**, with his role more like a winger in the attacking phase.

Granit Xhaka (defensive midfielder) and **Jonas Hofmann (attacking midfielder)** provided crucial stability and creativity in midfield, with **Hofmann scoring 5 goals and contributing 7 assists**.

Despite injuries, the centre forward **Victor Boniface was very impressive with 14 goals and 8 assists in 23 appearances**.

Collectively, these players helped Bayer Leverkusen set records, culminating in a historic unbeaten German league title.

"The football he [Alonso] is playing, the teams he sets up, the transfers he did, it was absolutely exceptional.

I played a long time in my life in the Bundesliga, that is super-impressive. Not only the points tally but the way they play."

Jürgen Klopp

Xabi Alonso's Incredible Success at Bayer Leverkusen

Bayer Leverkusen's Historic 51 Match Unbeaten Run

Bayer Leverkusen's Results in All Competitions
(12th August 2023 - 18th May 2024)

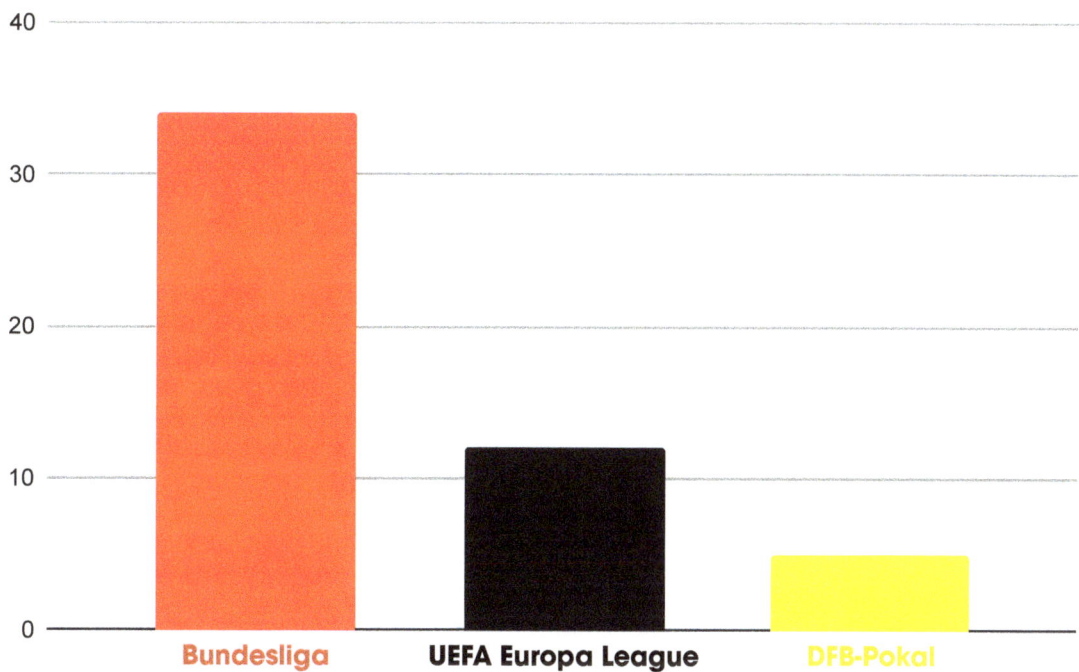

Here is the breakdown of Bayer Leverkusen's incredible 51 game unbeaten run during the 2023-2024 season:

- **Bundesliga:** 34 matches unbeaten *(28 wins, 6 draws)*
- **DFB-Pokal (German Cup):** 5 matches unbeaten *(5 wins)*
- **UEFA Europa League:** 12 matches unbeaten *(9 wins, 3 draws)*
- **Total:** 51 matches unbeaten *(42 wins, 9 draws)*

Key Aspects of Bayer Leverkusen's Record Breaking Unbeaten Run

Creating History

Xabi Alonso and Bayer Leverkusen's 51 match unbeaten run during the 2023-2024 season is a monumental achievement and stands tall as a remarkable football milestone. It is **one of the longest unbeaten records in football history**, placing them alongside legendary teams. It mirrors the unbeaten runs of the great AC Milan team (58 Serie A matches in 1991-93) and Arsenal's "Invincibles" (49 Premier League matches in 2003-04). This extraordinary run demonstrates the team's exceptional consistency, tactical intelligence, and mental resilience, setting a new benchmark in the sport, and establishing Bayer Leverkusen as a formidable force in the game.

Unprecedented Consistency

Achieving a 51 match unbeaten run in the highly competitive era of modern football is spectacular and highlights **Bayer Leverkusen's ability to maintain peak performance across all competitions**, including the **Bundesliga**, **DFB-Pokal**, and **UEFA Europa League**. It is a testament to their teamwork, discipline, focus, adaptability, and the tactical acumen of their manager, Xabi Alonso.

Dominance Across Competitions

Bayer Leverkusen's dominance was evident in their flawless Bundesliga campaign, where they remained unbeaten for the entire season, a rare accomplishment in one of the world's toughest leagues. Additionally, their unbeaten runs in the DFB-Pokal (5 matches) and UEFA Europa League (12 matches) further demonstrated the ability, depth, and versatility of the squad, and their extremely high consistent performance levels.

Tactical Innovations and Youth Development

Under Alonso's guidance, Leverkusen adopted a dynamic, fluid playing style characterised by build up play from the back, ball possession, midfield control, attacking wing backs, high pressing, and quick transitions. His emphasis on integrating young talents like **Florian Wirtz** and **Jeremie Frimpong** not only enhanced the team's immediate performance but also ensured a bright future for the club. This **combination of tactical innovation and youth development** was crucial to sustaining such a remarkable run.

Winning Mentality

"The mental aspect of football is as important as the physical. Building a strong, resilient mindset in players can be the difference between winning and losing."

Xabi Alonso

Key Aspects of Xabi Alonso's Success at Bayer Leverkusen

Xabi Alonso: From World Class Player to Elite Manager

Xabi Alonso is widely acknowledged as one of the best central midfielders of his era. His transition from player to manager has been seamless, with his second season at Bayer Leverkusen showcasing his ability to elevate the team to a level where they compete with the elite European teams. Alonso has crafted an **innovative playing style that has consistently delivered outstanding performances**. Bayer Leverkusen, under his management, play an **attractive and exciting brand of football with a relentless and effective attack**.

Formation, Control, the Double Pivot Midfield, and Key Players

Xabi Alonso's strategy emphasises possession, achieved through a **versatile 3-4-2-1 formation adaptable to different scenarios**.

The defence includes a trio of tall, quick, and athletic players i.e. **Jonathan Tah**, **Edmond Tapsoba**, and **Odilon Kossounou**. The wing backs **Alex Grimaldo** and **Jeremie Frimpong** contribute impressively to both attack and defence.

In midfield, a double pivot featuring **Granit Xhaka** and **Robert Andrich** (or Exequiel Palacios), combines high levels of passing ability with defensive strength. This duo ensures stability and smooth transitions between defence and attack.

The attack is very versatile, with **Florian Wirtz**, **Jonas Hofmann**, and **Victor Boniface** (or Patrik Schick) providing a dynamic and powerful threat.

Possession and Precision Play

Alonso's possession-focused strategy is not merely about retaining the ball but also about leveraging it to generate scoring opportunities. Bayer Leverkusen led the Bundesliga in passing accuracy and successful take-ons, reflecting their **technical skill and tactical intelligence**.

High Intensity Counter-pressing

Defensively, **Alonso's team excels with aggressive counter-pressing**, swiftly regaining possession and disrupting the opposition's play. This high energy approach is supported by a well organised and strong defensive line, and a midfield adept at breaking up attacks, and intercepting attempted through passes.

Efficient Attacking Transitions / Counter Attacks

Bayer Leverkusen's attacking transitions are fast and effective, often catching opponents off guard with their coordinated movements. Alonso's tactics ensure a compact defence while enabling explosive counter attacks, creating many goal scoring opportunities.

Xabi Alonso's Bayer Leverkusen: Tactical Philosophy

Xabi Alonso's Bayer Leverkusen: Tactical Philosophy

Team Organisation

"Success in football is not just about individual brilliance. It's about creating a team where each player understands their role and works together towards a common goal."

Xabi Alonso

Xabi Alonso's Bayer Leverkusen: Tactical Philosophy

Xabi Alonso's Bayer Leverkusen: 3-4-2-1 Formation

- **Hradecky (GK):** Goalkeeper
- **Tapsoba (LCB):** Left Centre Back
- **Tah (CB):** Middle Centre Back
- **Kossounou (RCB):** Right Centre Back
- **Grimaldo (LWB):** Left Wing Back
- **Frimpong (RWB):** Right Wing Back
- **Xhaka (DM):** Defensive Midfielder
- **Andrich (DM):** Defensive Midfielder
- **Hofmann (AM):** Attacking Midfielder
- **Wirtz (AM):** Attacking Midfielder
- **Boniface (CF):** Centre Forward
- **Other Notable Players Used:** Hincapié, Stanisic, Palacios, Adli, Tella, and Schick.

Xabi Alonso's Bayer Leverkusen: Key Attacking Tactics

1. Tactical Philosophy and Style of Play

- **Xabi Alonso blends positional play and relational play** with strict positional discipline, while emphasising coordinated movements and interactions to create fluid and dynamic team play.
- Utilise relational concepts, **position players around ball**, exploit **1v1 situations**, and ensure readiness for counter-pressing.
- **Hybrid strategy** = Fluid and unpredictable attacking unit.

2. Innovative 3-4-2-1 Formation with Wing Backs

- **Xabi Alonso's key tactics are based on the 3-4-2-1 formation** and utilising 2 wing backs in different heights of the pitch.
- One wing-back can join the defensive line and the other in attack (**4-2-4 shape**) or they both push forward (**3-2-5 / 2-3-5 shape**).
- This **strategic imbalance and fluidity confuses opponents**, which creates space and openings (goal scoring opportunities).

3. Focus for Possession and Midfield Control

- **Xabi Alonso emphasises controlling the midfield area to dominate** Bayer Leverkusen's opponents and matches.
- *"If you have control of the midfield, you have control of the game, and you have more chances to win. If you win the midfield, you probably win the game."* - **Xabi Alonso**.
- This **focus on midfield dominance** has been a key central factor to Bayer Leverkusen's success and tactical evolution.

Xabi Alonso's Bayer Leverkusen: Tactical Philosophy

Relational Play and Positional Play: A Big Influence on Xabi Alonso's Style

Switching of Positions

- In relational play, players constantly switch positions.
- Creates unpredictability in attack making it harder for opponents to mark.
- Example: LWB Grimaldo will often rotate into attacking midfielder position.

Triangle and Diamond Shapes

- Triangle and diamond shapes create passing lines all over the pitch.
- Maintained during play to ensure multiple passing options.
- Facilitates fast ball circulation and support play.

Positional Play (Juego de Posición)

- Players occupy specific zones on the pitch to control space.
- Focus on maintaining balance.
- Ensure optimal spacing and maximising the amount of passing options.

Rotations and Overloads

- Players rotate positions to overload certain areas of the pitch.
- Creates a numerical superiority around the ball to progress the play.
- Disorganise the opposition's defensive organisation.

Third Man Runs

- Players make runs that are not directly involved in the initial play.
- These players become available as the third option.
- This opens up space and creates new passing lanes for the player/s in possession.

Xabi Alonso's Tactical Philosophy and Style of Play

Xabi Alonso's Tactical Philosophy

By combining relentless pressing intensity, structured positional play, and possession play, **Xabi Alonso has created an innovative tactical style** which has made Bayer Leverkusen one of the best teams in Europe, punching well above their weight.

Alonso's coaching philosophy emphasises **control and tactical flexibility**. He blends a fast-paced, possession focused approach with triangle passing shapes and direct forward passing alongside a strong defensive organisation, high pressing, and fast counter attacks.

Bayer Leverkusen play with a **high speed and attractive attacking style of play**. Here we have outlined some of the key elements of Alonso and Bayer Leverkusen's tactical philosophy.

3-4-2-1: Dominance and Fluidity

Bayer Leverkusen primarily use the 3-4-2-1 formation. This setup emphasises ball control and counter-pressing, allowing the team to dominate possession, quickly regain the ball after losing it, and maintain an organised and solid defence. They start in a 3-4-2-1 formation, but this often shifts to resemble a 4-2-4 in practice.

Jeremie Frimpong, the right wing back, most often acts as a right winger, and the left wing back **Alex Grimaldo** is more like a traditional full back. The **wing backs are not restricted or confined to fixed positions** and are free to rotate, making sure that they are constantly moving, producing a fluidity that is crucial for effective build up play and applying consistent pressure on opposing players/teams.

Game Principles and Tactical Adaptability

Xabi Alonso's Bayer Leverkusen team is characterised by its clear principles of play, and a well-defined game model. They have the ability to adapt their tactics based on the characteristics of their specific opponents. This has enabled them to be competitive in all their matches and create an unmatched consistency to compete with Bayern Munich and other elite teams in Europe.

During the 2023-24 season, Xabi Alonso used a **variety of build-up shapes such as 4-2-4**, **3-2-5**, and **2-3-5**, each of which is analysed later in the book. This tactical versatility **enables Bayer Leverkusen to adjust to varying game situations**, allowing them to modify their formation as required to the flow of the match and capitalise on their opponent's vulnerabilities.

Structured and Patient Build Up Play

Bayer Leverkusen build up play from the back with **short and accurate passing**. The aim is to move the ball from the defensive area into the attacking areas of the pitch whilst maintaining control, and without losing possession of the ball.

There is a comprehensive analysis of Bayer Leverkusen's build up play in a later section of the book "*Xabi Alonso's Bayer Leverkusen: Build Up Play Tactics.*"

Xabi Alonso's Bayer Leverkusen: Tactical Philosophy

Possession Play, Midfield Control, and Initiating Attacks

Xabi Alonso prioritises control through sustained ball possession. The team methodically **develops play from the back, even under pressure**, with defenders playing a key role in launching attacks. **Controlling possession is crucial for Xabi Alonso**, who is focused on patient build up play, waiting for the right moment to make incisive passes and create scoring opportunities. This allows Bayer Leverkusen to **dictate the tempo of matches and prevents them from losing possession**.

Midfield control is vital for Xabi Alonso. The Bayer Leverkusen midfielders are skilled at keeping the ball, distributing with precise and accurate passing, breaking the opposition's midfield line, and progressing the play into open spaces and/or in behind their opponents. Players such as attacking midfielder **Florian Wirtz** and right wing back **Jeremie Frimpong** excel at taking advantage of these openings that they create.

Positional Play and Passing Combinations

With Xabi Alonso's Bayer Leverkusen, there is a big focus on positional play. The team is organised in a way that ensures players are **optimally positioned to create numerous passing choices**, establishing triangles and clear passing channels. This attention to detail allows them to maintain control of the ball under pressure and break through their opponent's midfield and defensive lines.

Their playing style is adaptable but is centred around using passing sequences to progress the ball. Players often stay close to one another, enabling swift one-two combinations with many passing channels.

Florian Wirtz's Key Playmaker Role for Bayer Leverkusen

Attacking midfielder and key attacking player **Florian Wirtz** excelled during the 2023-24 season with 37 goal involvements in all competitions (18 goals and 19 assists).

Bayer Leverkusen's achievements owe much to the technical skill and inventiveness of Wirtz, who had an incredible individual season. He **constantly positions himself in the pockets between the opposition's midfield and defensive lines**, so he is able to receive the ball and turn quickly away from his direct opponents. From these positions, he is very adept at playing correctly timed and weighted through passes for teammates making forward runs (in behind), creating a lot of goal scoring chances for the team.

Unique Role of Dynamic Wing Backs

In the way he uses wing backs, Alonso's tactics are different to traditional roles. **Bayer Leverkusen are more flexible and less predictable**. With a focus on central build up play, **Florian Wirtz** and **Jonas Hofmann** operate as inside forwards, creating space for the wing backs **Alejandro Grimaldo** and **Jeremie Frimpong** to attack in advanced wide areas. The latter often adopts a very attacking "winger" position, which is outlined later in the book.

With these two attacking wing backs, **Bayer Leverkusen's formation changes to a 3-2-5 or 2-3-5 shape** in the attacking phase, which makes the team more unpredictable and dangerous for their opponents, often **creating overloads to finish attacks in the final third**.

Diagram Key

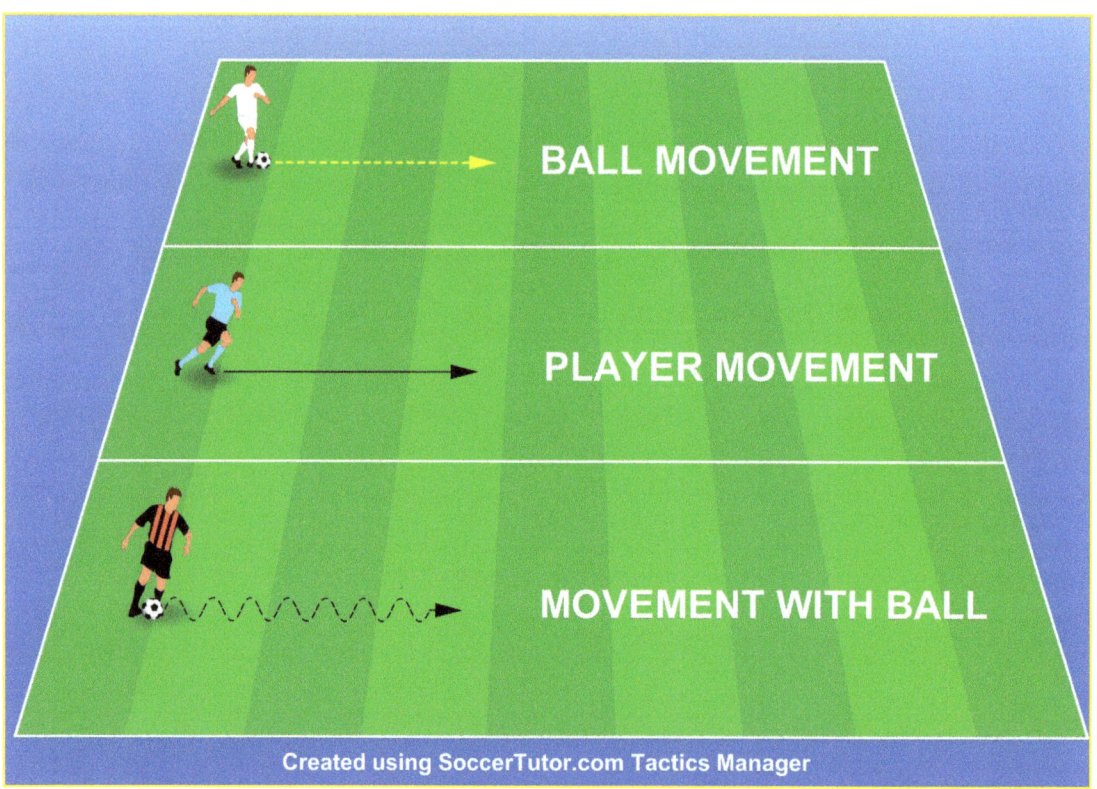

Practice and Tactics Format

- All of the practices in this book are **taken directly from Xabi Alonso's Bayer Leverkusen training sessions** between 2022 and 2024.

- Each practice includes the practice topic/name and clear diagrams with a detailed description.

- The tactical examples presented in the book represent consistent tactics and patterns of play observed in Bayer Leverkusen matches during the 2023-24 season.

Xabi Alonso's Coaching Style During Bayer Leverkusen Training Sessions

1. **Xabi Alonso carries notes, and everything is preplanned** to ensure attention to each player's positioning, movement angles, support options, and receiving areas in build up combinations, positional possession games, patterns of play, and training games in the book.

2. **Xabi Alonso is actively involved in his Bayer Leverkusen training sessions**, pausing his practices to highlight key coaching points.

3. There is a **strong focus from the coaching staff and players throughout** the sessions, with constant praise and encouragement for the players.

4. A **positive atmosphere** is also maintained amongst the players before, during, and after training.

5. Please **see Page 111 for specific details on how Xabi Alonso coached Positional Possession Games**.

Warm Ups

Direct from Xabi Alonso's Training Sessions

Xabi Alonso Practices: Warm Ups

1. Dribble, Pass, and Switch Positions Activation Warm Up

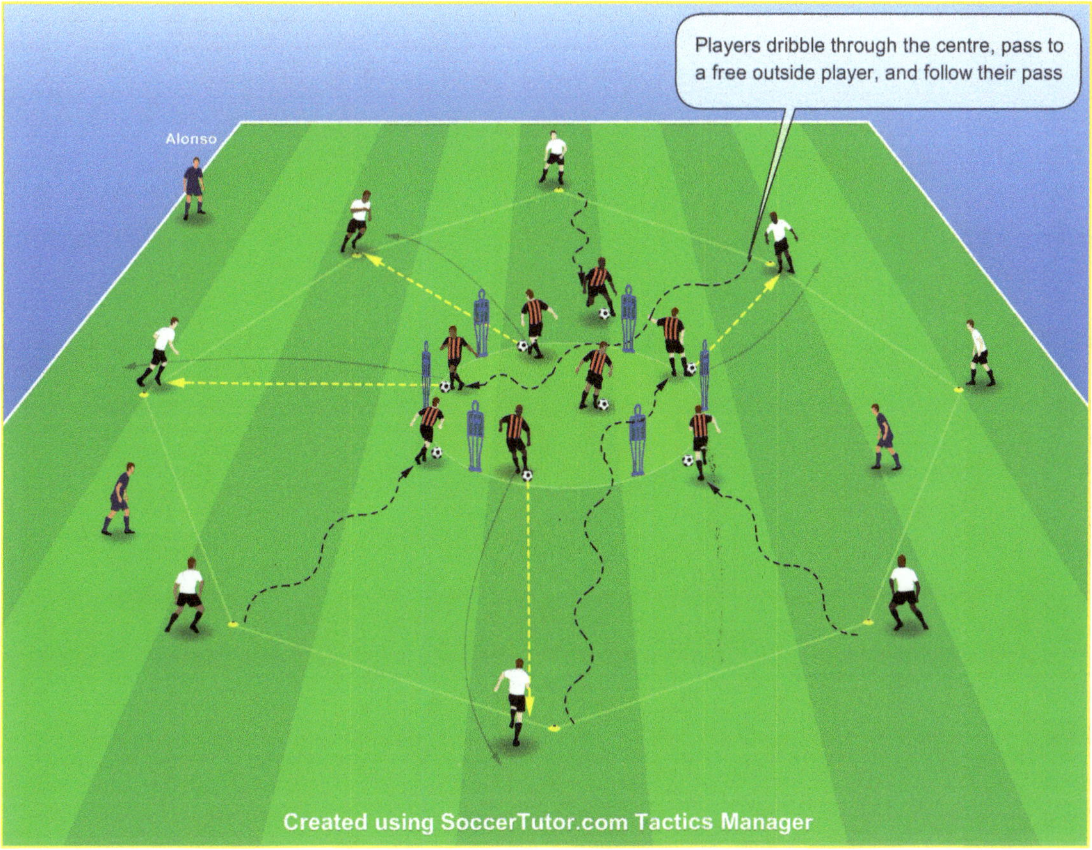

Players dribble through the centre, pass to a free outside player, and follow their pass

Practice Description

- In the octagon shape marked out, all of the players start outside of the area.
- 8 players (reds in diagram) dribble through the centre circle marked out by mannequins and pass to a free outside player.
- After playing their pass, they follow their pass to move back outside of the area. They then wait to receive a pass.

Coaching Points

1. When dribbling into the centre, the players must avoid their teammates and keep the ball very close to their feet.
2. The players show good awareness and vision by looking up to spot a free teammate to pass to.

Source: Xabi Alonso's Bayer Leverkusen training session at Bayer 04 Leverkusen Training Ground - 9th May 2024

Xabi Alonso Practices: Warm Ups

2. Dribble, One-Two, and Lay-off to Switch Positions Activation Warm Up

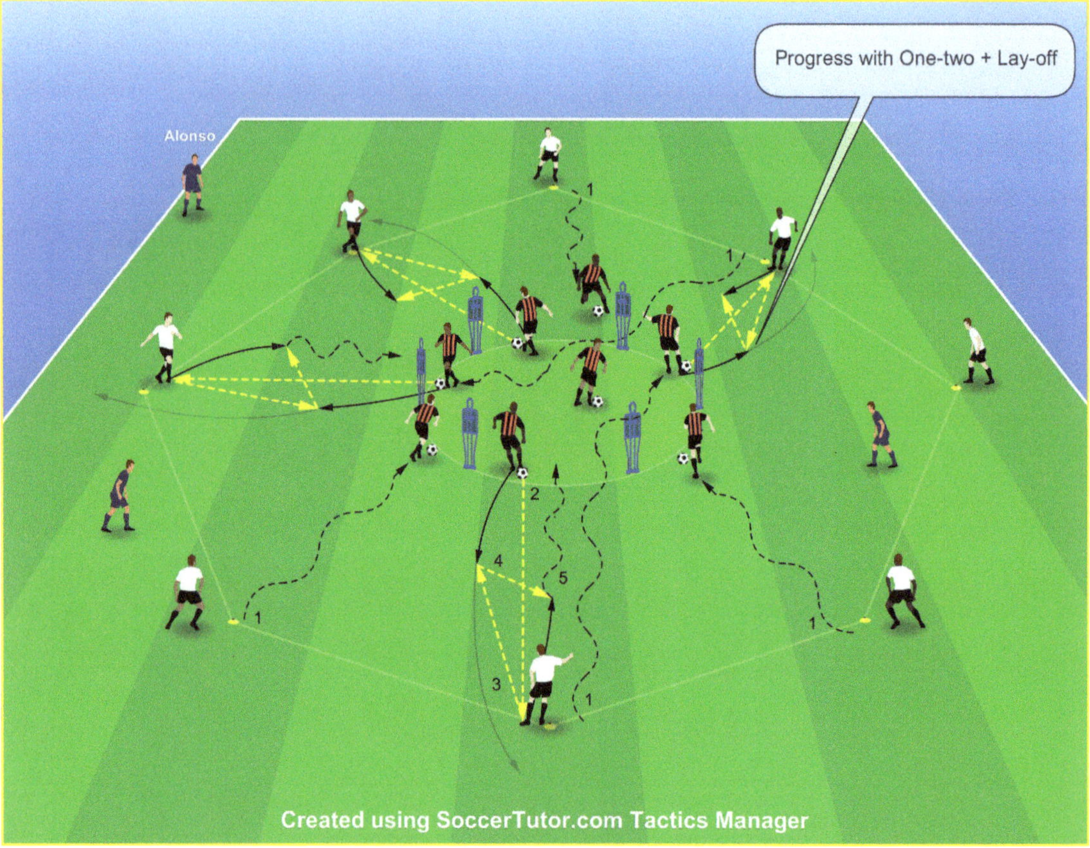

This is a progression of previous practice.

Practice Description

1. The 8 red players still start by dribbling the ball through the centre circle.

2-3. **Red** plays a one-two with free outside **White** player, moving to receive return.

4. **Red** sets the ball (lay-off) for **White** to move forward and receive. After playing their pass, **Red** players move outside of the area, waiting to receive.

5 → The **White** players dribble through the centre circle and then pass a to a free **Red** outside player (continuous warm up practice).

Source: Xabi Alonso's Bayer Leverkusen training session at Bayer 04 Leverkusen Training Ground - 9th May 2024

Xabi Alonso Practices: Warm Ups

3. Speed Work, Dynamic Movements, and Quick Return Passing Warm Up

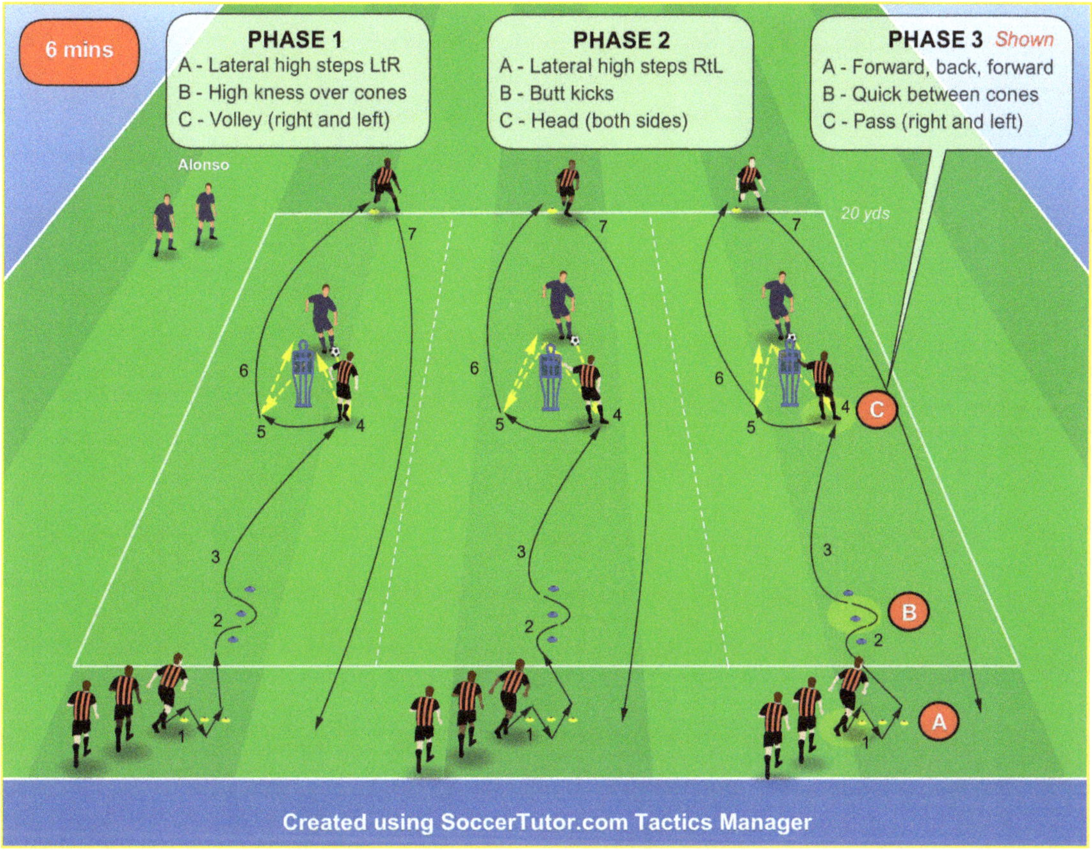

6 mins

PHASE 1
A - Lateral high steps LtR
B - High knees over cones
C - Volley (right and left)

PHASE 2
A - Lateral high steps RtL
B - Butt kicks
C - Head (both sides)

PHASE 3 *Shown*
A - Forward, back, forward
B - Quick between cones
C - Pass (right and left)

Phase 3 is displayed in the diagram example.

Practice Description (Phase 3)

1. Quick feet forward, backward, forward, in and out of the 3 yellow cones.
2. Quick feet through the 3 blue cones.
3. Run to the mannequin.
4-5. The coach feeds the ball (ground) to one side of mannequin for a pass back and repeats to other side (2 x one-twos).
6. Sprint to end.
7. Jog back to start.

Practice Description (Phases 1 & 2)

Phase 1. Lateral high steps through yellow cones, butt kicks through blue cones, and return headers with coach.

Phase 2. Lateral high steps through yellow cones, high knees over blue cones, and return volleys alternate feet with coach.

Source: Xabi Alonso's Bayer Leverkusen training session at Bayer 04 Leverkusen Training Ground - 15th Feb 2023

Xabi Alonso Practices: Warm Ups

4. Technical Pass, Receive and Dribble Speed and Agility Warm Up

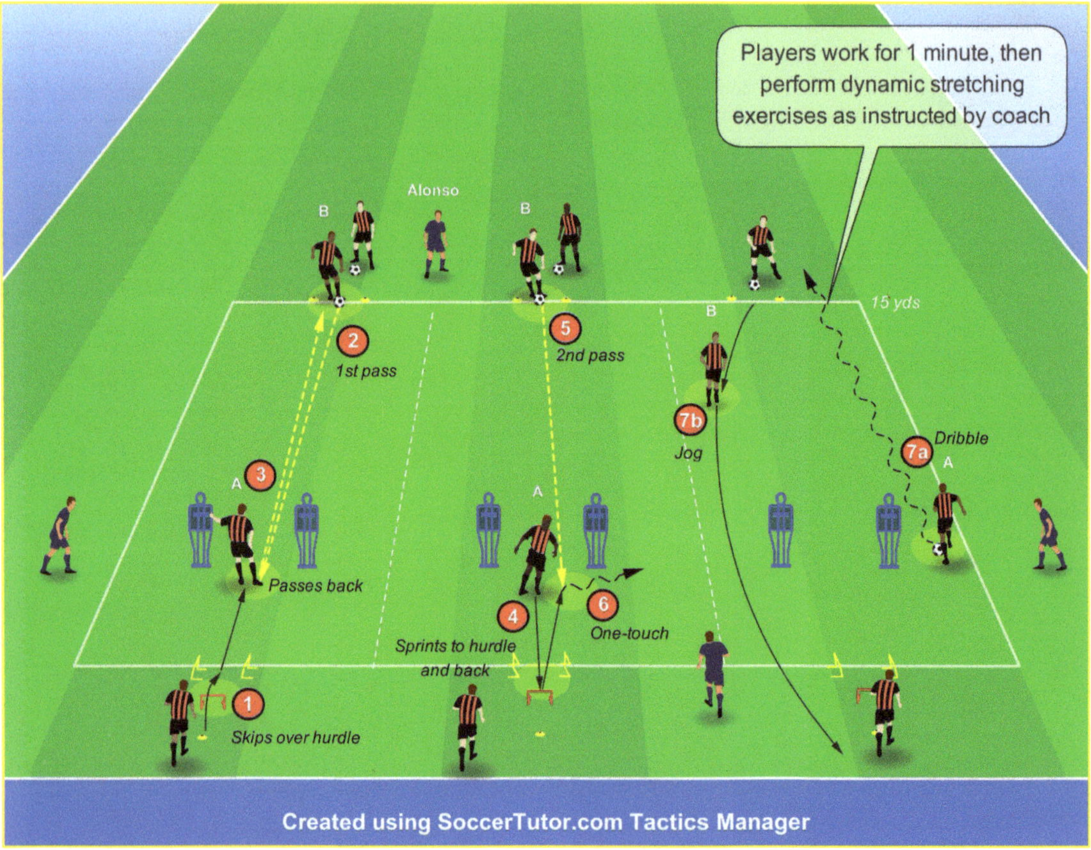

The players work in channels in groups of 4.

Practice Description

1. **A** skips over the red hurdle and runs forward.
2. **B** passes the ball in between the mannequins to **A**.
3. **A** has timed his movement forward to meet the ball and pass back to **B**.
4. **A** sprints back to the red hurdle and then back towards the mannequins.
5. **B** passes the ball in between the mannequins again to **A**.
6. **A** takes a directional first touch to the side of one of the mannequins.
7. **A** dribbles to the end and **B** jogs to the opposite side to switch ends. The other 2 players waiting repeat the same sequence.

Source: Xabi Alonso's Bayer Leverkusen training session at Bayer 04 Leverkusen Training Ground - 17th May 2024

Xabi Alonso Practices: Warm Ups

5. Technical One-Two, Move to Receive, and Dribble Speed and Agility Warm Up

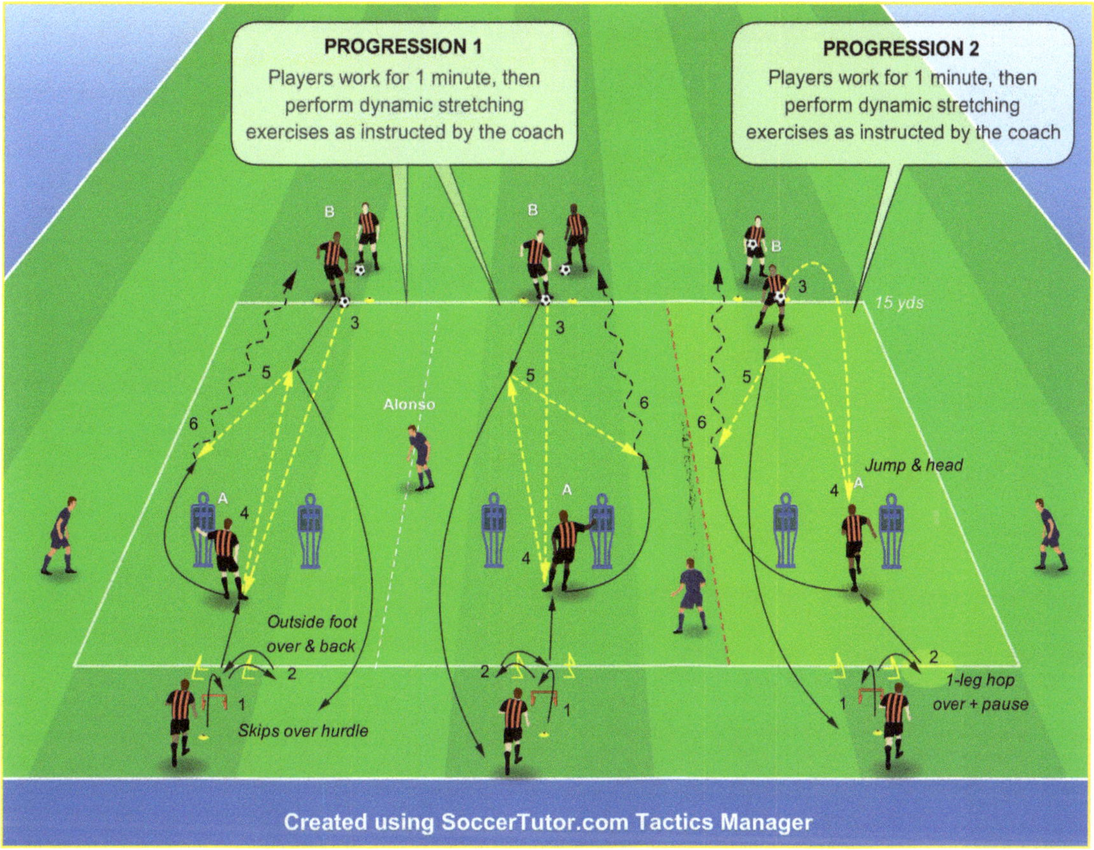

This is a progression of the previous practice.

Progression 1

1-2. **A** skips over the red hurdle and moves his outside foot over and back over one of the yellow hurdles.

3. **B** passes in between the mannequins to **A**, who has moved forward.

4-6. **A** passes back to **B**, who sets the ball for **A** to run around the mannequin, receive, and dribble to the end.

Progression 2

1-2. **A** skips over the red hurdle and performs a one-leg hop + pause.

3-4. **B** throws the ball to **A**, who jumps to head the ball back to **B**.

5-6. **B** sets the ball for **A** to run around the mannequin, receive, and dribble to end.

→ **B** jogs to the opposite side to switch ends. The other 2 players waiting repeat the same sequence.

Source: Xabi Alonso's Bayer Leverkusen training session at Bayer 04 Leverkusen Training Ground - 17th May 2024

Xabi Alonso Practices: Warm Ups

6. Technical Skill Variations to Pass, Volley, and Dribble Speed and Agility Warm Up

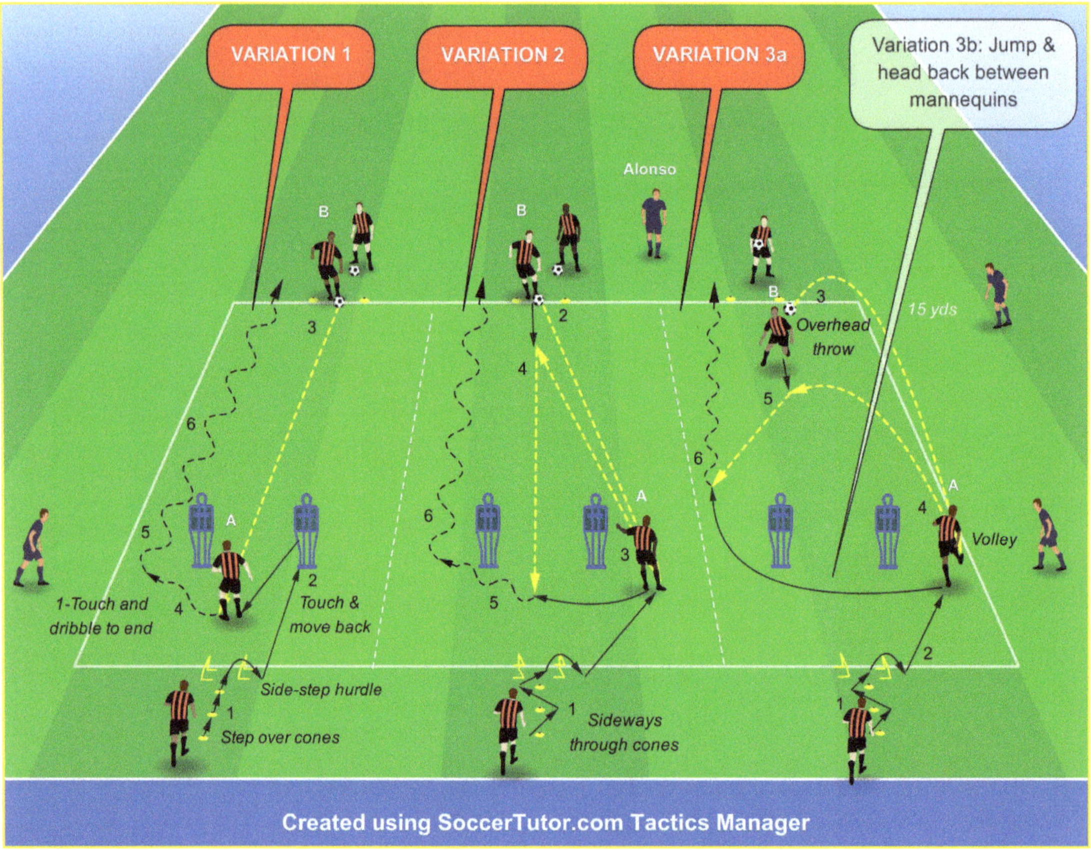

Variation 1
- A steps over 3 cones and side-steps a hurdle, runs to touch mannequin, and moves back at angle. B passes to A, who takes a touch wide of the other mannequin, and dribbles to the end.

Variation 2
- A moves sideways through cones and hurdle, and moves to side of mannequin to play a 3 pass combination with B.

- A receives the third pass, takes a touch wide of the other mannequin, and dribbles to the end.

Variation 3
- Steps 1+2 same as Variation 2. B throws the ball for A to volley back. B then sets the ball for A to run around mannequin to receive, and dribble to the end.

→ B jogs to opposite side to switch ends. The other 2 players waiting go.

Source: Xabi Alonso's Bayer Leverkusen training session at Bayer 04 Leverkusen Training Ground - 17th May 2024

XABI ALONSO: PRACTICES DIRECT FROM SESSIONS

Xabi Alonso Practices: Warm Ups

7. Pass and Receive, One-Two, and Run With the Ball Warm Up Circuit

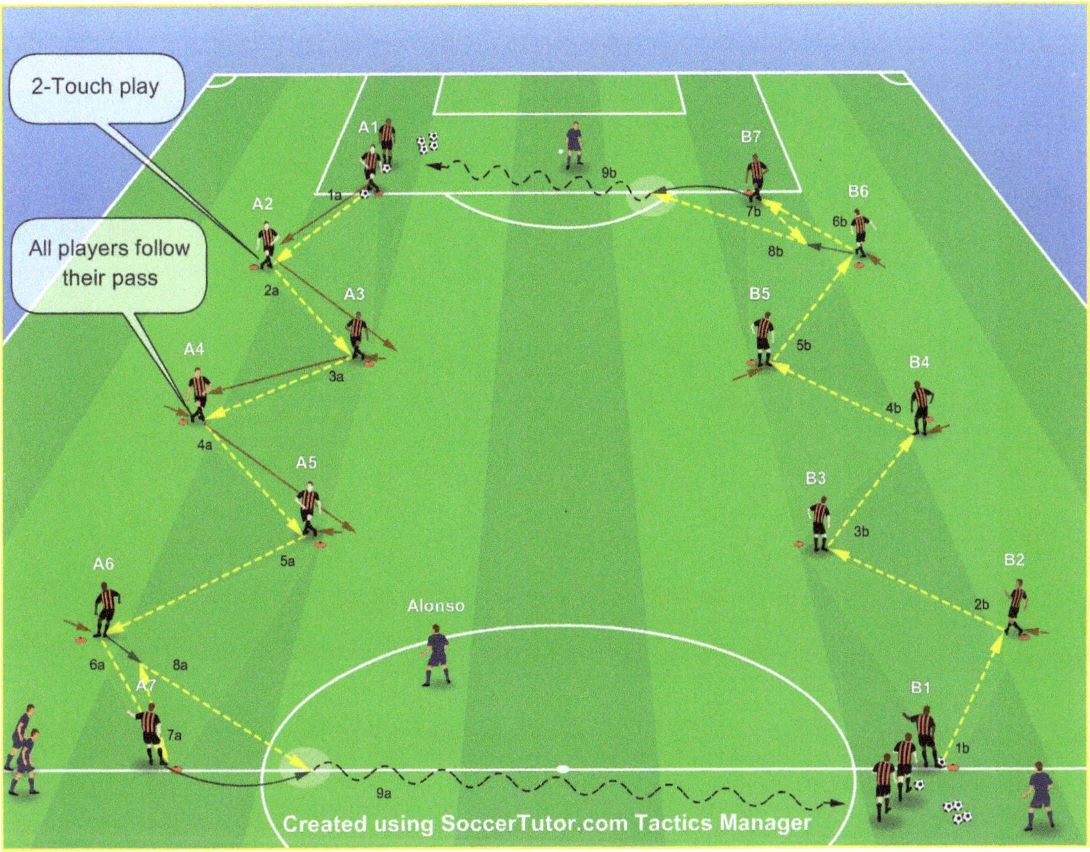

This practice has 7 cones marked out on each side of the pitch, creating 2 groups, who play simultaneously (2 balls).

Practice Description

1-5. Players pass to the next cone and then move to that cone. The receiving players take 2 touches to receive and pass.

6-8. At the sixth cone **(A6/B6 in diagram)**, a one-two is played with **A7/B7**, who then moves to receive the return.

9. That receiving player **(A7/B7)** then runs with the ball to the start point of the opposite group, as shown.

Coaching Points

1. The players move slightly forward off their cone before receiving.

2. They use 2 touches throughout to receive and then pass to the next cone.

3. Always sharp + follow pass to next cone.

Source: Xabi Alonso's Bayer Leverkusen training session at Bayer 04 Leverkusen Training Ground - 2023

Xabi Alonso Practices: Warm Ups

8. One Touch Passing Triangle with Coordination Exercise

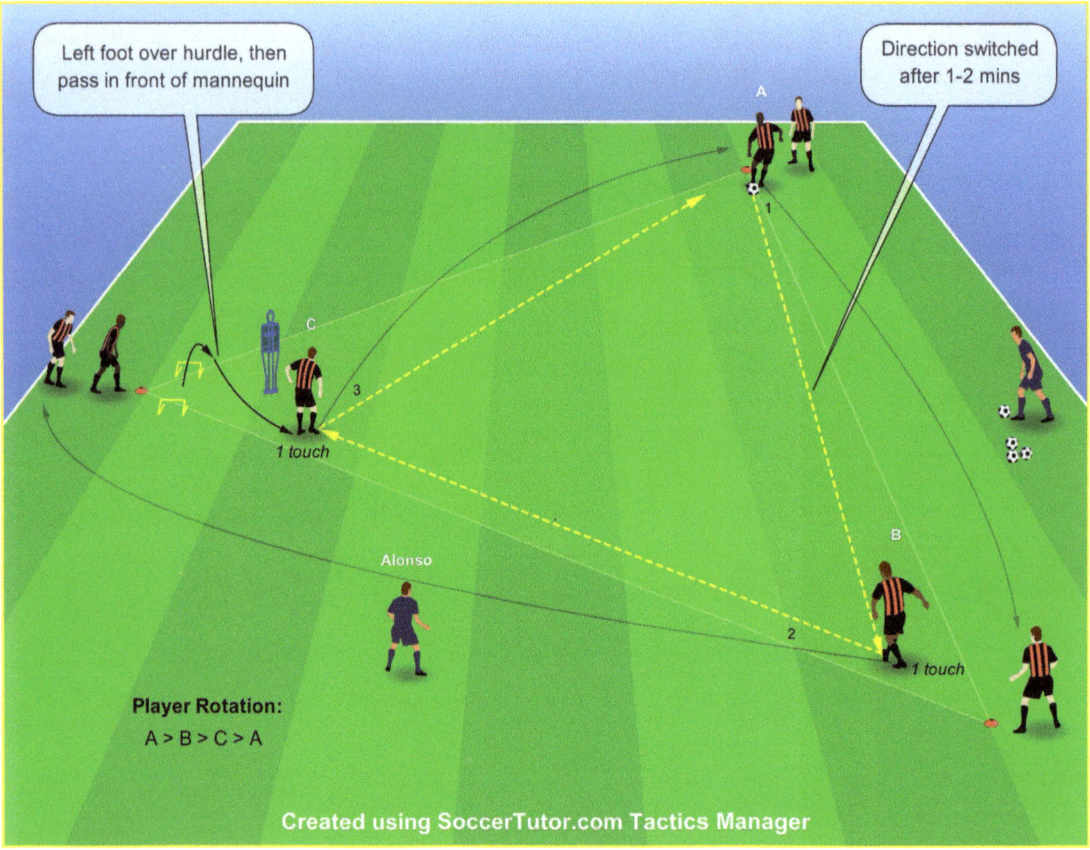

The players were observed working in groups of 7, as shown.

Practice Description

1. **A** passes to **B**.
2. **B** passes to **C** first time with 1 touch.
3. **C** has performed quick steps, lifted his left foot over the left hurdle to touch the ground, and back over, before moving in front of the mannequin to meet **B's** pass and pass first time back to the start.

→ The next player waiting at Position A continues and all players rotate to the next position: **A → B → C → A**.

→ After 1 to 2 minutes, the direction is switched to anti-clockwise.

Coaching Point

- The players use 1 touch throughout and always have their body position facing the way they are passing.

Source: Xabi Alonso's Bayer Leverkusen training session at Bayer 04 Leverkusen Training Ground - 2nd Dec 2023

Xabi Alonso Practices: Warm Ups

9. Passing Triangle with Coordination Exercise and Directional First Touch

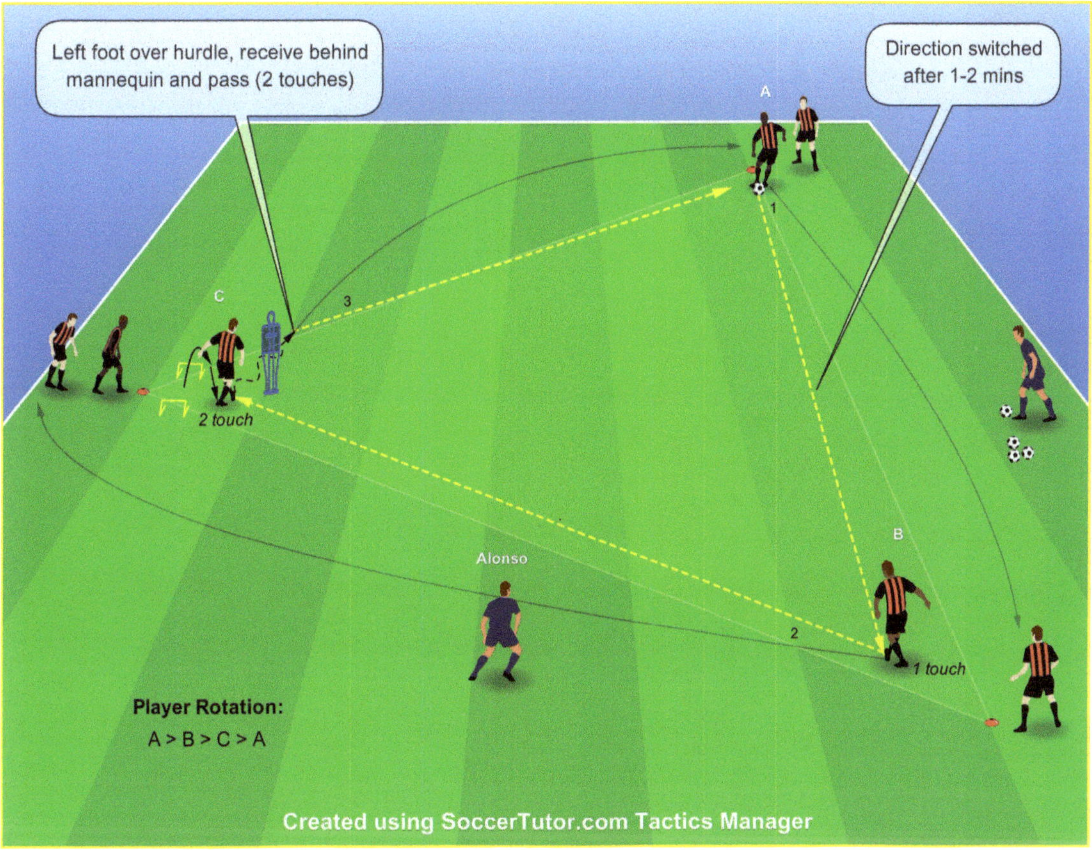

This is a variation of the previous practice.

Practice Description

1. **A** passes to **B**.
2. **B** passes to **C** first time with 1 touch.
3. **C** performs quick steps, lifts his left foot over the left hurdle to touch the ground, and back over, receives **B's** pass with a directional touch (1st touch), and then passes back to the start (2nd touch).

→ The next player waiting at Position A continues and all players rotate to the next position: **A → B → C → A**.

→ After 1 to 2 minutes, the direction is switched to anti-clockwise.

Source: Xabi Alonso's Bayer Leverkusen training session at Bayer 04 Leverkusen Training Ground - 2nd Dec 2023

Xabi Alonso Practices: Warm Ups

10. One Touch Passing Triangle with Coordination Exercise and Give & Go with Defensive Pressure

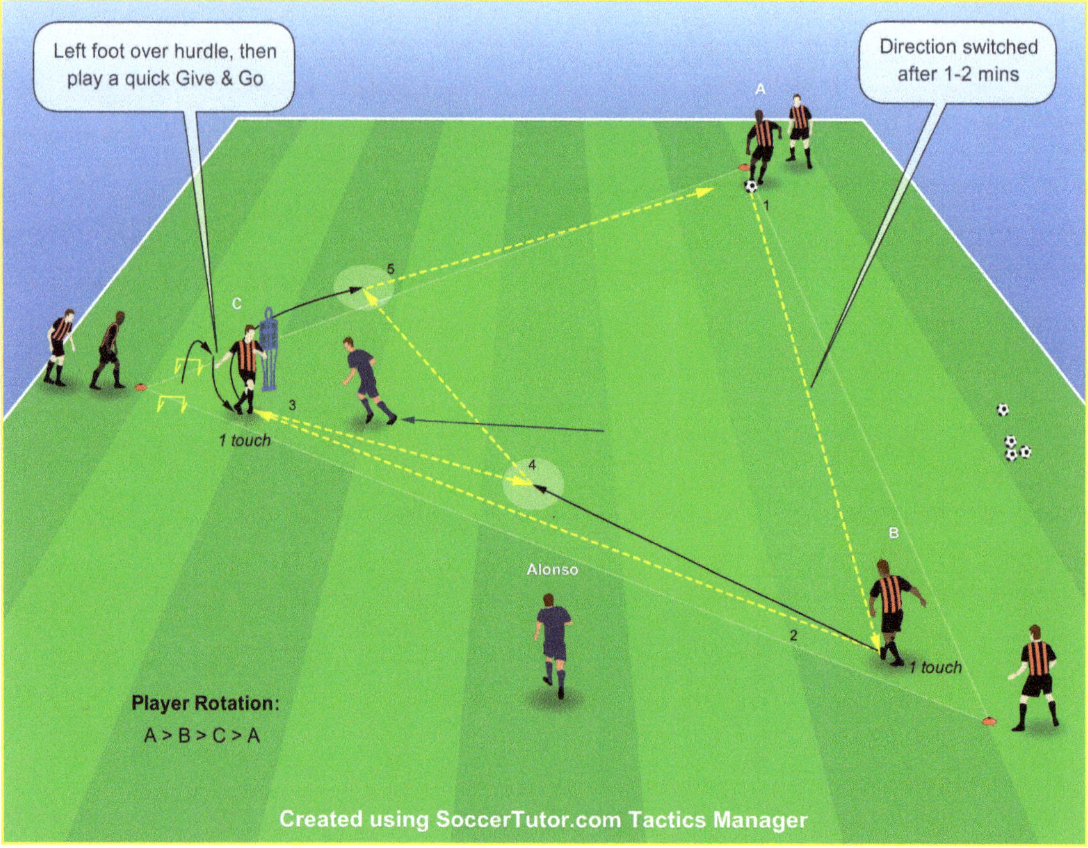

This is a progression of previous practice.

Practice Description

1. **A** passes to **B**.
2. **B** passes to **C** first time with 1 touch.
3. **C** performs quick steps, lifts his left foot over the left hurdle to touch the ground, and back over, then moves in front of the mannequin to set the ball back for **B** to move forward onto (under passive pressure from the coach).
4-5. **B** moves to meet **C's** set back and passes for **B** to receive after running around the mannequin. This completes **C's** give & go, and he passes to the start.

→ The next player waiting at <u>Position A</u> continues and all players rotate to the next position: **A → B → C → A**.

→ After 1 to 2 minutes, the direction is switched to anti-clockwise.

Source: Xabi Alonso's Bayer Leverkusen training session at Bayer 04 Leverkusen Training Ground - 2nd Dec 2023

Xabi Alonso Practices: Warm Ups

11. Dynamic Speed, Agility, and Movement Passing Warm Up Circuit

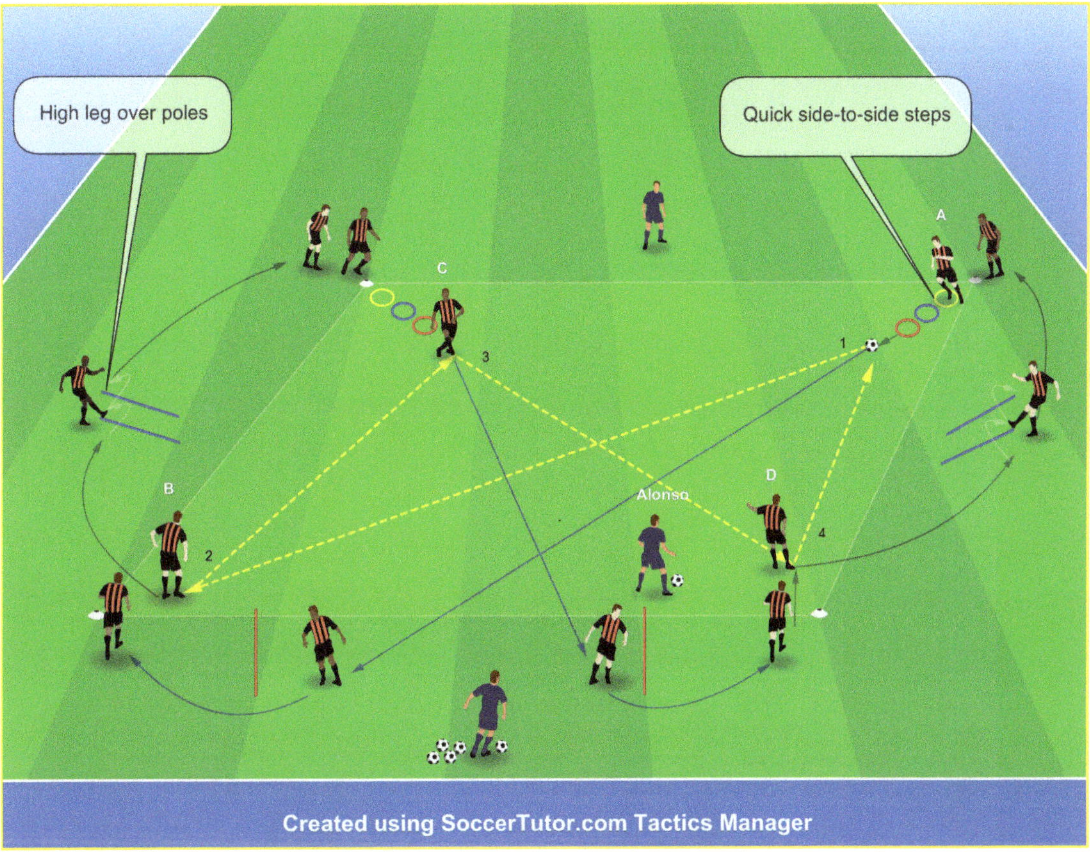

There are 4 starting positions (A, B, C, and D).

Practice Description

1. **A** uses side-to-side steps through the speed rings and passes to **B**. He then runs diagonally and around the pole to Position B.

2. **B** passes to **C**, runs to the 2 poles which are at a 45° angle, and lifts one leg over both of them alternately. He then jogs to Position C.

3. **C** uses side-to-side steps through the speed rings and passes to **D**. He then runs diagonally and around the pole to Position D.

4. **B** passes to Position A, runs to the 2 poles which are at a 45° angle, and lifts one leg over both of them alternately. He then jogs to Position A.

→ The next player waiting continues and all players are constantly rotating to the next position: **A → B → C → D → A**.

Source: Xabi Alonso's Bayer Leverkusen training session at Bayer 04 Leverkusen Training Ground - 12th April 2023

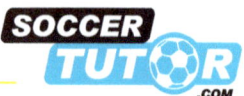

12. Speed, Agility and Quickness (SAQ) Circuit

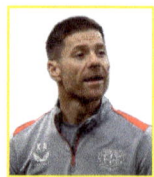

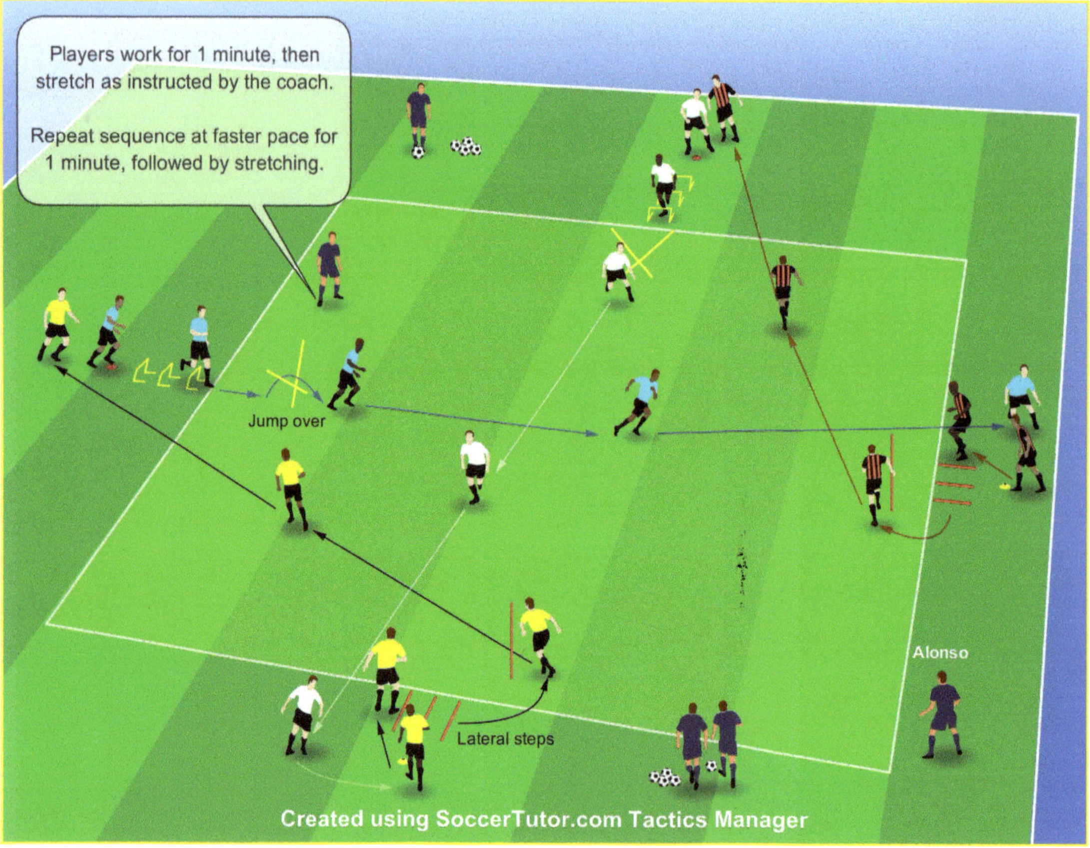
Players work for 1 minute, then stretch as instructed by the coach.
Repeat sequence at faster pace for 1 minute, followed by stretching.
Jump over
Lateral steps
Alonso
Created using SoccerTutor.com Tactics Manager

The different colours is illustrated just to distinguish between the 4 different stations.

Practice Description

- 4 players start at the same time from the 4 stations. They perform their set exercise and move to another group.
- **YELLOW:** Lateral steps through ground poles, run to the right of pole, make a sharp change of direction to the left, and run to Blue Station.
- **BLUE:** Steps over hurdles, jump over crossed "X" poles, run to Red Station.
- **WHITE:** Same as Blues, then run to Yellow Station.
- **RED:** Same as Yellow, but with pole to left side, then run to White Station.
- *Note: Players make sure to avoid each other in the middle of the area. They then move onto a practice progression with 2 balls added (see next page).*

Source: Xabi Alonso's Bayer Leverkusen training session at Bayer 04 Leverkusen Training Ground - 12th Dec 2023

Xabi Alonso Practices: Warm Ups

13. Speed, Agility and Quickness (SAQ) Circuit With a Ball

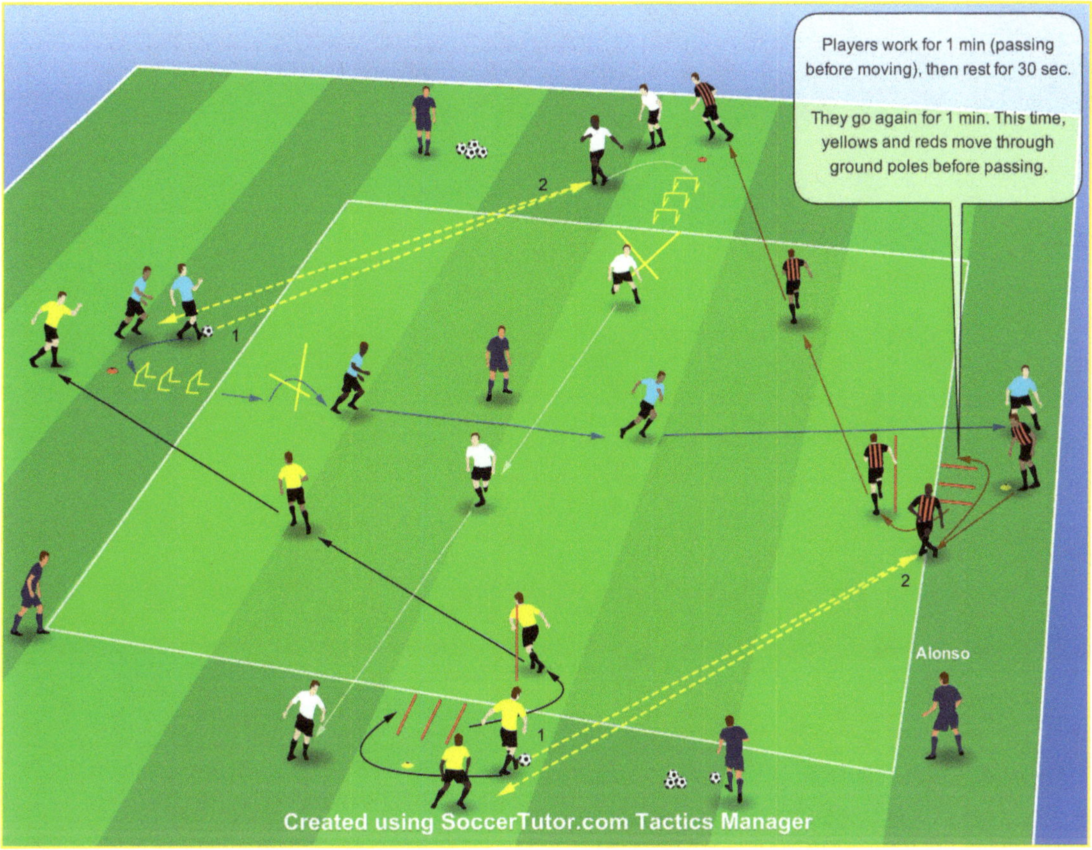

This is a progression of previous practice.

Practice Description

- Start at same time from 4 stations.
- **YELLOW:** Pass to Red player, lateral steps through ground poles, run to right of pole, and sharp change of direction to the left (run to Blue Station).
- **BLUE:** Pass to White player, steps over hurdles, jump over crossed "X" poles, and run to Red Station.
- **WHITE:** Pass ball to the next Blue player waiting, perform the same exercises as Blues, then run to Yellow Station.
- **RED:** Pass ball to the next Yellow player waiting, perform the same exercises as Yellows, then run to White Station.
- *Note: For the first phase, all players pass before any exercises. In the second phase, the red and yellow players move through ground poles before passing.*

Source: Xabi Alonso's Bayer Leverkusen training session at Bayer 04 Leverkusen Training Ground - 12th Dec 2023

Xabi Alonso Practices: Warm Ups

Variation: Adjusted Floor and Upright Pole Exercises

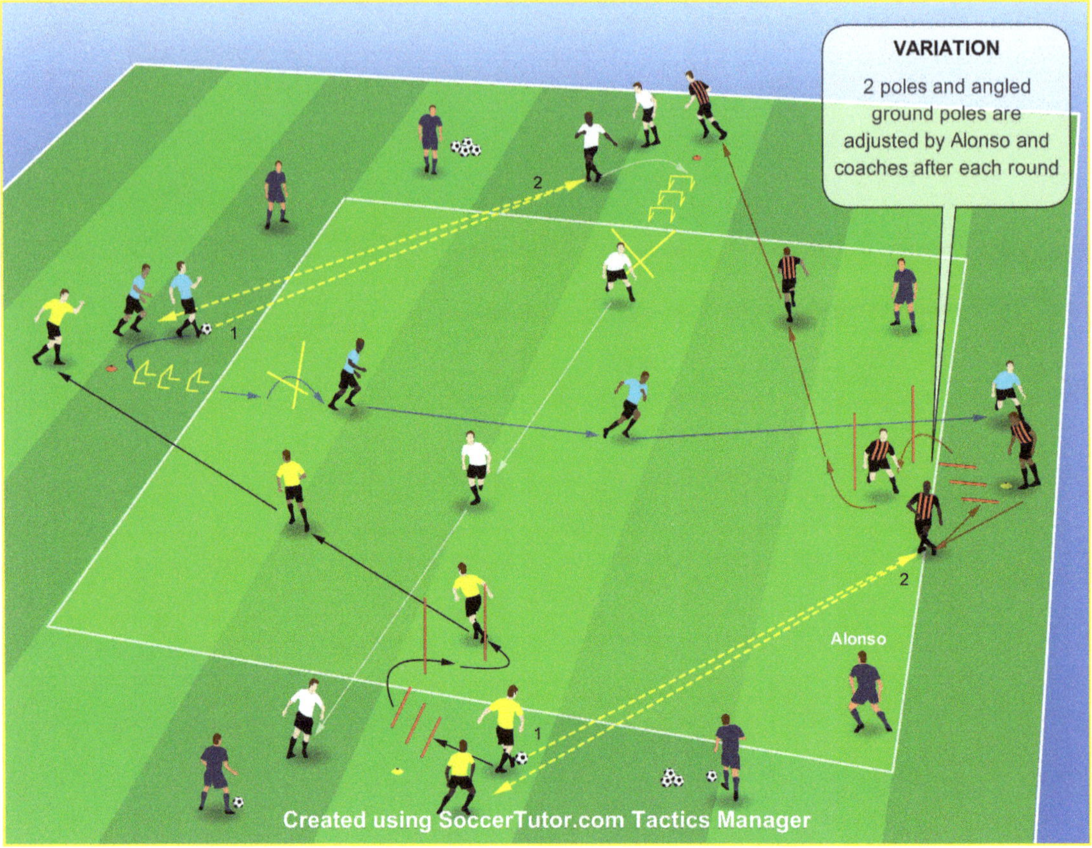

[Diagram with callout: **VARIATION** — 2 poles and angled ground poles are adjusted by Alonso and coaches after each round]

Practice Description

- This practice is the same as the variation shown on the previous page with some minor changes.
- The ground pole angles and positions for the Red and Yellow players are changed after each phase (repetition) of the practice.
- There are also 2 upright poles instead of 1 for the red and yellow players, for which the angles and positions are changed after each repetition.

- **BLUE + WHITE:** The Blues and Whites pass before moving to perform steps through hurdles and jump over crossed "X" poles.
- **YELLOW + RED:** The reds and yellows perform lateral steps through the ground poles and slalom through the 2 upright poles before passing.

Source: Xabi Alonso's Bayer Leverkusen training session at Bayer 04 Leverkusen Training Ground - 25th Oct 2023

Xabi Alonso Practices: Warm Ups

14. Technical Pass, Volley, and Heading Warm Up Conditioning Circuit

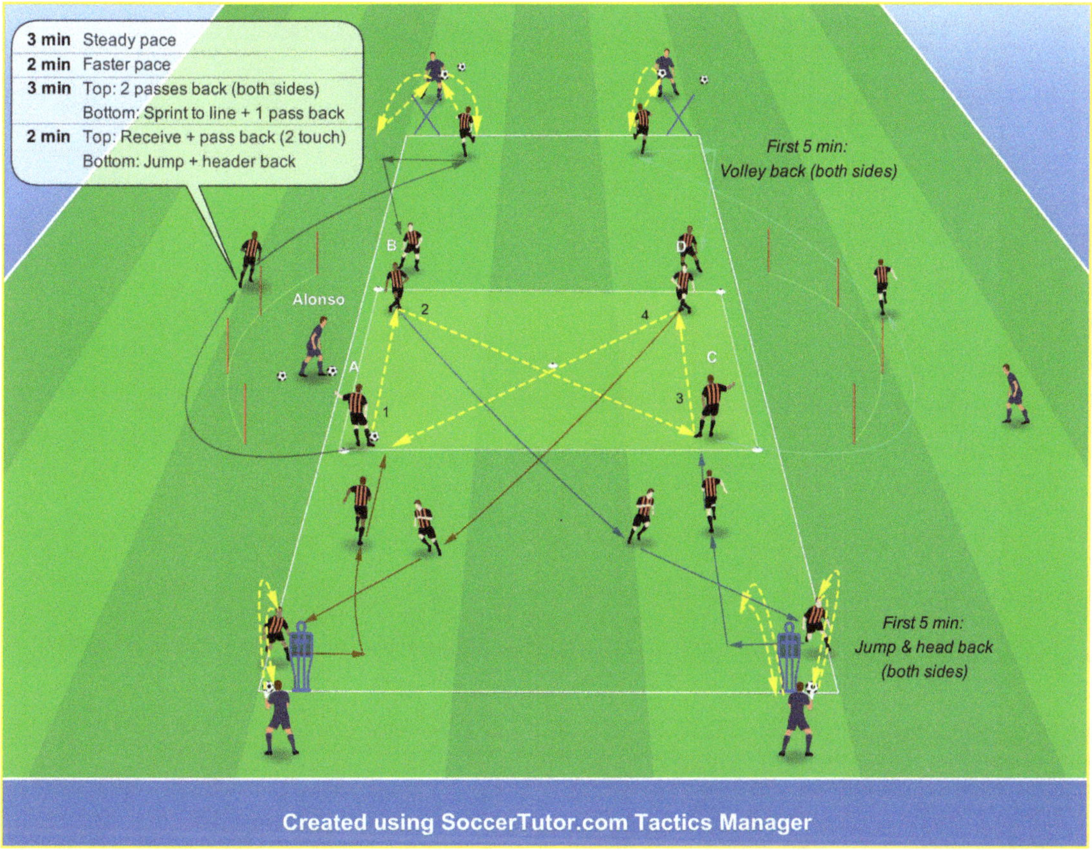

Practice Description

- **A** passes to **B** and runs around the red poles towards the crossed "X" blue poles. The coach alternates throwing the ball to the left and right for **A** to volley back, who then **A** jogs to Position B. Movements shown with **black arrows**.

- **B** passes to **C** and runs diagonally to the mannequin. The coach alternates throwing the ball to the left and right for **B** to jump up and head back.

- **B** jogs to Position C. Movements shown with **blue arrows**.

- **C** passes to **D**, replicates **A's** actions on the opposite side, and jogs to Position D. Movements shown with **sky blue arrows**.

- **D** passes to **A**, replicates **B's** actions on the opposite side, and jogs to Position A. Movements shown with the **red arrows**.

- *Note: Timings and variations are fully described in diagram.*

Source: Xabi Alonso's Bayer Leverkusen training session at Bayer 04 Leverkusen Training Ground - 23rd Jan 2024

Xabi Alonso Practices: Warm Ups

*Images taken from **Technical Pass, Volley, and Heading Warm Up Conditioning Circuit** practice on the previous page. Top - **Alejandro Grimaldo** volley back to coach. Bottom - **Xabi Alonso** observes.*

Passing Combinations

Direct from Xabi Alonso's Training Sessions

Xabi Alonso Practices: Passing Combinations

Passing

"I always say that passing the ball well is like conducting an orchestra. You have to find the right rhythm and timing to bring out the best in your teammates. It's about vision, precision, and understanding the flow of the game."

Xabi Alonso

Xabi Alonso Practices: Passing Combinations

1. Timing of Movement and Support Play Passing Combination

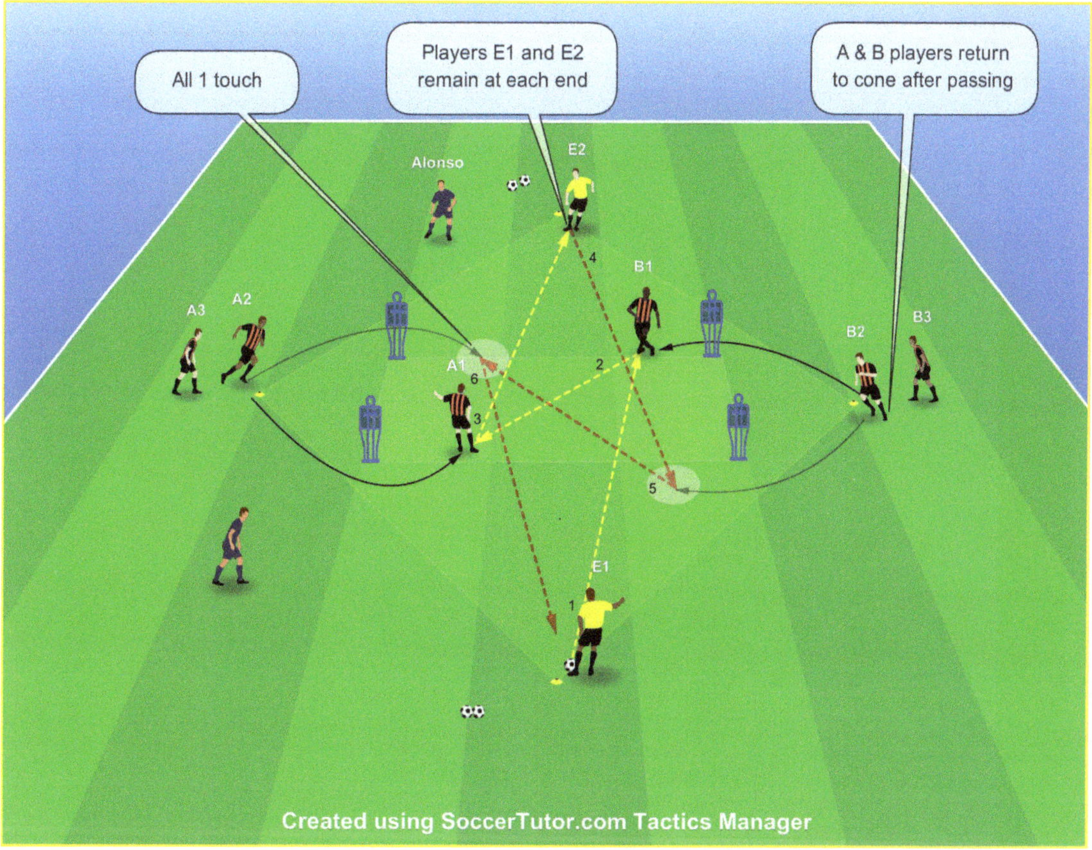

E1 and E2 remain at each end. The other players move into the centre to pass and then move back out to the same starting position behind the yellow cone.

Practice Description

1. **E1** passes to **B1**, who runs around the mannequin to meet the pass.

2-3. **B1** passes to **A1**, who runs around the mannequin and passes to **E2**. **B1** and **A1** move back outside to their cones.

4-6. **E2** passes to **B2**, who runs around the other mannequin on that side. **B2** passes to **A2**, who passes to **E1**. **B2** and **A2** move back outside to their cones.

→ The same combination continues with:
E1 → B3 → A3 → E2 → B1 → A1 → E1.

Note: The players use 1 touch throughout.

Source: Xabi Alonso's Bayer Leverkusen training session at Bayer 04 Leverkusen Training Ground - 6th March 2024

Xabi Alonso Practices: Passing Combinations

2. Timing of Movement and Support Play Passing Combination with Defensive Pressure (Variation 1)

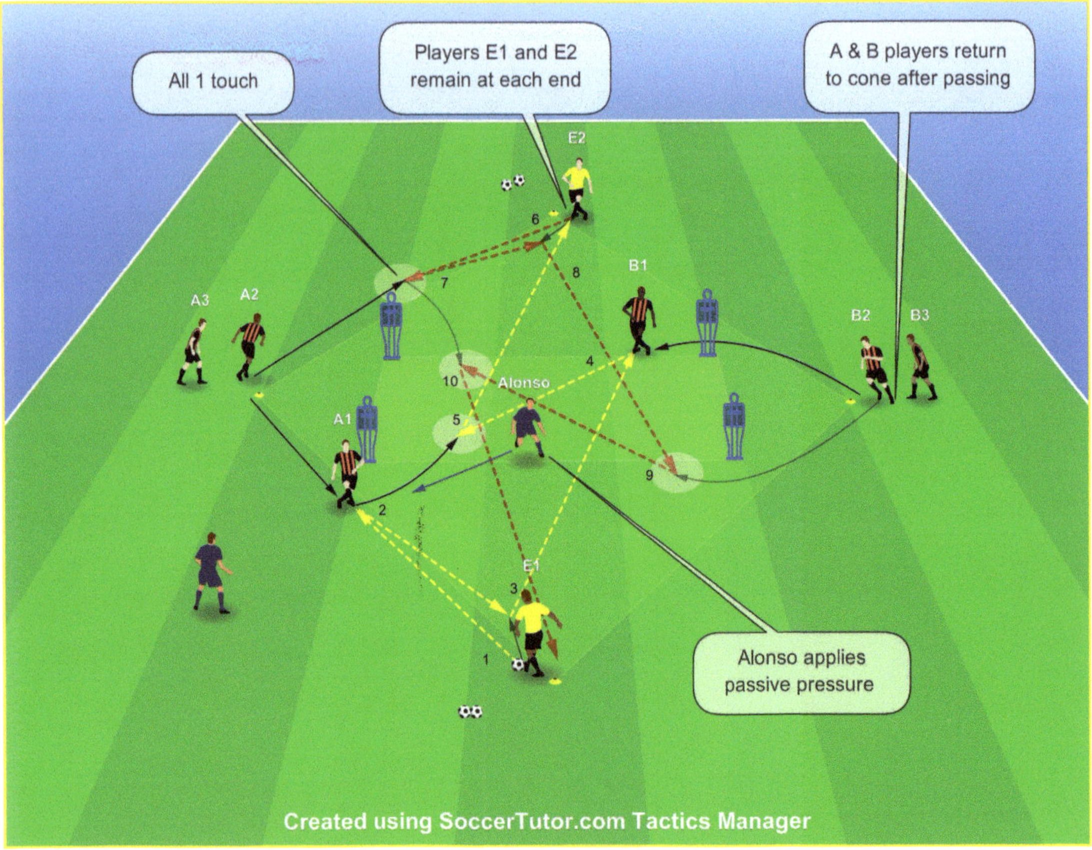

This is a progression of previous practice.

Practice Description

1-2. E1 plays a one-two with **A1**, who drops to meet the pass and is pressed by the coach (**Alonso**).

3-5. E1 passes to **B1**, who runs around the mannequin and sets the ball for **A1** to move onto. **A1** then passes to **E2**.

→ **A1** and **B1** move back outside to their cones.

6-7. E2 plays a one-two with **A2**, who moves to meet the pass.

8-10. E2 passes to **B2**, who runs around the mannequin and sets the ball for **A2** to move onto. **A2** then passes to **E1**.

→ **A2** and **B2** move back outside to their cones.

→ The same combination is repeated starting with **E1** passing to **A3**.

Note: The players use 1 touch throughout.

Source: Xabi Alonso's Bayer Leverkusen training session at Bayer 04 Leverkusen Training Ground - 8th May 2024

Xabi Alonso Practices: Passing Combinations

3. Timing of Movement and Support Play Passing Combination with Defensive Pressure (Variation 2)

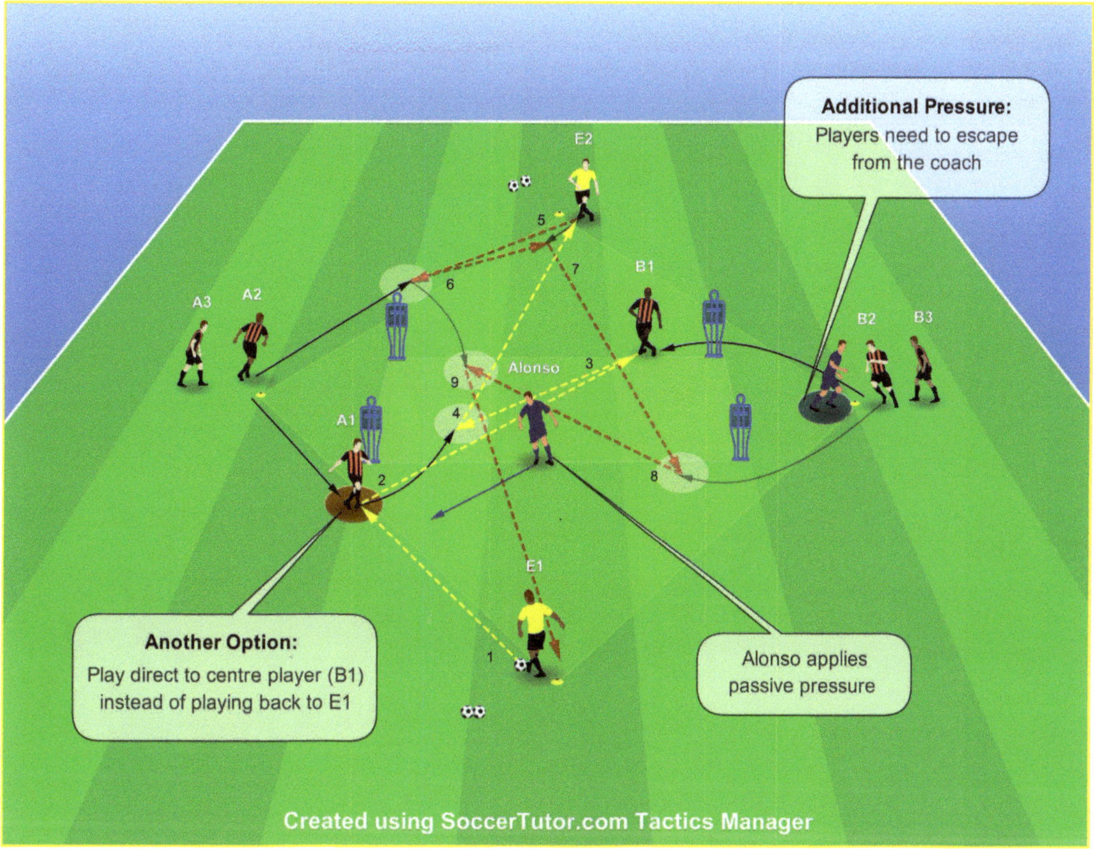

This is a variation of the previous practice.

Practice Description

1. **E1** passes to **A1**, who drops to meet the pass and is pressed by the coach (**Alonso**).

2-4. **A1** plays a one-two with **B1**, who runs around the mannequin to set the ball for **A1** to move onto. **A1** then passes to **E2**.

→ **A1** and **B1** move back outside to their cones.

5-6. **E2** plays a one-two with **A2**, who moves to meet the pass.

7-9. **E2** passes to **B2**, who runs around the mannequin and sets the ball for **A2** to move onto. **A2** then passes to **E1**.

→ **A2** and **B2** move back outside to their cones.

→ The same combination is repeated starting with **E1** passing to **A3**.

Note: The players use 1 touch throughout.

Source: Xabi Alonso's Bayer Leverkusen training session at Bayer 04 Leverkusen Training Ground - 8th May 2024

Xabi Alonso Practices: Passing Combinations

4. Pass and Move with Central Player Support and Combination Play

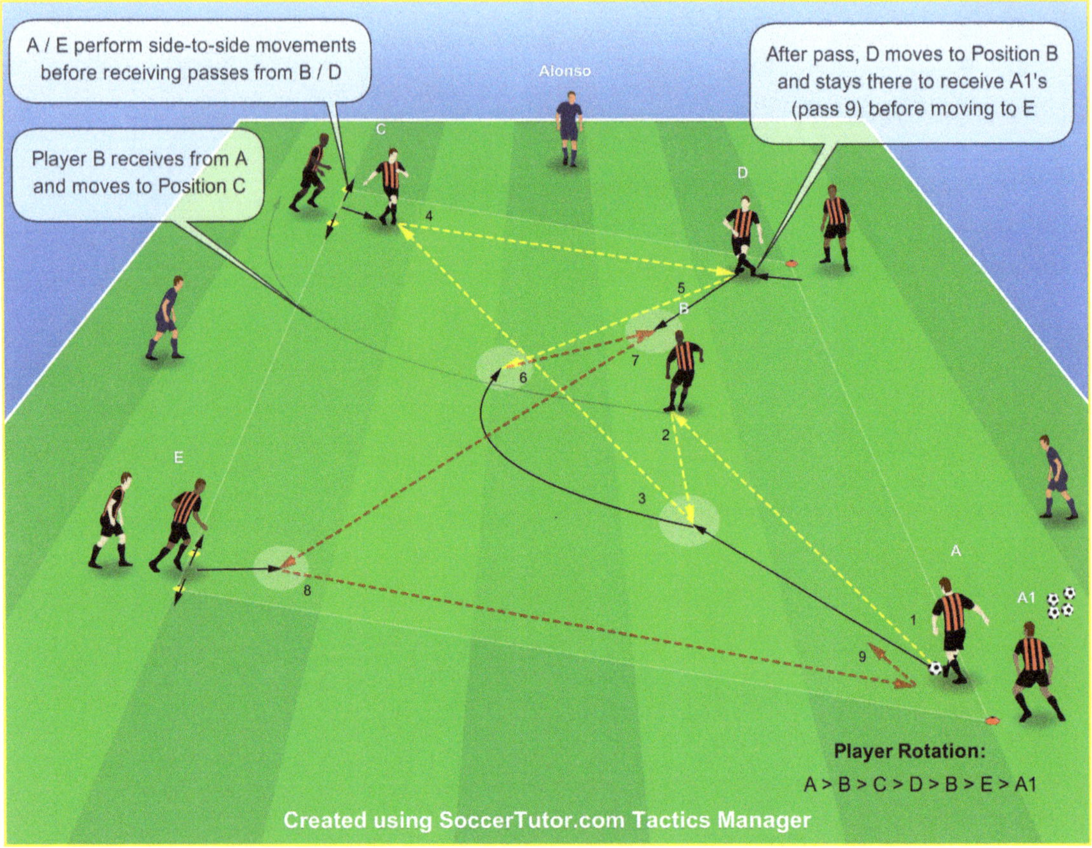

A / E perform side-to-side movements before receiving passes from B / D

Player B receives from A and moves to Position C

After pass, D moves to Position B and stays there to receive A1's (pass 9) before moving to E

Player Rotation:
A > B > C > D > B > E > A1

Created using SoccerTutor.com Tactics Manager

The yellow arrows show the first few passes with all players in their original positions. The red arrows show the passes after A has taken over B's role as the central player.

Practice Description

1-3. A plays a one-two with **B**, and then passes to **C**. A becomes the new central player and **B** moves to Position C.

4-5. C passes to **D** - he passes to **A**, who is the new central player in Position B.

6-7. A sets the ball back for **D**, who passes to **E**. A moves to Position C and **D** stays in the centre in Position B.

8-9. E passes to the next player waiting (**A1**), who passes to **D** in Position B in the centre. **D** moves to **E**, A1 moves to **B**.

→ The players rotate their positions:
A → B → C → D → B → E → A1.

Note: C and E perform side-to-side feet movements before receiving.

Source: Xabi Alonso's Bayer Leverkusen training session at Bayer 04 Leverkusen Training Ground - 20th Sep 2023

Xabi Alonso Practices: Passing Combinations

5. One-Two, Give & Go, and Directional First Touch Diamond Passing Circuit with Defensive Pressure

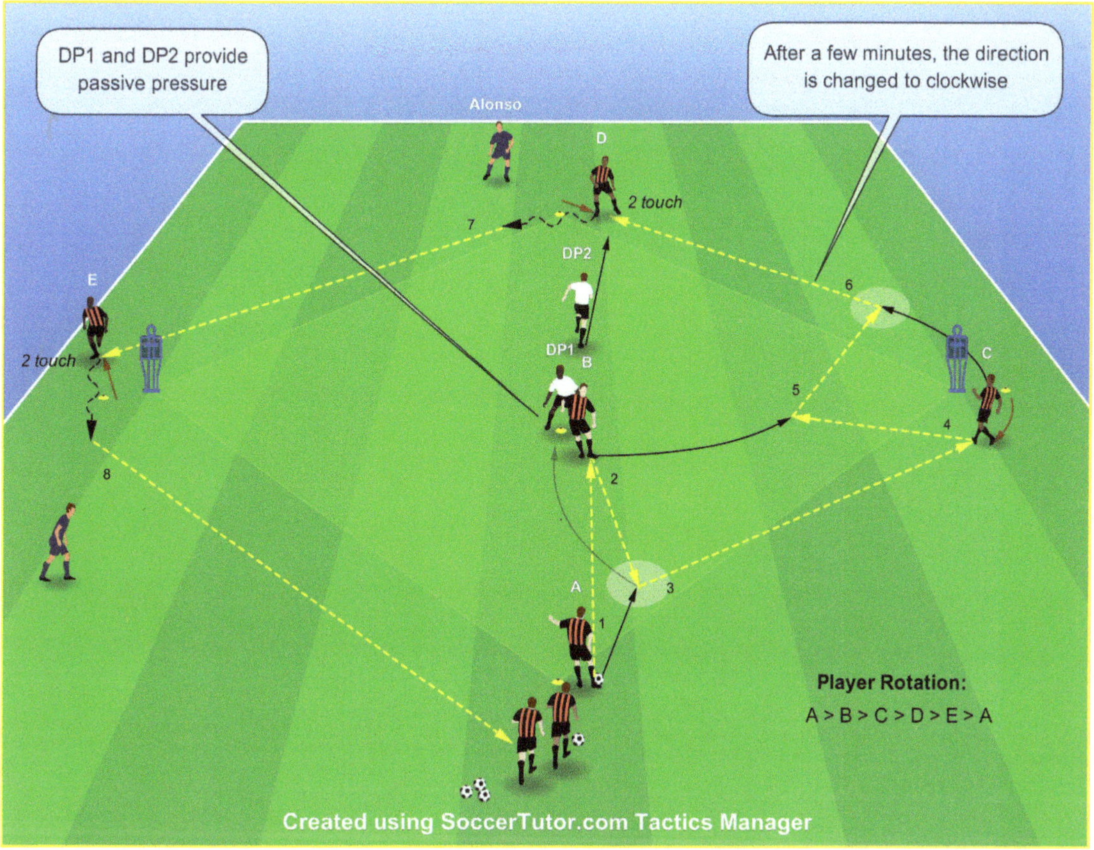

The 2 yellow players apply passive pressure to make the actions more game realistic.

Practice Description

1-2. **A** passes to **B**, who passes back for **A** to move forward onto as he is pressed from behind by **DP1**.

3. **B** passes wide to **C**, who drops off the cone to receive.

4-5. **C** plays a give and go with **B**, who moves across to play the return pass.

6. **C** passes to **D**, who is pressed by **DP2**. He takes the ball away from pressure with a good directional first touch.

7. With his second touch, **D** passes to **E**, who drops off the cone to receive.

8. **E** also takes a good directional first touch and then passes to the start position to the next player waiting.

→ The players rotate their positions:
A → B → C → D → E → A.

Source: Xabi Alonso's Bayer Leverkusen training session at Bayer 04 Leverkusen Training Ground - 20th Sep 2023

Xabi Alonso Practices: Passing Combinations

6. One-Two, Give & Goes, and Switch of Play Diamond Passing Circuit with Defensive Pressure

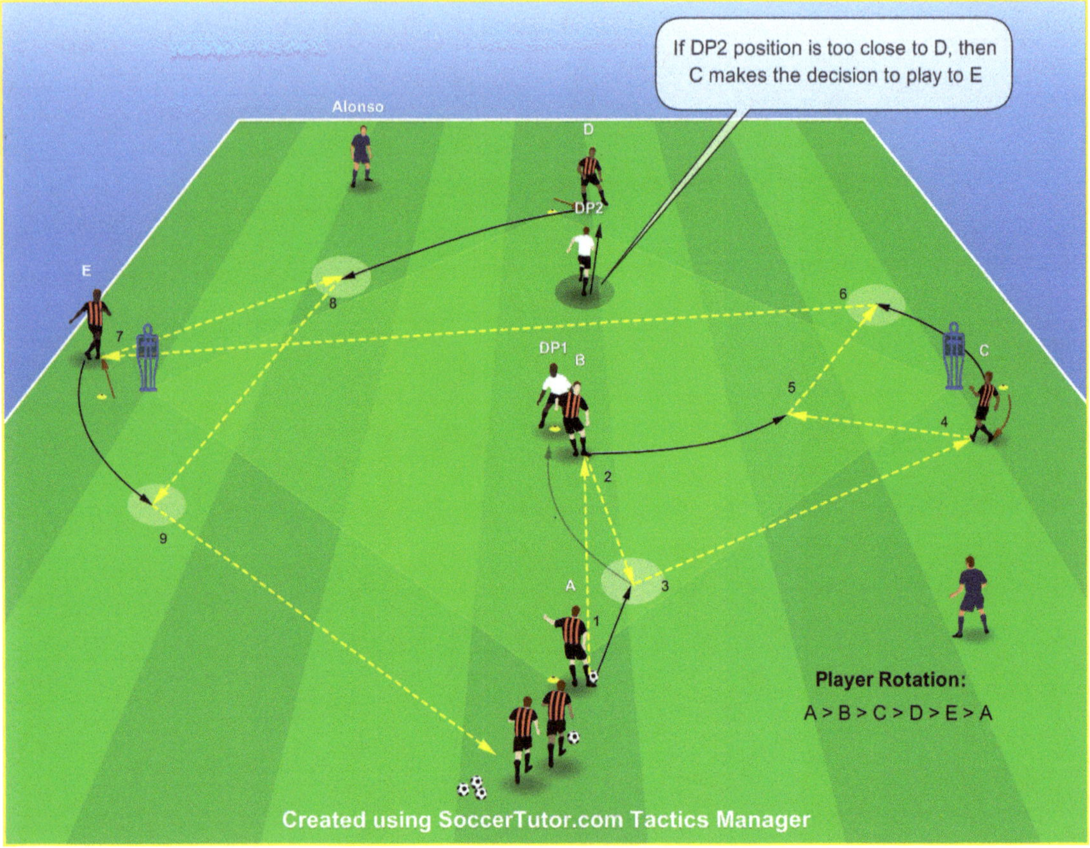

This is a variation of the previous practice.

Practice Description

1-2. **A** passes to **B**, who passes back for **A** to move forward onto as he is pressed from behind by **DP1**.

3. **B** passes wide to **C**, who drops off the cone to receive.

4-5. **C** plays a give and go with **B**, who moves across and away from his marker to play the return pass.

6-7. **C** passes across the diamond to switch the play to **E**, who sets the ball for **D**. **D** has checked off his cone to draw pressure from **DP2**, and then changes direction to receive the pass from **E**.

8-9. **D** passes to **E**, who runs around the mannequin to receive the return and complete the second give & go. **E** passes to the start position to the next player.

→ The players rotate their positions:
A → B → C → D → E → A.

Source: Xabi Alonso's Bayer Leverkusen training session at Bayer 04 Leverkusen Training Ground - 20th Sep 2023

Xabi Alonso Practices: Passing Combinations

7. Two Ball Passing Circuit with Central Link Players and Defensive Pressure (Variation 1)

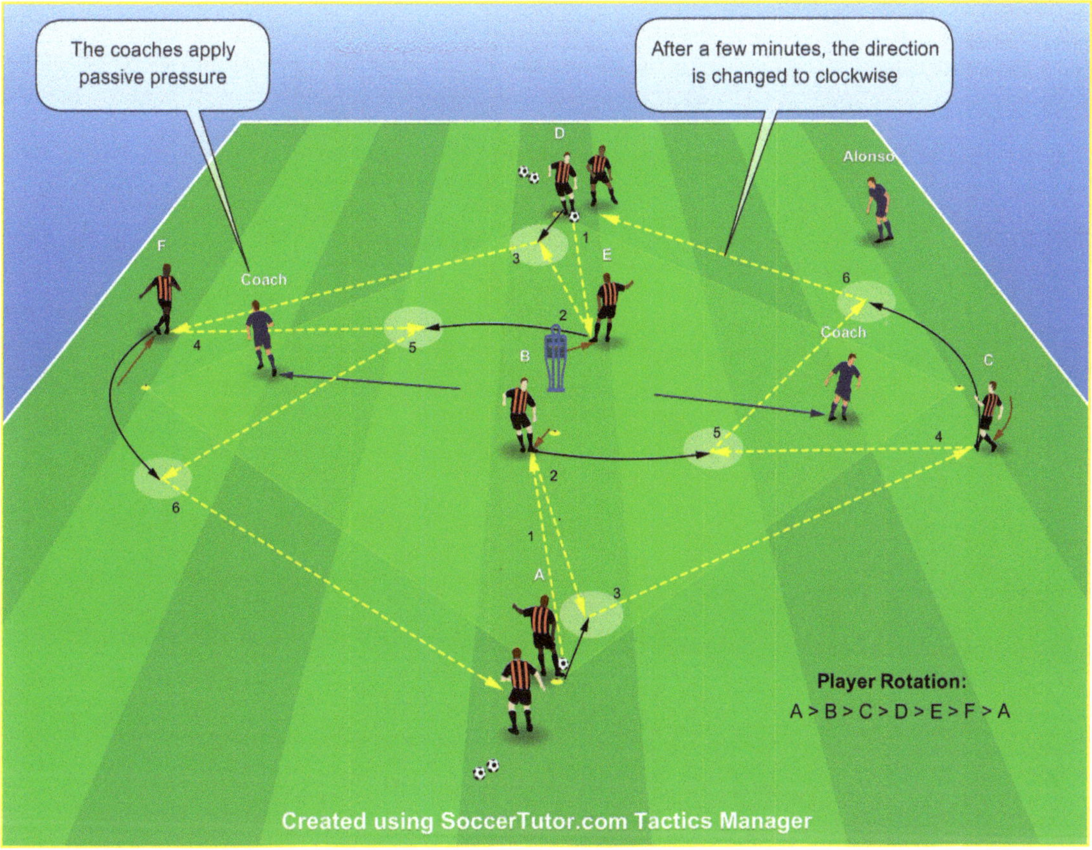

The practice starts with 2 balls from A and D simultaneously.

Practice Description

1-3. A/D play a one-two with **B/E**, and then pass wide to **C/F**.

4-5. C/F are put under passive pressure by a coach, then play a give & go with **B/E**, who move across.

6. C/F pass to the next player waiting at Position D/A as the circuit continues.

→ The players rotate their positions: A → B → C → D → E → F → A.

Note: The players in positions C and F check away from their cone before moving to receive, as they are put under pressure by a coach.

Source: Xabi Alonso's Bayer Leverkusen training session at Bayer 04 Leverkusen Training Ground - 2024

Xabi Alonso Practices: Passing Combinations

8. Two Ball Passing Circuit with Central Link Players and Defensive Pressure (Variation 2)

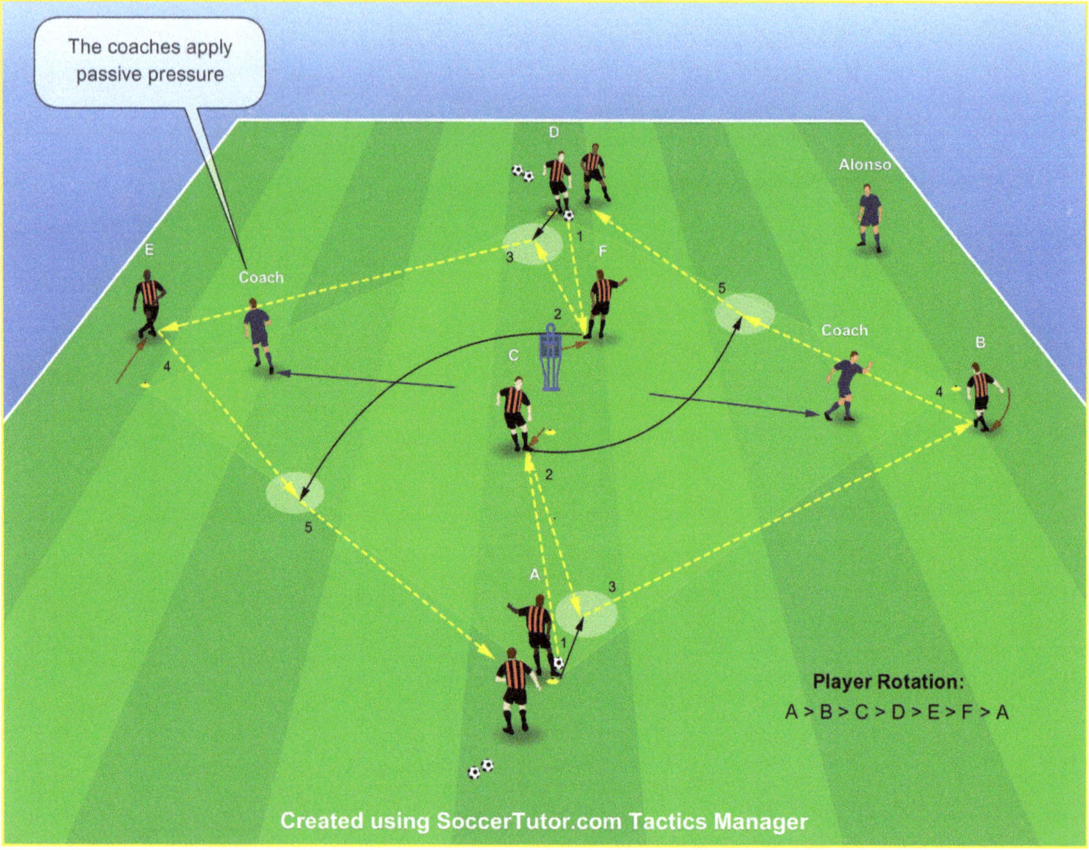

This is a variation of the previous practice.

Practice Description

1-3. **A/D** play a one-two with **C/F**, and then pass wide to **B/E**.

4. **B/E** check off their cone, are put under passive pressure by a coach, then open up and pass (correct weight) for the forward curved run of **C/F**.

5. **C/F** pass to the next player waiting at Position D/A as the circuit continues.

→ The players rotate their positions:
A → B → C → D → E → F → A.

Note: The players in positions B and E check away from their cone before moving to receive, as they are put under pressure by a coach.

Source: Xabi Alonso's Bayer Leverkusen training session at Bayer 04 Leverkusen Training Ground - 2024

Xabi Alonso Practices: Passing Combinations

9. End to End Passing Combinations and Support Play to Break the Lines (Variation 1)

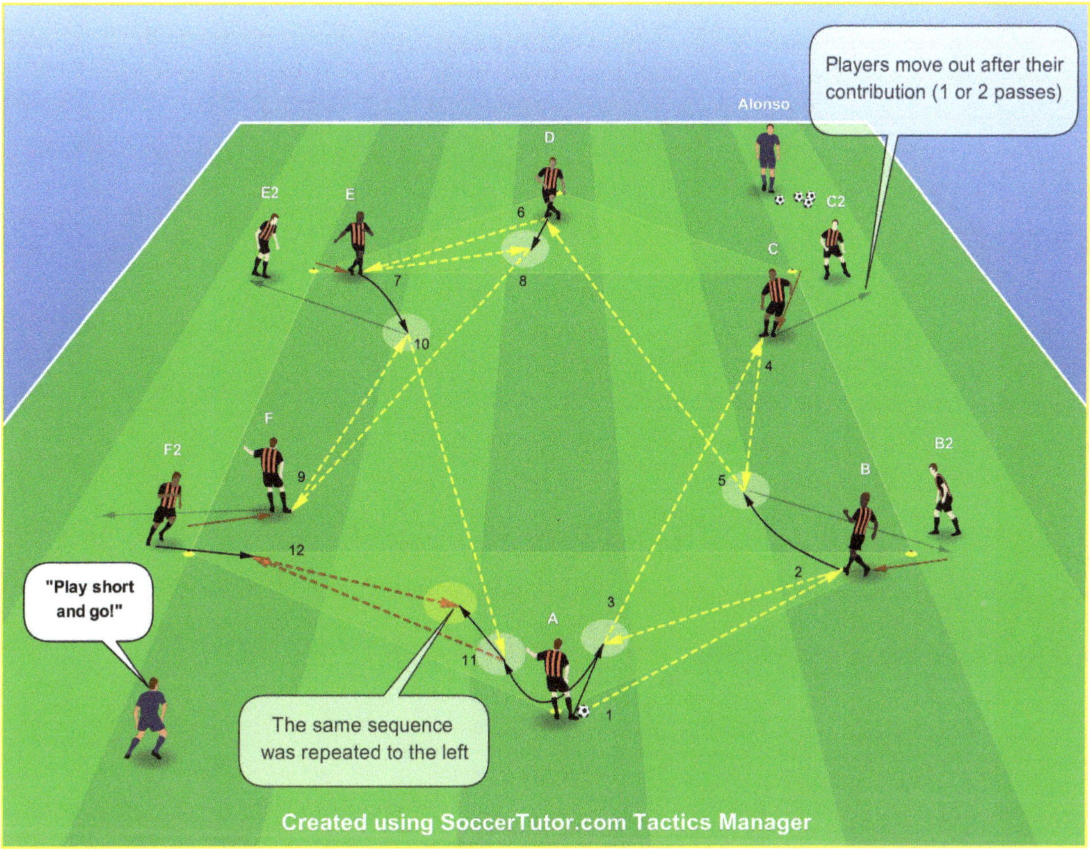

The players are labelled A to F to best illustrate the order of the passing sequence. There are 2 players in positions B, C, E, and F who all rotate in and out after their contribution within the passing sequence (1 or 2 passes) is complete.

Practice Description

1-3. **A** plays a one-two with **B**, and then passes forward to **C**, who drops back.

4-5. **C** sets the ball back for **B** to pass to **D**.

6-8. **D** plays a one-two with **E**, and then passes forward to **F**, who moves to meet the pass.

9-10. **F** sets the ball back for **E** to complete the sequence with the final pass to **A**.

11-12 → The same sequence is repeated as a mirror image starting on the left with **A** playing a one-two combination with **F2**, then passing to **E2**.

Source: Xabi Alonso's Bayer Leverkusen training session at Bayer 04 Leverkusen Training Ground - 2024

Xabi Alonso Practices: Passing Combinations

10. End to End Passing Combinations and Support Play to Break the Lines (Variation 2)

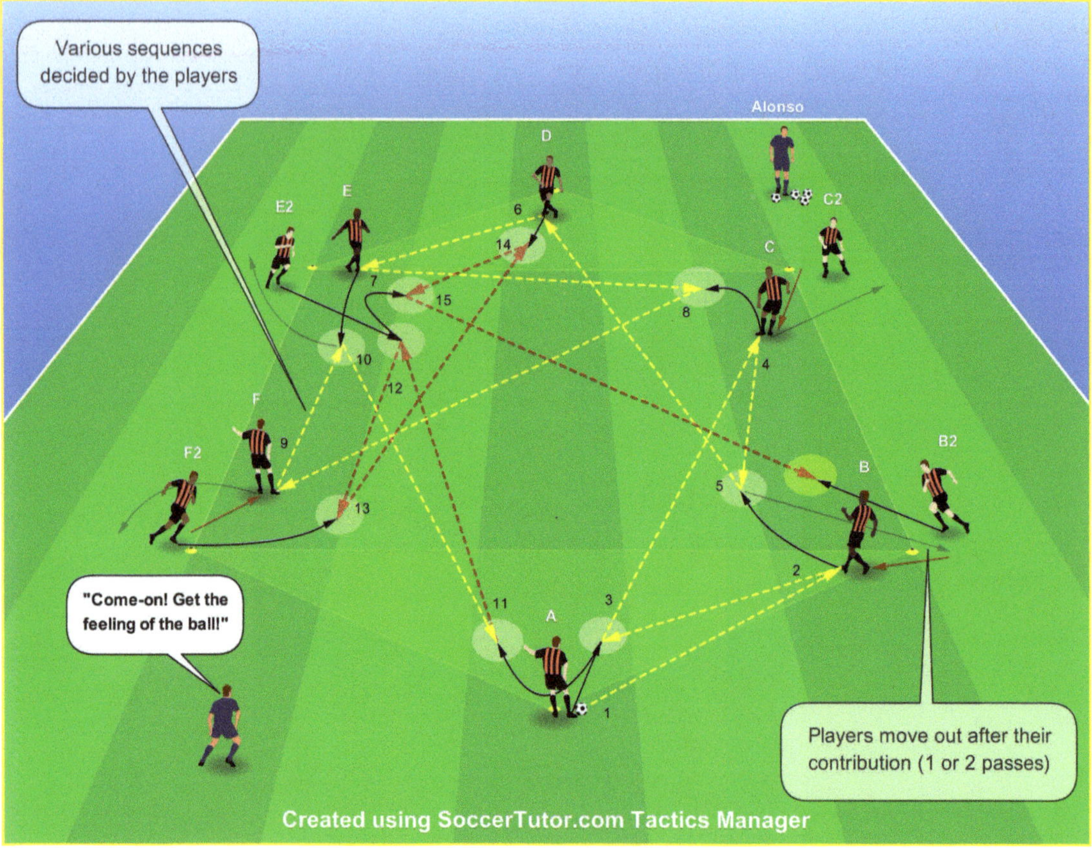

Various sequences decided by the players

"Come-on! Get the feeling of the ball!"

Players move out after their contribution (1 or 2 passes)

This is a variation of the previous practice where the players were seen using various sequences with free decision making - the diagram shows 2 of the patterns which were observed.

Practice Description

1-3. **A** plays a one-two with **B**, and then passes forward to **C**, who drops back.

4-5. **C** sets the ball back for **B** to pass to **D**.

6-7. **D** passes to **E**, who passes back to **C**.

8-10. **C** passes diagonally to **F**, who sets the ball back for **E** to complete the sequence with the final pass to **A**.

11-13. **A** passes to **E2**, who sets the ball back for **F2** to pass to **D**.

14-15. **D** passes short to **E2**, who plays a diagonal pass to **B2**.

16 → The practice is continuous with the players creating their own passing sequences.

Source: Xabi Alonso's Bayer Leverkusen training session at Bayer 04 Leverkusen Training Ground - 2024

Xabi Alonso's Bayer Leverkusen: Build Up Play Tactics

Tactical Flexibility

"Football is a constantly evolving game. A good coach must be adaptable and ready to change tactics to suit the strengths of the team and counter the opponents."

Xabi Alonso

Xabi Alonso's Bayer Leverkusen: Build Up Play Tactics

Xabi Alonso's Bayer Leverkusen 3-4-2-1 Formation with Wing Backs

During the 2023-2024 season, **Xabi Alonso implemented the 3-4-2-1 as his primary formation for his Bayer Leverkusen team**.

This formation capitalises on the players' versatility, allowing for **smooth transitions between 3 or 4 player defences**.

In this section, we show how **different variations of build up play shapes were used effectively** by Xabi Alonso's Bayer Leverkusen team to play through pressure and break the lines to progress into the attacking phase.

- **GK:** Goalkeeper
- **CB:** Middle Centre Back
- **LCB:** Left Centre Back
- **RCB:** Right Centre Back
- **LWB:** Left Wing Back
- **RWB:** Right Wing Back
- **DM:** Defensive Midfielder
- **AM:** Attacking Midfielder
- **CF:** Centre Forward

Xabi Alonso's Bayer Leverkusen: Build Up Play Tactics

Xabi Alonso's Bayer Leverkusen 3-2-5 Build Up Play Shape

1. Wing Backs Push Up to Create 3-2-5 Build Up Shape

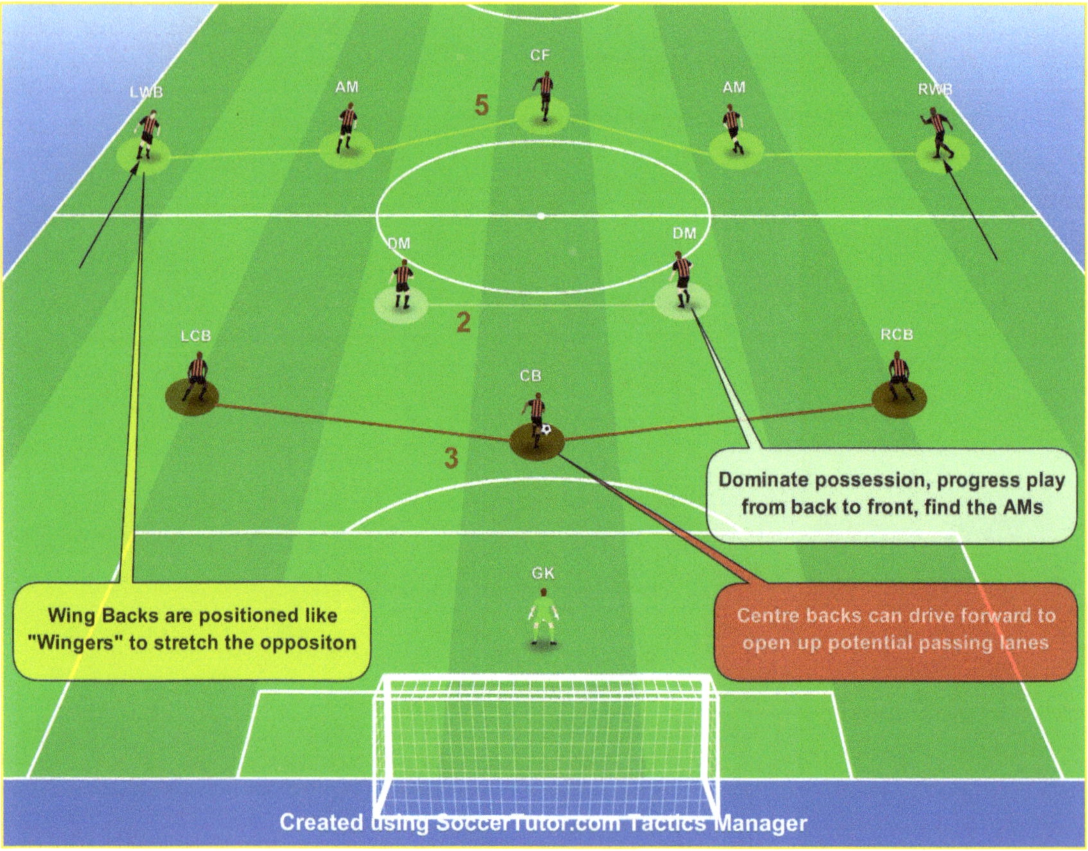

Dominate possession, progress play from back to front, find the AMs

Wing Backs are positioned like "Wingers" to stretch the opposition

Centre backs can drive forward to open up potential passing lanes

When building up play from the back with a **3 player defence**, Bayer Leverkusen use a **3-2-5 shape** with both wing backs (**LWB & RWB**) pushing up high into the midfield line and into attack to play as "wingers."

Xabi Alonso's strategy revolves around **controlling possession** and advancing the ball from defence to attack with **patience and calculated risk**. This 3-2-5 build up shape frees up space for the defensive midfielders (**DM**) and attacking midfielders (**AM**). The centre backs are comfortable to play out and can also carry the ball forward.

The aim is to create overloads and openings to progress play through the centre.

Once the ball is played into the attacking midfielders, the team can launch fast attacks to score, often with overloads.

©SOCCERTUTOR.COM   XABI ALONSO: PRACTICES DIRECT FROM SESSIONS

Xabi Alonso's Bayer Leverkusen: Build Up Play Tactics

2. Tactical Example of 3-2-5 Build Up Shape vs 2 Forwards

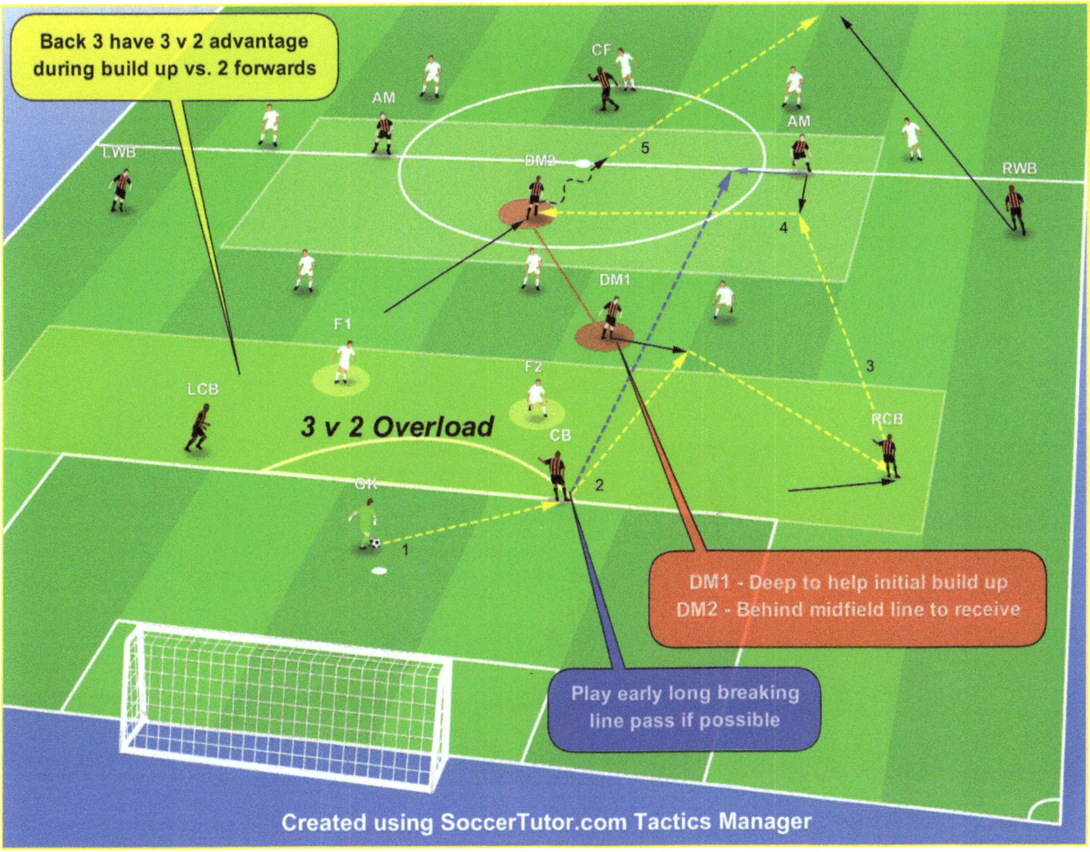

The key point to highlight here is that the **defensive midfielders (DM) can vary their play between vertical and horizontal passes/movement** to maintain unpredictability and disrupt the opposition as much as possible. In this tactical example against a 3-5-2 formation, **Bayer Leverkusen counter the 2 opposing forwards' pressing by using 3 players in their build-up phase (3 v 2 overload)**. Their 3-2-5 build up shape allows them to **progress play through the centre**, which is the team's main aim during this phase.

The wing backs (**LWB** & **RWB**) maintain width. The defensive midfielders (**DM**) position themselves behind the first line of pressure (behind F1 & F2), adjusting their roles based on which side the ball is played out. Here, **DM1** drops deeper to help in the build up, while **DM2** pushes forward behind the opposition's midfield line, ready to receive passes between the lines.

DM2 is able to receive after **DM1's** bounce pass to **RCB**, and **AM** dropping to act as a link player. From here, Bayer can move into attack with a potential 6 v 5 overload.

Note: If there is a clear passing line and the risk is not too great, the defenders will always look to play a long pass from back to front to a free player if they can, as shown by the blue arrow in the diagram.

Xabi Alonso's Bayer Leverkusen: Build Up Play Tactics

3. Tactical Example of 3-2-5 Build Up Shape vs 1 Forward

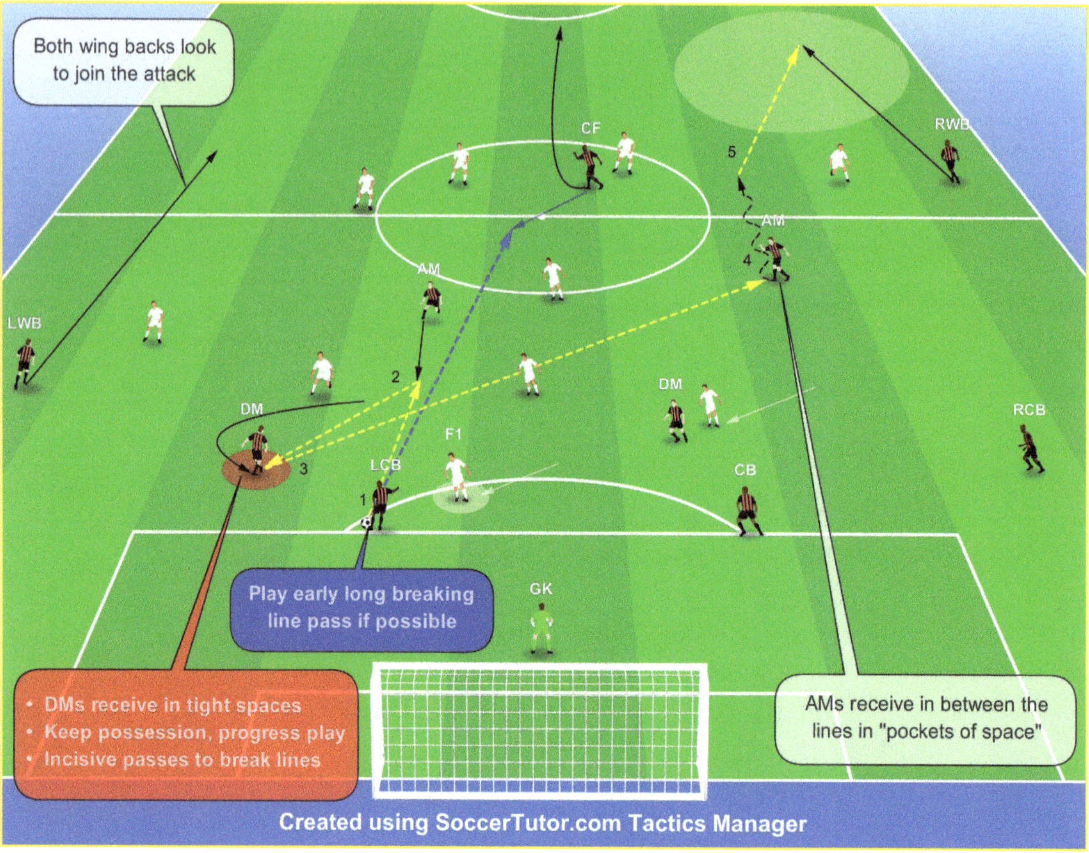

In this tactical example against the 4-3-3 formation, Bayer Leverkusen focus on playing out from the back with **incisive passing under pressure**.

The defensive midfielders (**DM**) are crucial, receiving the ball in tight spaces, maintaining possession, and **progressing play with sharp, line-breaking passes**. These passes are aimed at finding the **attacking midfielders (AM) positioned between the lines** in "pockets of space."

This effectively neutralises 5 or 6 opposing players, creating opportunities to release the right wing back (**RWB**) or centre forward (**CF**) in dangerous areas.

Both wing backs can join the attack, potentially creating an advantageous 4v4 situation in the final third.

If no such option materialises around the ball, the **DMs** have the backup option to reset the play, maintaining control and fluidity in their build up.

Note: If there is a clear passing line and the risk is not too great, the defenders will always look to play a long pass from back to front to a free player if they can, as shown by the blue arrow in the diagram.

Xabi Alonso's Bayer Leverkusen 2-3-5 Build Up Play Shape (Variation)

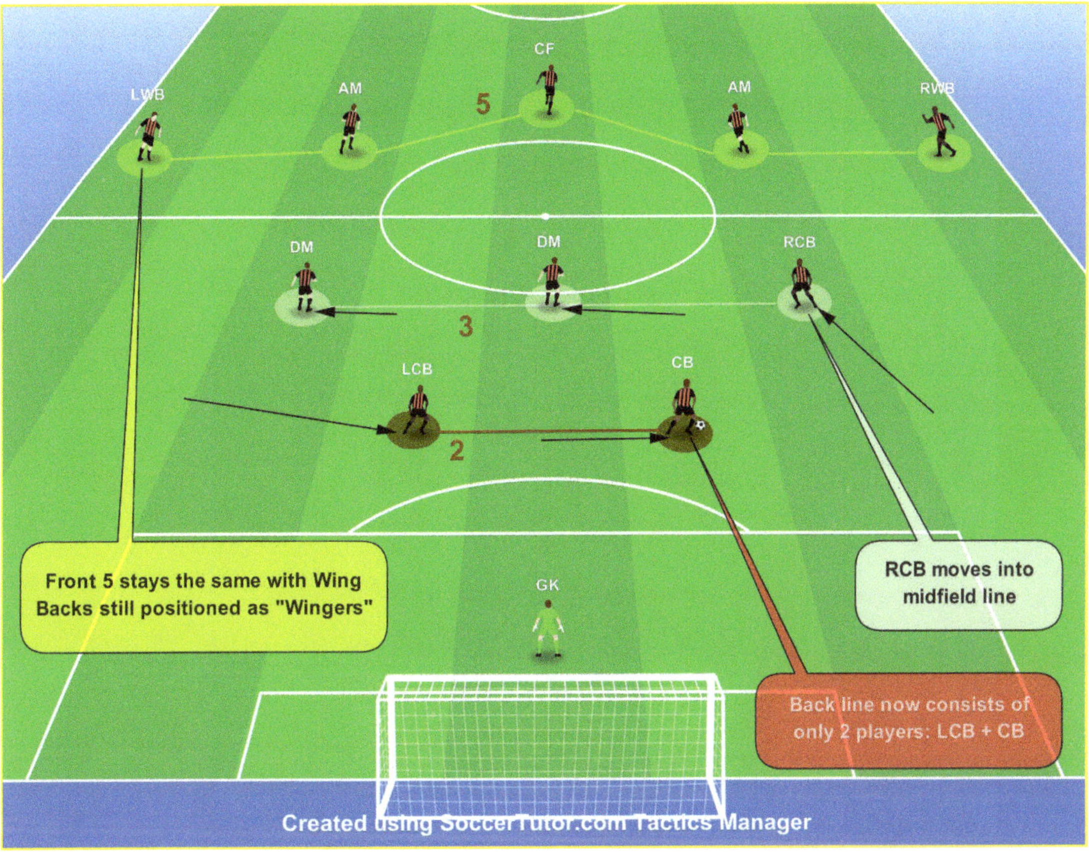

In this tactical variation, Bayer Leverkusen are able to create a 2-3-5 build up shape.

The **right centre back (RCB) pushes up into the midfield line**, forming a temporary 3 with the 2 defensive midfielders (**DM**).

This rotation alters the team's shape, creating a more compact and dynamic midfield presence. The **RCB's** movement into the midfield line adds an extra layer of support, allowing the team to maintain possession more easily under pressure against certain opponents and systems.

This adjustment also provides flexibility in playmaking, as the **RCB's advanced position can help overload the midfield**, disrupt the opposition's structure, and facilitate smoother transitions from defence to attack.

Xabi Alonso's Bayer Leverkusen 4-2-4 Build Up Play Shape

1. 4-2-4 Build Up Shape with Right Wing Back Advanced

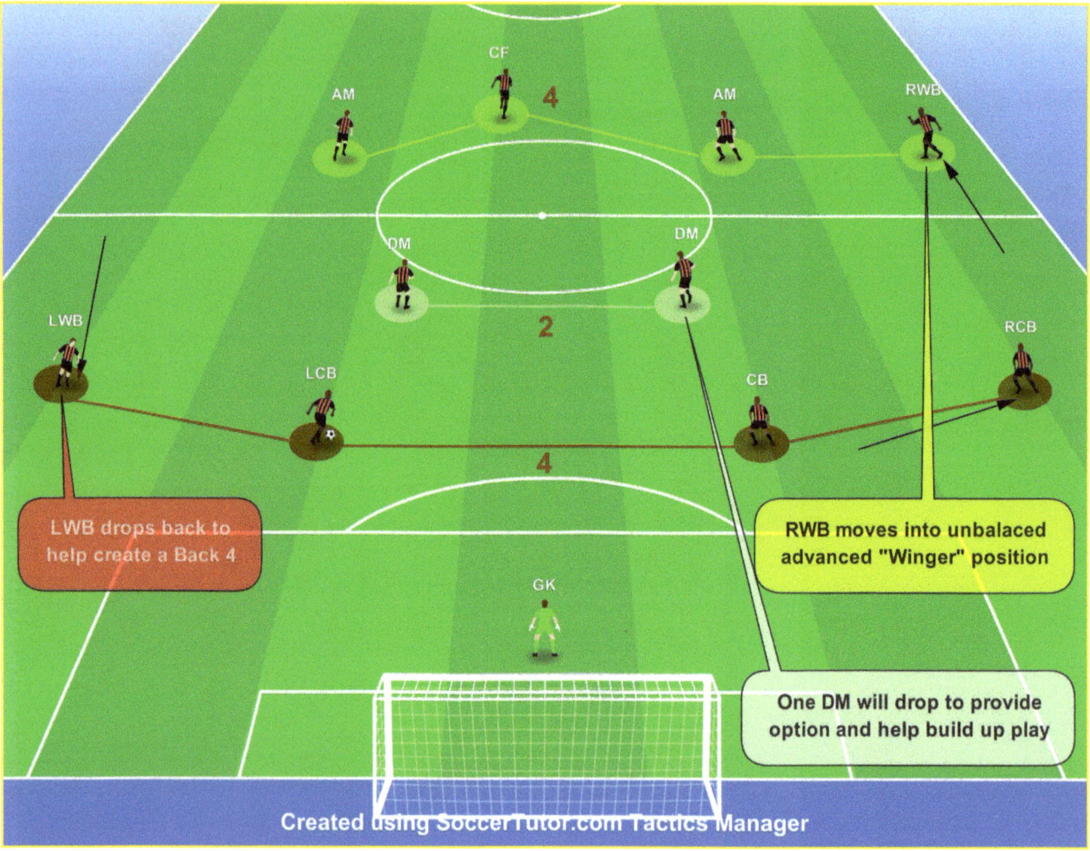

When building up play with a **4 player defence**, the team use a **4-2-4 shape** with the left wing back (**LWB**) dropping back, and right wing back (**RWB**) pushing forward.

To change from the starting 3-4-2-1 shape into a 4-2-4 shape, the right centre back (**RCB**) shifts into the right back position, and the **LWB** drops back into a left back position, as shown.

The defensive midfielders (**DM**) are still in the same positions. The **RWB** moves forward into a right winger position and the attacking midfielder (**Left AM**) moves into a more central position as part of a front 4.

Note: Versatile players allow Leverkusen to adjust their shape during build up play, creating adaptable passing options against different opponents' pressing.

Xabi Alonso's Bayer Leverkusen: Build Up Play Tactics

2. Tactical Example of 4-2-4 Build Up Shape vs 2 Forwards

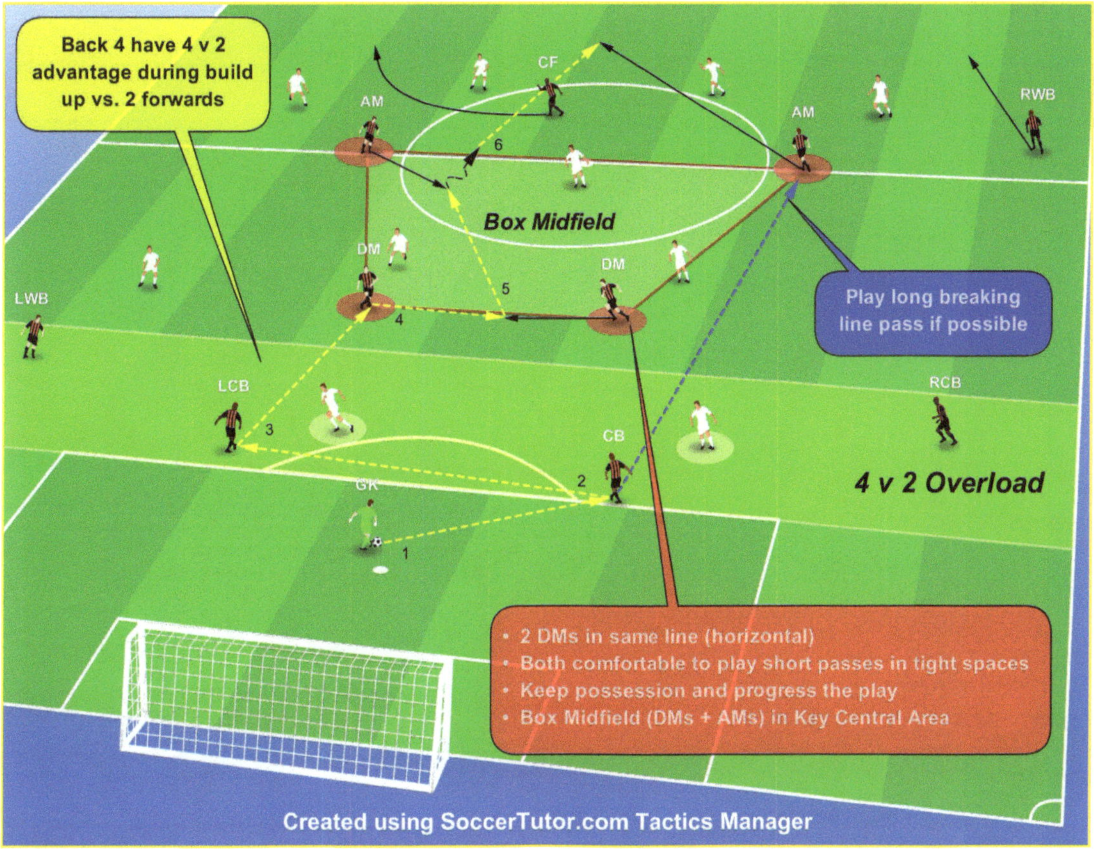

Diagram annotations:
- Back 4 have 4 v 2 advantage during build up vs. 2 forwards
- Box Midfield
- Play long breaking line pass if possible
- 4 v 2 Overload
- 2 DMs in same line (horizontal)
- Both comfortable to play short passes in tight spaces
- Keep possession and progress the play
- Box Midfield (DMs + AMs) in Key Central Area

Created using SoccerTutor.com Tactics Manager

Within their 3-4-2-1 formation, Xabi Alonso's Bayer Leverkusen can shift to a back 4 during build-up play, as shown on the previous page. This adjustment is particularly effective against teams pressing with 2 forwards, creating a **4 v 2 advantage in the initial phase of build up**.

The double pivot of the 2 defensive midfielders (**DM**) can vary between horizontal and vertical alignments - this example highlights the horizontal setup.

The middle centre back (**CB**) receives from the GK and initiates play, with the **RCB** positioned as a right back and the **DMs** supporting behind the first line of pressure.

The **DMs** are aligned horizontally, enabling short, controlled passes in tight spaces. The defenders and **DMs** work together to maintain possession and progress the play through the centre.

The **"Box Midfield" setup in central areas offers an additional 4 v 3 advantage** once Bayer Leverkusen progress past the initial press.

Note: If there is a clear passing line and the risk is not too great, the defenders will always look to play a long pass from back to front to a free player if they can, as shown by the blue arrow in the diagram.

Xabi Alonso's Bayer Leverkusen: Build Up Play Tactics

Creating Overload on Right Side of Pitch and then Switching Play

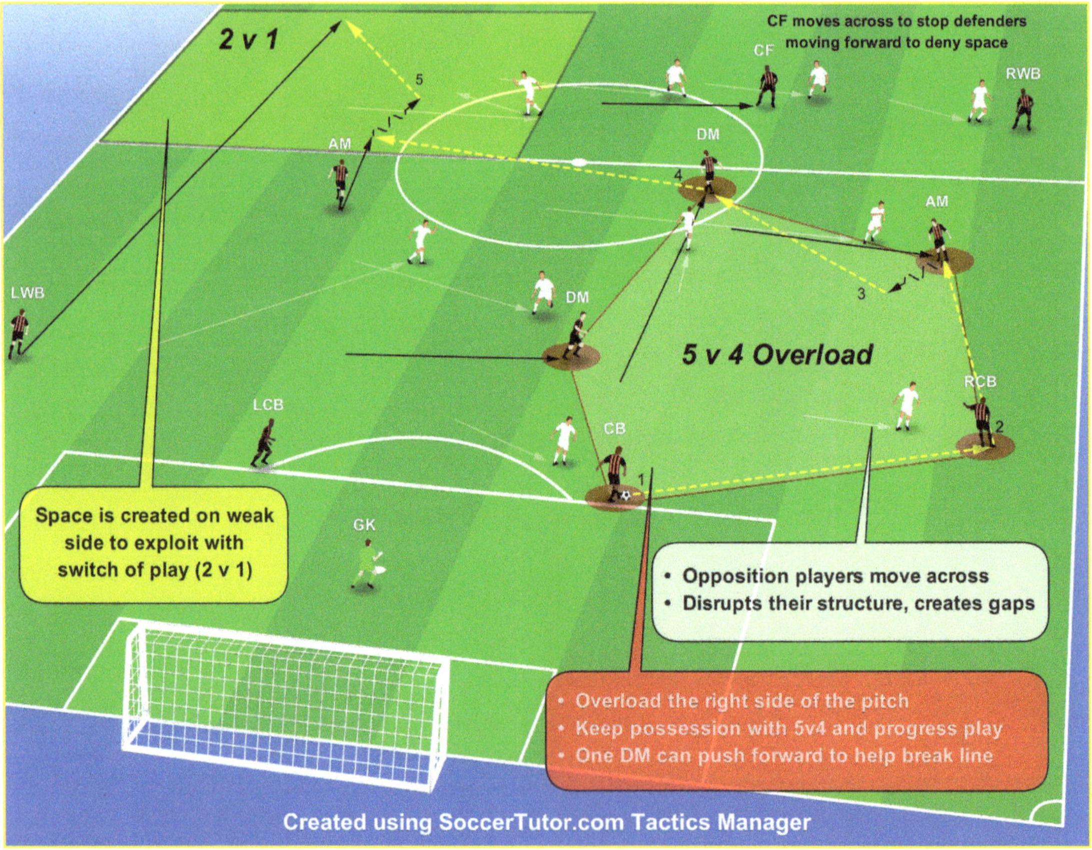

This example shows how Xabi Alonso's Bayer Leverkusen team overload the right side of the pitch during build up play from the back.

Their aim is to **create a 5v4 overload (highlighted) to maintain possession and progress play** into attack.

The 2 defensive midfielders (**DM**) can align horizontally or vertically. In this example, they start deep and parallel, adjusting based on the opponent's press. **One DM pushes forward while the other stays back**.

This tactic disrupts the opposition's defensive structure and forces them to adjust which opens up exploitable spaces. Bayer's flexibility helps control the game's tempo and break down defensive structures effectively.

In the diagram, the **opposition are dragged across to one side of the pitch**. The **5v4 overload allows Bayer to play through the right into the centre, and then switch play** to the weak side where there is a favourable **2v1 situation to exploit**.

©SOCCERTUTOR.COM   XABI ALONSO: PRACTICES DIRECT FROM SESSIONS

Xabi Alonso's Bayer Leverkusen 4-2-4 Build Up Play Shape from Goal Kicks

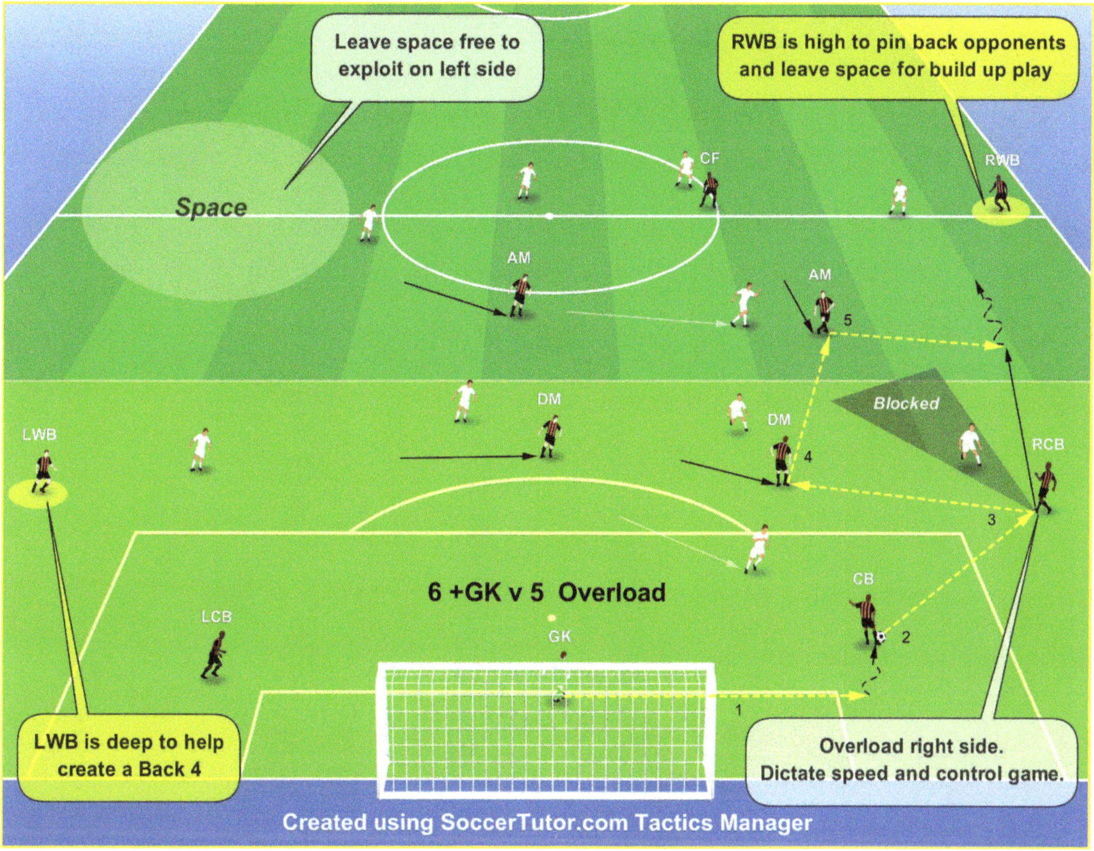

In this tactical example, Bayer Leverkusen are playing against the 4-3-3 formation, and adopt a 4-2-4 build-up shape to build up play from their goal kick.

The left wing back (**LWB**) is deep as part of the back 4 and the right wing back (**RWB**) is pushed high to pin back the opposition and create space for the build up phase.

This approach is **similar to tactics used by Roberto De Zerbi**. It involves 6 players plus the goalkeeper to create a 6 (+GK) v 5 numerical advantage.

When building up from goal kicks, the focus is often on overloading the right side of the pitch, which helps Xabi Alonso's team to break through the press and advance the ball, while dictating the rhythm, speed, and control of the game from the back.

As the **opposing team shifts across to counter this overload**, **space opens on the left side**, ideal for a long switch of play to the left wing back (**LWB**).

Positional Build Up Play Combinations

**Direct from
Xabi Alonso's
Training Sessions**

Xabi Alonso Practices: Positional Build Up Play Combinations

1. Build Up and Breaking Midfield Line End to End Combination Circuit (Variation 1)

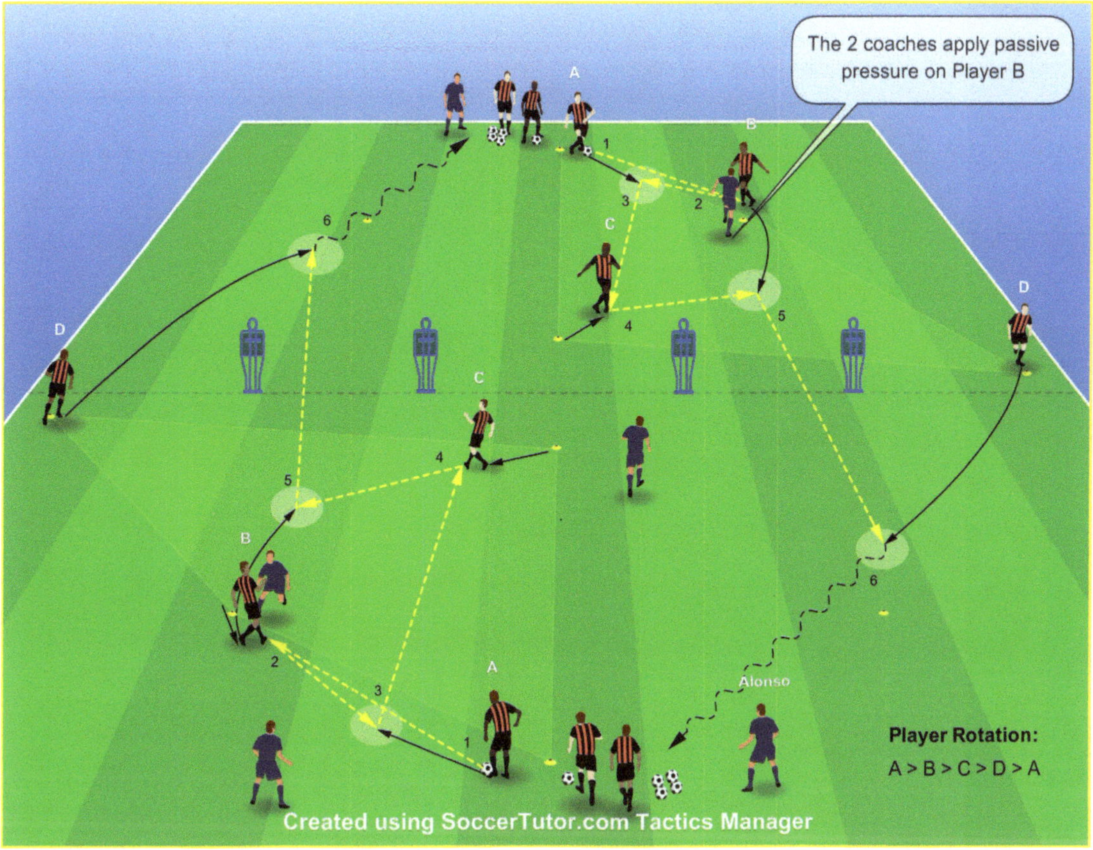

Practice Description

The sequence starts simultaneously with 2 balls (one at each end with player A).

1-2. **A** plays a one-two with **B**. The coach applies passive pressure to **B** to force the return pass back to **A**.

3-4. **A** passes forward to **C**, who moves off the cone to set the ball for the forward movement of **B**.

5. **B** plays a through pass in between the mannequins, weighted for the forward run of **D** in behind the midfield line.

6. **F** receives and dribbles to Position A at the opposite end.

→ The players continuously rotate their positions: A → B → C → D → A.

→ The same sequence is repeated as the next players go.

Source: Xabi Alonso's Bayer Leverkusen training session at Bayer 04 Leverkusen Training Ground - 1st May 2024

©SOCCERTUTOR.COM   XABI ALONSO: PRACTICES DIRECT FROM SESSIONS

Xabi Alonso Practices: Positional Build Up Play Combinations

2. Build Up and Breaking Midfield Line End to End Combination Circuit (Variation 2)

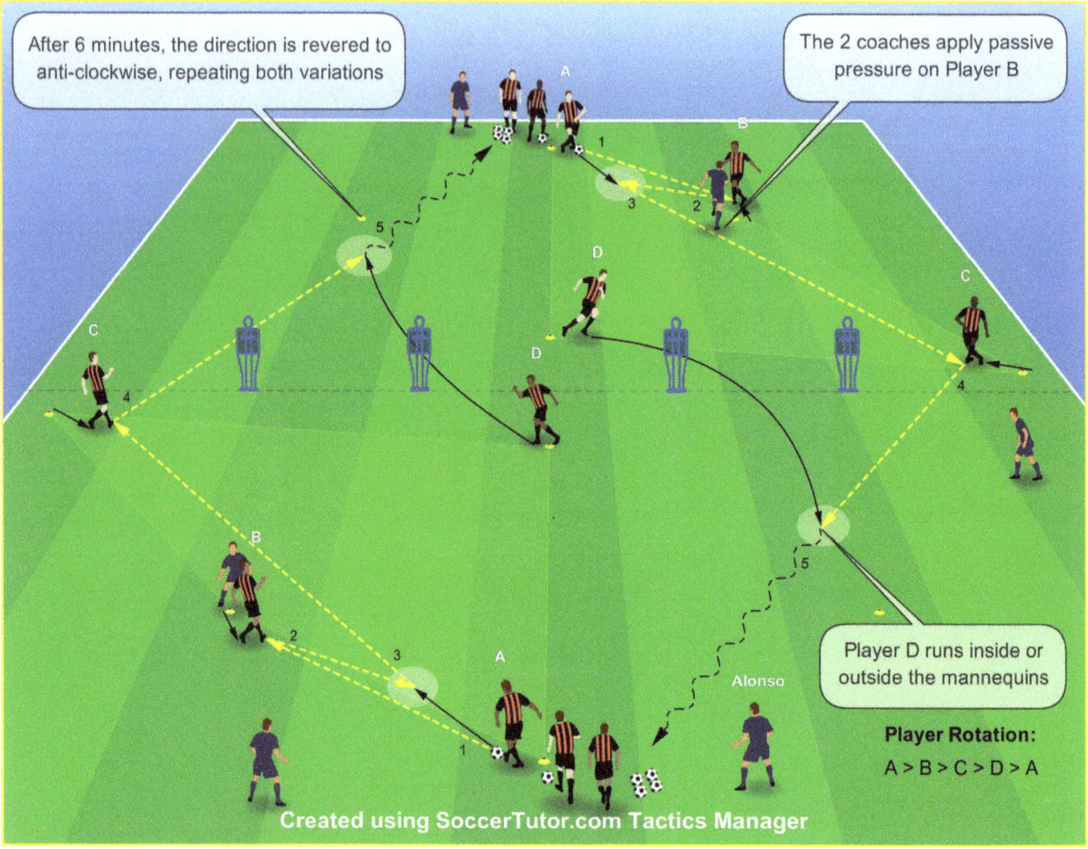

This is a variation of the previous practice.

Practice Description

1-2. **A** plays a one-two with **B**. The coach applies passive pressure to **B** to force the return pass back to **A**.

3-4. **A** passes wide to **C**, who plays in behind the midfield line for the well timed run of **D**.

5. **D** receives and dribbles to <u>Position A</u> at the opposite end.

<u>Note:</u> D can run inside or outside the mannequins to receive C's pass in behind.

→ The players continuously rotate their positions: **A → B → C → D → A**.

→ The same sequence is repeated as the next players go.

→ After 6 minutes, the direction of play is switched to anti-clockwise - the variation on the previous page and this one are repeated in reverse.

Source: Xabi Alonso's Bayer Leverkusen training session at Bayer 04 Leverkusen Training Ground - 1st May 2024

Xabi Alonso Practices: Positional Build Up Play Combinations

3. Build Up Combinations, Through Pass to Break Midfield Line, and Dribble Passing Circuit

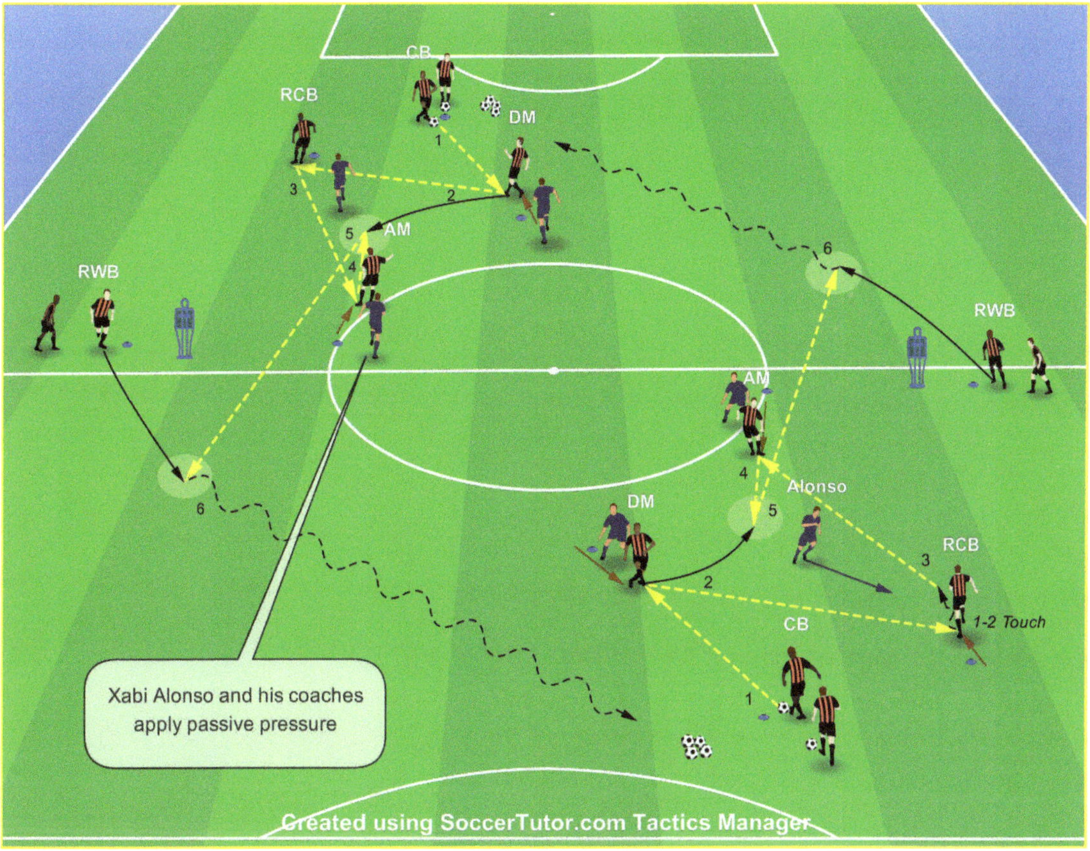

Practice Description

The sequence starts simultaneously with 2 balls (one at each end with CB).

1. **CB** passes to **DM** and the coach applies passive pressure from behind.
2-3. **DM** passes to **RCB** and another coach applies pressure. **RCB** uses 1 touch to receive and another to pass to **AM**.
4. **AM** also has a coach applying pressure from behind, so sets the ball for **DM**.
5. **DM** plays a through pass into the other half of the pitch (breaking midfield line), weighted for the forward run of **RWB**.
6. **RWB** receives the pass and dribbles to Position CB at the opposite end.

→ The players rotate their positions: **CB → DM → RCB → AM → RWB → CB.**

→ The same sequence is repeated as the next players go.

Source: Xabi Alonso's Bayer Leverkusen training session at Bayer 04 Leverkusen Training Ground - 2024

4. Build Up Play Combinations and Breaking Midfield Line (Through Pass) Circuit

Practice Description

The sequence starts simultaneously with 2 balls (one at each end with CB).

1. **CB** passes to **DM** and the coach applies passive pressure from behind.
2-3. **DM** passes to **LCB** and a coach applies passive pressure. **LCB** uses 1 touch to receive and another to pass to **AM**.
4. **AM** also has a coach applying pressure from behind, so sets the ball for **DM**.
5. **DM** plays a through pass into the other half of the pitch (breaking midfield line), weighted for the forward run of **LWB**.
6. In contrast to the previous variation, **LWB** passes first time to Position CB at the opposite end (instead of dribbling).

→ The players rotate their positions:
CB → DM → LCB → AM → LWB → CB.

→ The same sequence is repeated as the next players go.

Source: Xabi Alonso's Bayer Leverkusen training session at Bayer 04 Leverkusen Training Ground - 2024

Xabi Alonso Practices: Positional Build Up Play Combinations

5. Build Up Combinations, Switch Play, and Give & Go to Break Midfield Line Passing Circuit

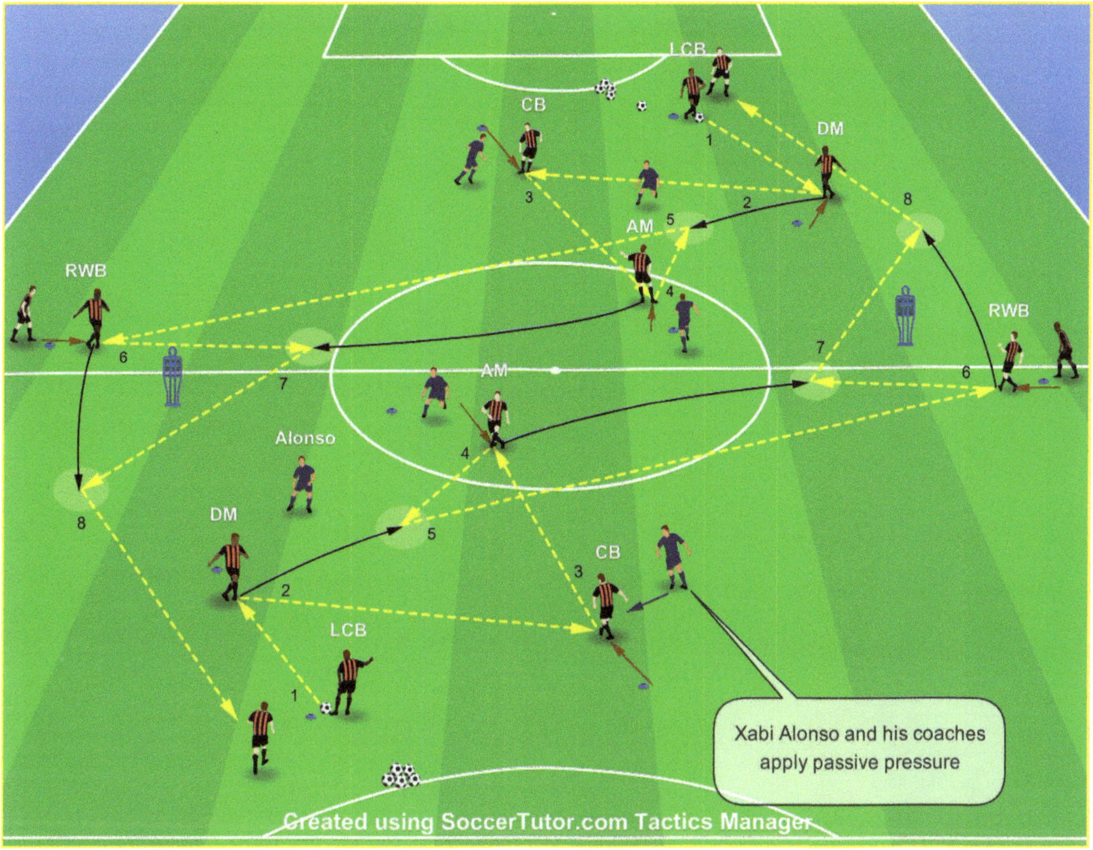

Xabi Alonso and his coaches apply passive pressure

Practice Description

The sequence starts simultaneously with 2 balls (one at each end with LCB).

1-2. LCB passes to **DM**, who passes across to **CB**. The coach applies pressure.

3-4. CB passes forward to **AM** and another coach applies pressure from behind. **AM** sets the ball back for **DM** to move onto.

5. DM switches play with a pass to **RWB** in front of the mannequin.

6-7. RWB plays a give & go with **AM** (who shifts across) and receives back after moving around the mannequin.

8. RWB passes to Position **LCB** at the opposite end to complete the sequence.

→ The players rotate their positions: **LCB** → **DM** → **CB** → **AM** → **RWB** → **LCB**.

→ The same sequence is repeated as the next players go.

Source: Xabi Alonso's Bayer Leverkusen preseason training session in Donaueschingen, Germany - 29th July 2024

Xabi Alonso Practices: Positional Build Up Play Combinations

6. Build Up and Break Midfield Line Passing Circuit with Pressing Variations (1)

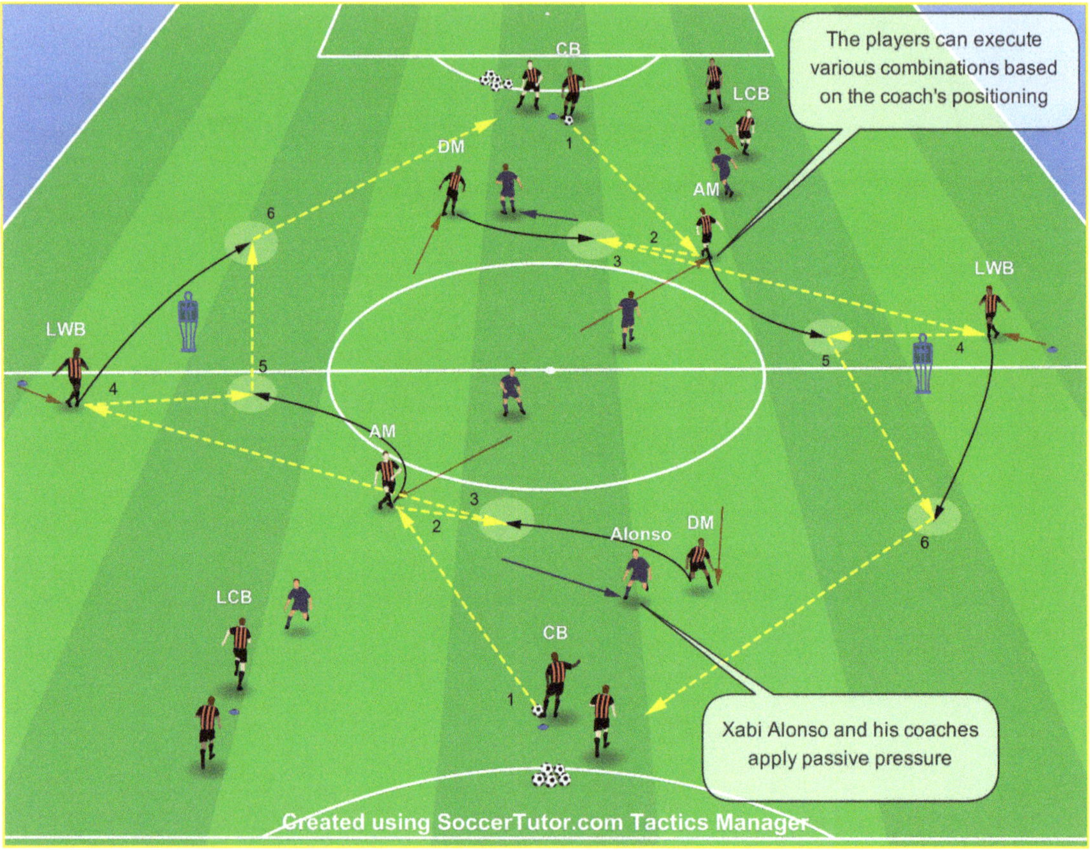

The players can execute various combinations based on the coach's positioning

Xabi Alonso and his coaches apply passive pressure

Practice Description

In this progression of the previous practices, players execute combinations based on the type of pressing applied by the coaches.

1-2. The coach blocks the pass to **DM**, so **CB** passes to **AM**, and then **DM** moves to receive the next pass.

3-6. **DM** passes wide to **LWB**, who plays a give & go with **AM**, then passes to Position CB at the opposite end.

→ The players rotate their positions: **CB → DM → LCB → AM → LWB → CB**.

→ The next players go.

→ Many different combinations are observed and 2 more examples are shown on the next page.

Source: Xabi Alonso's Bayer Leverkusen training session at Bayer 04 Leverkusen Training Ground - 2nd Dec 2022

Xabi Alonso Practices: Positional Build Up Play Combinations

7. Build Up and Break Midfield Line Passing Circuit with Pressing Variations (2)

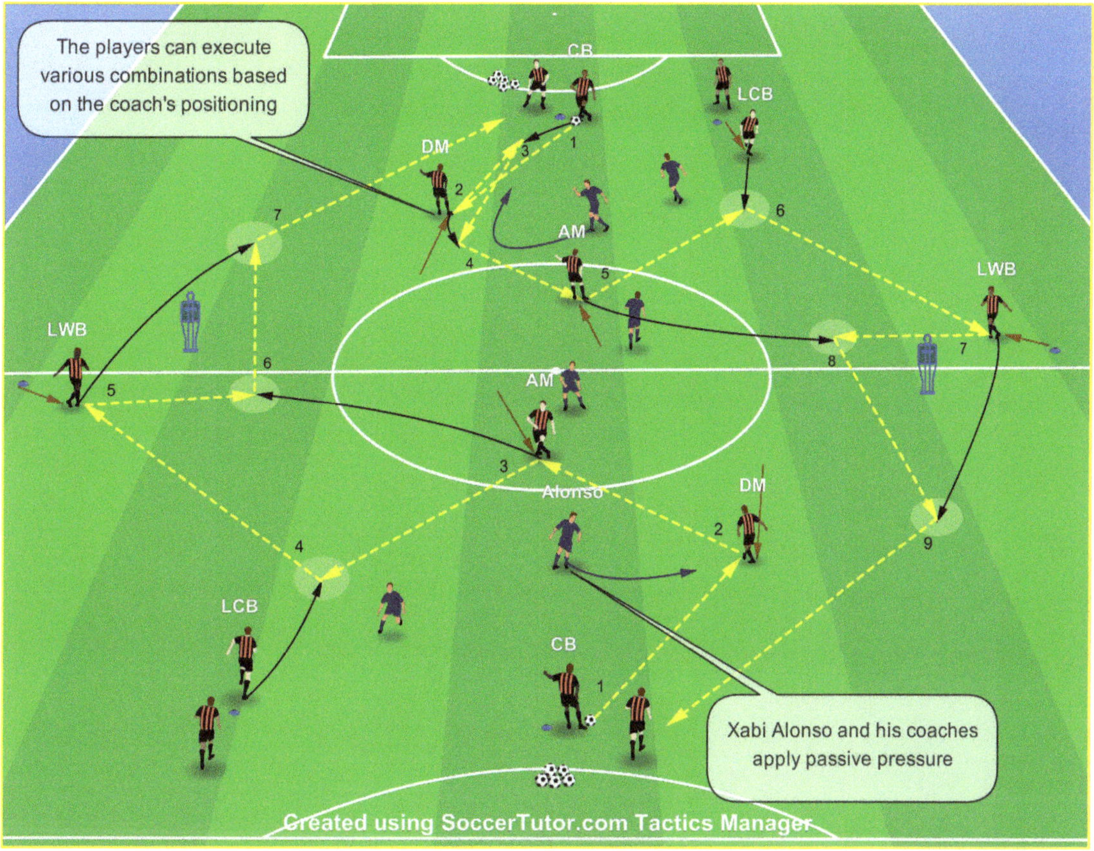

The players can execute various combinations based on the coach's positioning

Xabi Alonso and his coaches apply passive pressure

Practice Description

This diagram shows 2 variations of the practice on the previous page.

BOTTOM 1-2. **Alonso** blocks the pass to **AM**, so **CB** passes to **DM**, who then passes to **AM**.

3-4. **AM** passes back for **LCB** to move forward onto and pass wide to **LWB**.

5-7. **LWB** plays a give & go with **AM**, then passes to Position CB at opposite end.

TOP 1-4. The coach presses with a curved movement, which forces **CB** and **DM** to play 4 passes to move the ball to **AM**.

5-6. **AM** passes back for **LCB** to move forward onto and pass wide to **LWB**.

7-9. **LWB** plays a give & go with **AM**, then passes to Position CB at opposite end.

→ The players rotate their positions:
CB → DM → LCB → AM → LWB → CB.

→ The next players go.

Source: Xabi Alonso's Bayer Leverkusen training session at Bayer 04 Leverkusen Training Ground - 2nd Dec 2022

Xabi Alonso Practices: Positional Build Up Play Combinations

8. Positional Build Up / Combinations Through Blocked Lanes Passing Circuit (Variation 1)

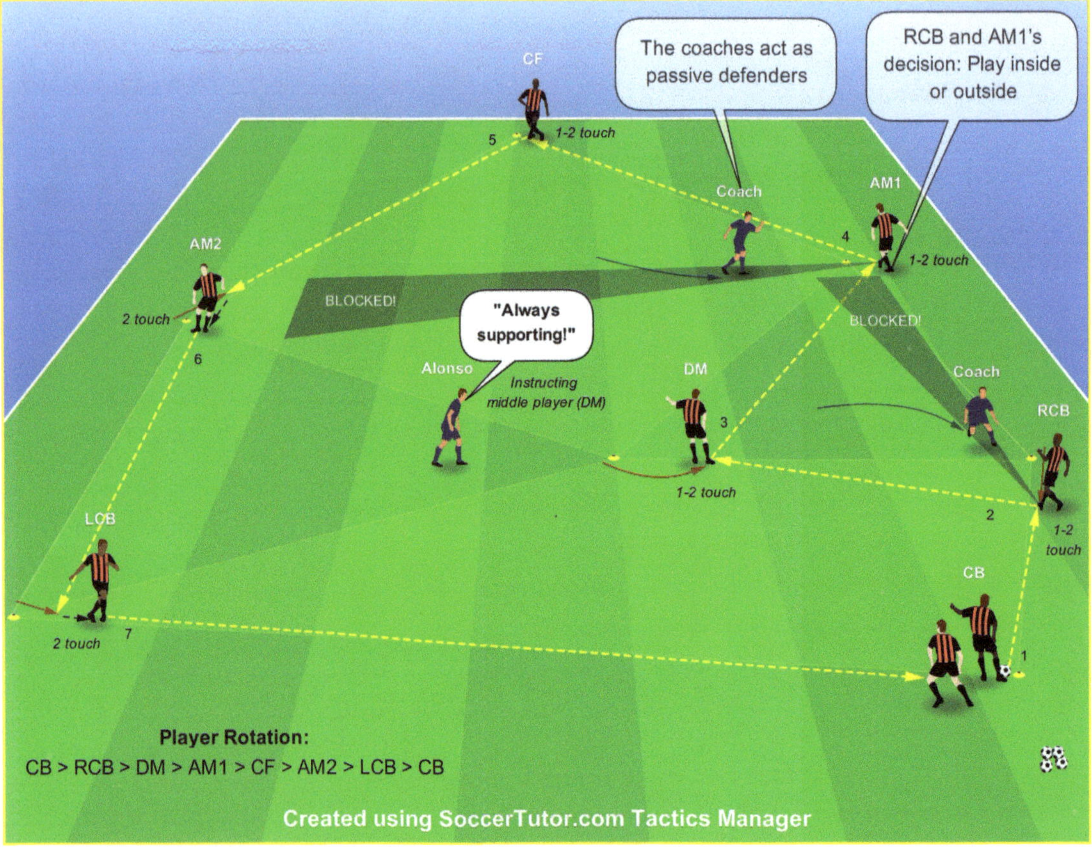

The **Positional Roles** are 3 centre backs (LCB, CB, & RCB), 1 defensive midfielder (DM), 2 attacking midfielders (AM), and the centre forward (CF) from Bayer's 3-4-2-1.

Practice Description

1. **CB** passes to **RCB** and a coach presses in a way that blocks the pass to **AM1**.

2-4. **RCB** passes inside to **DM**, who shifts to meet the pass, and passes to **AM1**. **AM1** is pressed by a coach which blocks a switch of play pass, so he passes to **CF**.

5-7. **CF** passes to **AM2**, who passes back to **LCB**. **LCB** passes to the next player waiting at <u>Position CB</u>.

→ The same sequence is repeated as the players rotate their positions: **CB** → **RCB** → **DM** → **AM1** → **CF** → **AM2** → **LCB** → **CB**.

Key Point: **DM** acts as a link player to move the ball to **AM1** to play around the blocked passing lane.

Source: Xabi Alonso's Bayer Leverkusen training session at Bayer 04 Leverkusen Training Ground - 2nd Dec 2022

Xabi Alonso Practices: Positional Build Up Play Combinations

9. Positional Build Up / Combinations Through Blocked Lanes Passing Circuit (Variation 2)

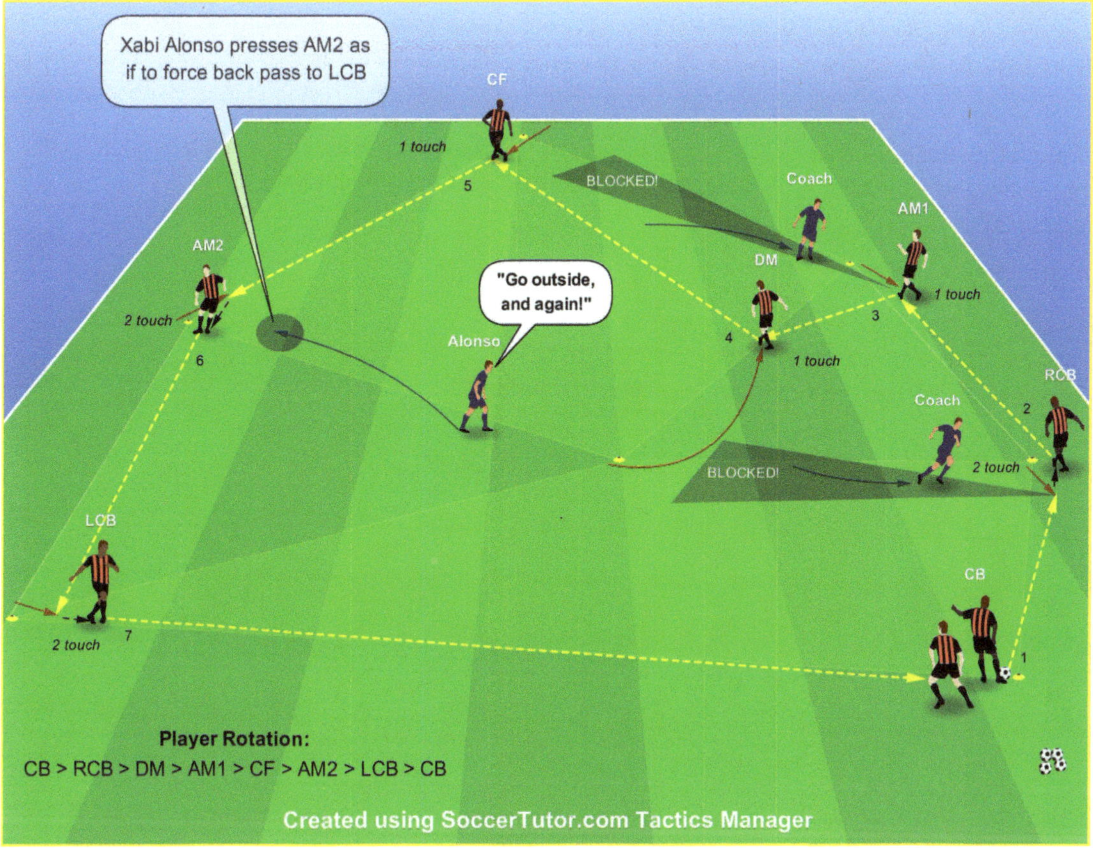

*The **Positional Roles** are 3 centre backs (LCB, CB, & RCB), 1 defensive midfielder (DM), 2 attacking midfielders (AM), and the centre forward (CF) from Bayer's 3-4-2-1.*

Practice Description

1. CB passes to **RCB** and a coach presses in a way that blocks the inside pass to **DM**.

2-4. RCB passes forward to **AM1**, who is also pressed to block a pass to **CF**. **AM1** sets the ball for **DM's** forward movement, who then passes to **CF**.

5-7. CF passes to **AM2** (pressed by **Alonso**), who passes back to **LCB**. **LCB** passes to the next player waiting at Position CB.

→ The same sequence is repeated as the players rotate their positions: **CB → RCB → DM → AM1 → CF → AM2 → LCB → CB**.

Key Point: AM1 acts as a link player to move the ball to **DM**, and **DM** acts as a link player to move the ball to **CF**.

Source: Xabi Alonso's Bayer Leverkusen training session at Bayer 04 Leverkusen Training Ground - 2nd Dec 2022

Xabi Alonso Practices: Positional Build Up Play Combinations

10. Positional Build Up / Combinations Through Blocked Lanes Passing Circuit (Variation 3)

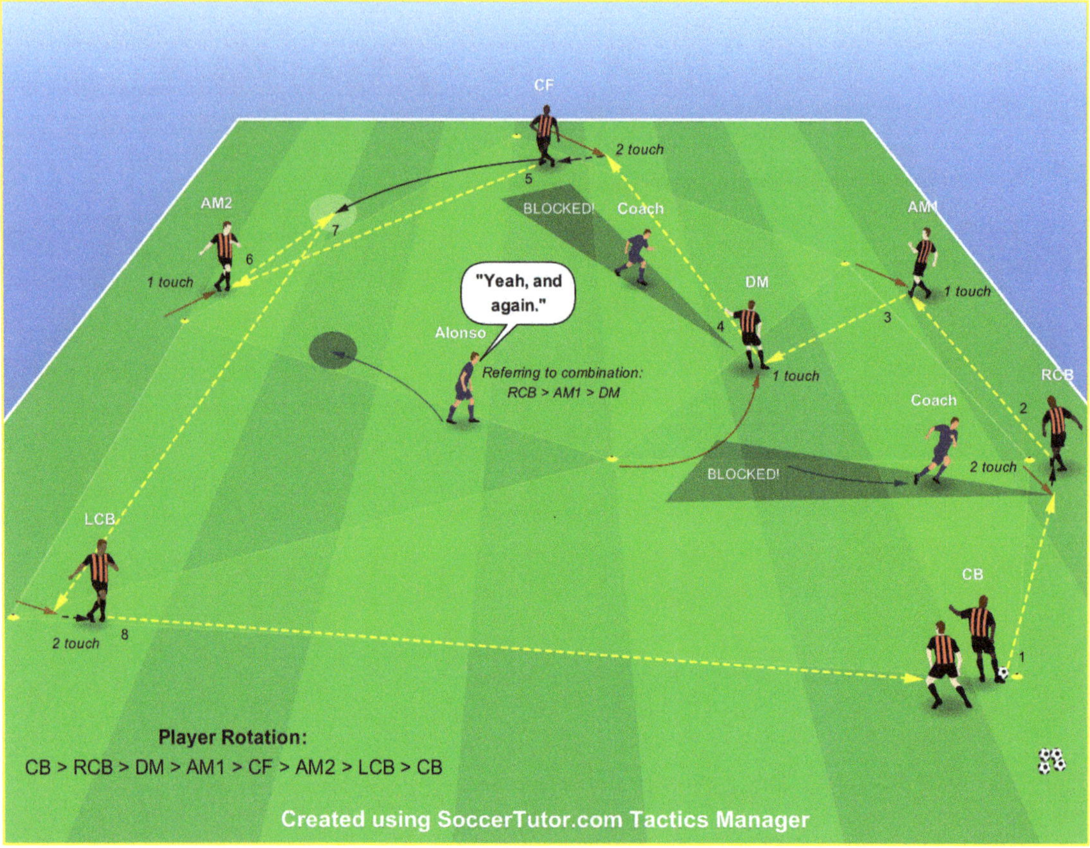

The **Positional Roles** are 3 centre backs (LCB, CB, & RCB), 1 defensive midfielder (DM), 2 attacking midfielders (AM), and the centre forward (CF) from Bayer's 3-4-2-1.

Practice Description

1. **CB** passes to **RCB** and a coach presses in a way that blocks the inside pass to **DM**.

2-3. **RCB** passes forward to **AM1**, who sets the ball for **DM's** forward movement. **DM** is pressed by the coach blocking the direct passing lane to **CF**. To solve this, **CF** moves across to create an angle to receive a forward pass.

4-8. **DM** passes to **CF**, who receives and then plays a one-two with **AM2**, before passing to **LCB**. **LCB** passes to the next player waiting at Position CB.

→ The same sequence is repeated as the players rotate their positions: **CB → RCB → DM → AM1 → CF → AM2 → LCB → CB**.

Source: Xabi Alonso's Bayer Leverkusen training session at Bayer 04 Leverkusen Training Ground - 2nd Dec 2022

Xabi Alonso Practices: Positional Build Up Play Combinations

11. Positional Build Up / Combinations Through Blocked Lanes Passing Circuit (Variation 4)

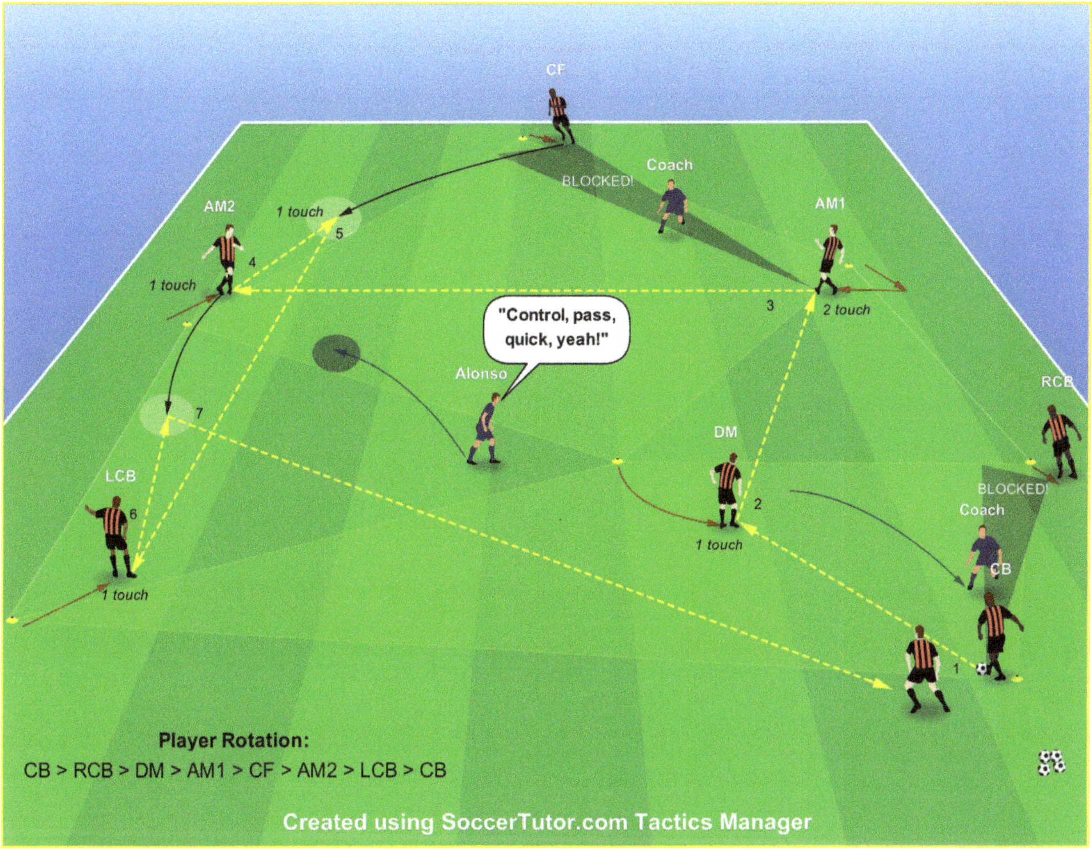

Player Rotation:
CB > RCB > DM > AM1 > CF > AM2 > LCB > CB

*The **Positional Roles** are 3 centre backs (LCB, CB, & RCB), 1 defensive midfielder (DM), 2 attacking midfielders (AM), and the centre forward (CF) from Bayer's 3-4-2-1.*

Practice Description

1. As the coach presses in a way that blocks the pass to **RCB**, **CB** passes to **DM**, who then plays forward to **AM1**.

2-3. The coach presses to block the pass to **CF**, so **AM1** passes across to **AM2**.

4-5. **AM2** sets the ball for **CF's** movement and he passes to **LCB**.

6-7. **LCB** sets the ball for **AM2's** movement and he passes to the next player waiting at Position CB.

→ The same sequence is repeated as the players rotate their positions: **CB → RCB → DM → AM1 → CF → AM2 → LCB → CB**.

Source: Xabi Alonso's Bayer Leverkusen training session at Bayer 04 Leverkusen Training Ground - 2nd Dec 2022

Xabi Alonso Practices: Positional Build Up Play Combinations

12. Positional Build Up / Combinations Through Blocked Lanes Passing Circuit (Variation 5)

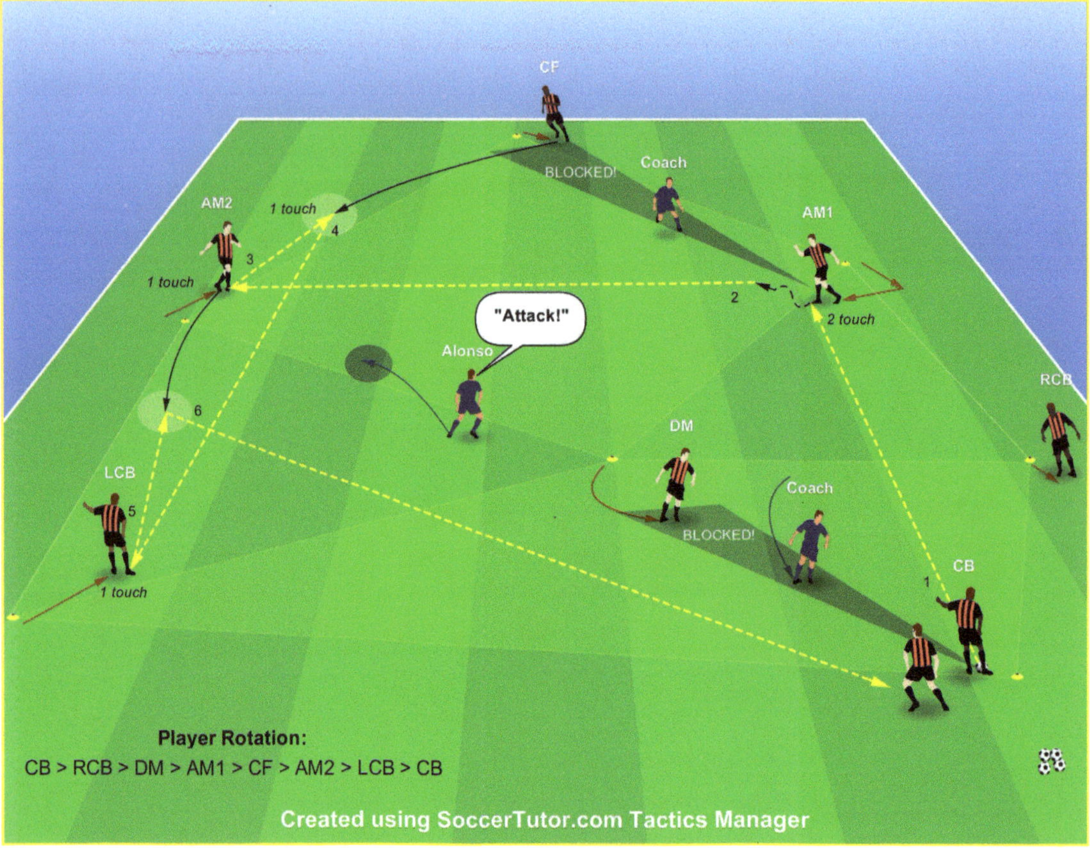

Player Rotation:
CB > RCB > DM > AM1 > CF > AM2 > LCB > CB

The **Positional Roles** are 3 centre backs (LCB, CB, & RCB), 1 defensive midfielder (DM), 2 attacking midfielders (AM), and the centre forward (CF) from Bayer's 3-4-2-1.

Practice Description

1. **CB** passes direct to **AM1** with the coach blocking the simple pass to **DM**.

2. Another coach presses to block the pass to **CF**, so **AM1** receives and passes across the area to **AM2**.

3-4. **AM2** sets the ball for **CF's** movement and he passes to **LCB**.

5-6. **LCB** sets the ball for **AM2's** movement and he passes to the next player waiting at Position CB.

→ The same sequence is repeated as the players rotate their positions: **CB → RCB → DM → AM1 → CF → AM2 → LCB → CB.**

Source: Xabi Alonso's Bayer Leverkusen training session at Bayer 04 Leverkusen Training Ground - 2nd Dec 2022

Xabi Alonso Practices: Positional Build Up Play Combinations

13. Positional Build Up / Combinations Through Blocked Lanes Passing Circuit (Variation 6)

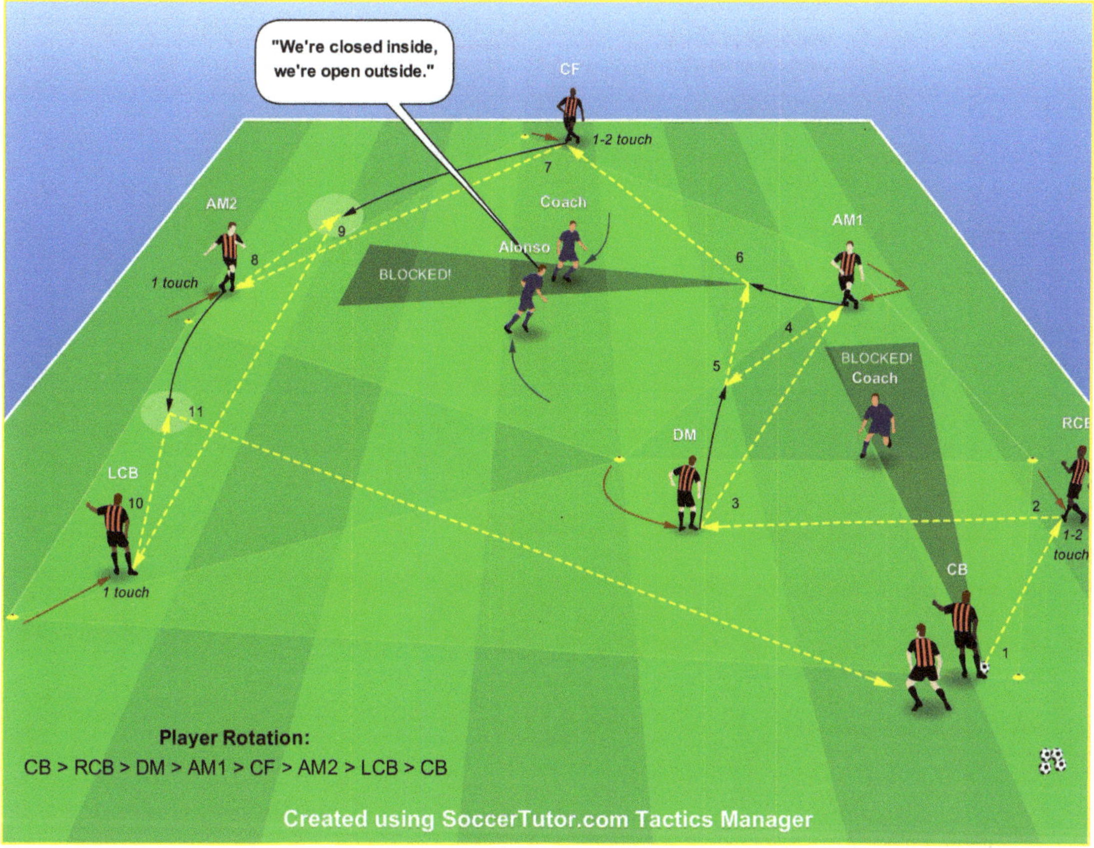

The **Positional Roles** are 3 centre backs (LCB, CB, & RCB), 1 defensive midfielder (DM), 2 attacking midfielders (AM), and the centre forward (CF) from Bayer's 3-4-2-1.

Practice Description

1-2. The coach is blocking the pass to **AM1**. **CB** passes to **RCB**, who then passes inside to **DM** as the coach approaches.

3-5. **DM** then has the space to play a 3 pass combination with **AM1**, as shown.

6. With the pass across to **AM2** blocked by 2 coaches, **AM1** passes to **CF**.

7-9. **CF** plays a one-two with **AM2** and then passes to **LCB**.

10-11. **LCB** sets the ball for **AM2's** movement and he passes to the next player waiting at Position CB.

→ The same sequence is repeated as the players rotate their positions: **CB → RCB → DM → AM1 → CF → AM2 → LCB → CB**.

Source: Xabi Alonso's Bayer Leverkusen training session at Bayer 04 Leverkusen Training Ground - 2nd Dec 2022

Xabi Alonso Practices: Positional Build Up Play Combinations

14. Positional Build Up / Combinations Through Blocked Lanes Passing Circuit (Variation 7)

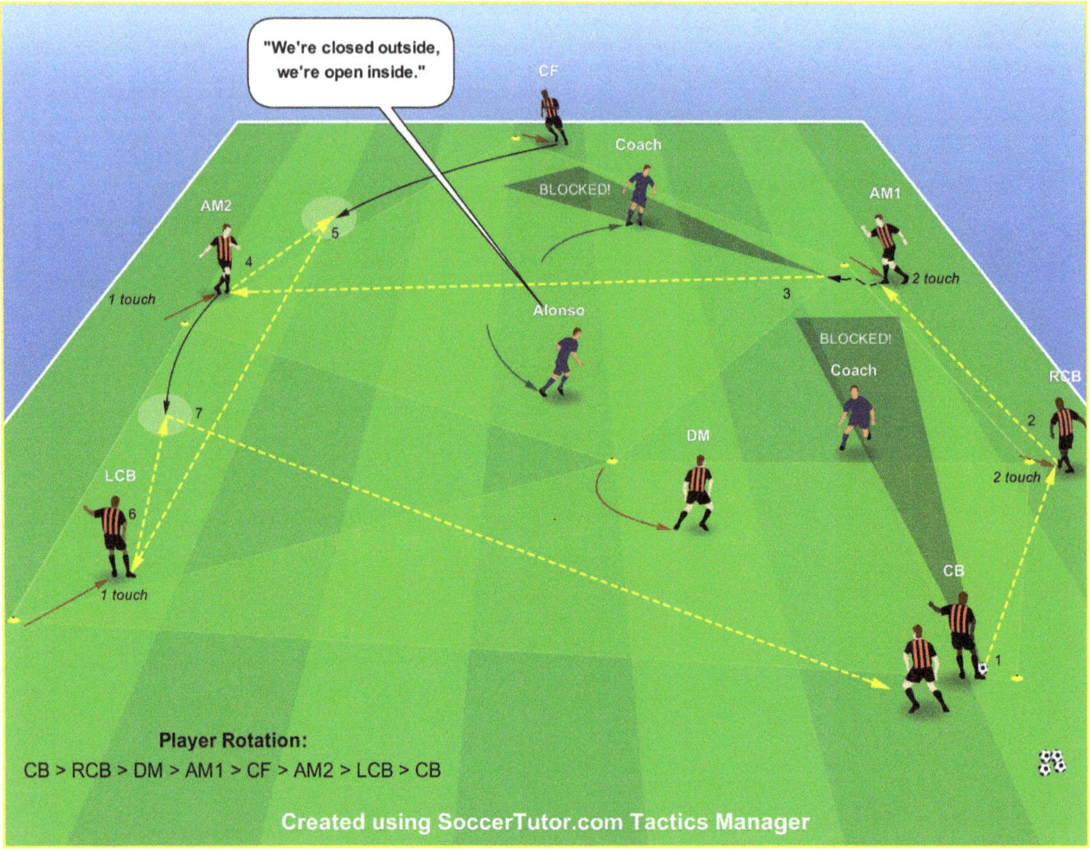

"We're closed outside, we're open inside."

Player Rotation:
CB > RCB > DM > AM1 > CF > AM2 > LCB > CB

*The **Positional Roles** are 3 centre backs (LCB, CB, & RCB), 1 defensive midfielder (DM), 2 attacking midfielders (AM), and the centre forward (CF) from Bayer's 3-4-2-1.*

Practice Description

1-2. The coach is blocking the direct pass to **AM1**, so **CB** uses **RCB** as a link player to move the ball forward to **AM1** instead.

3. The coach presses to block the pass to **CF**, so **AM1** receives and passes to **AM2**.

4-5. AM2 sets the ball for **CF's** movement and he passes to **LCB**.

6-7. LCB sets the ball for **AM2's** movement and he passes to the next player waiting at <u>Position CB</u>.

→ The same sequence is repeated as the players rotate their positions: **CB → RCB → DM → AM1 → CF → AM2 → LCB → CB**.

Source: Xabi Alonso's Bayer Leverkusen training session at Bayer 04 Leverkusen Training Ground - 2nd Dec 2022

Xabi Alonso's Bayer Leverkusen: Possession and Midfield Control Tactics

Xabi Alonso's Bayer Leverkusen: Possession and Midfield Control Tactics

Possession and Midfield Control

"If you have control of the midfield, you have control of the game, and you have more chances to win. If you win the midfield, you probably win the game."

Xabi Alonso

Xabi Alonso's Bayer Leverkusen 3-2-5 Possession Phase Shape

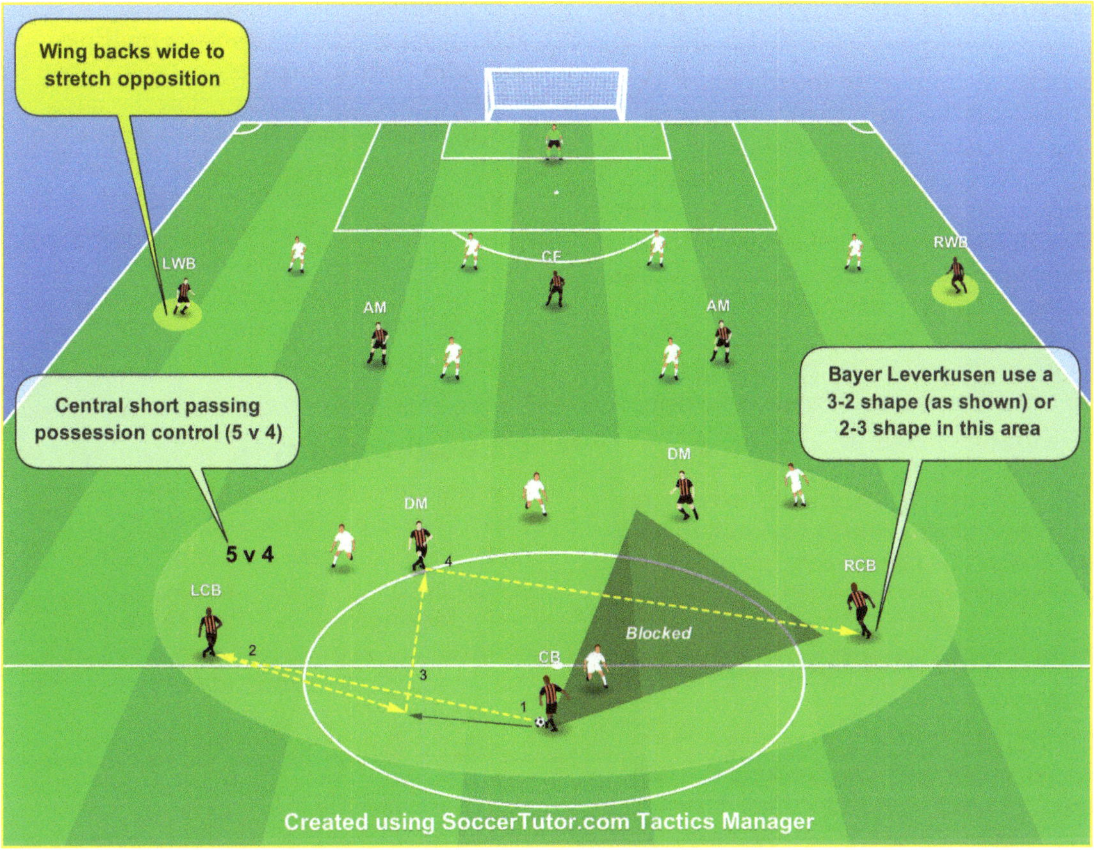

Xabi Alonso's **Bayer Leverkusen often adopt a 3-2 (shown) or 2-3 shape in central areas**, enabling them to maintain short passing possession with a 5v4 numerical advantage. This example shown is against the 4-2-3-1 formation.

The **wing backs position themselves high and wide**, pinning back the opposition and creating space in the centre to enhance possession control and progress play.

During the possession phase, **Alonso emphasises central control** by grouping many players in midfield, creating dense passing networks and shortening the length of passes.

This central dominance limits the opposition's ability to press effectively, allowing Bayer to dominate the game.

In this example, **short passes are used to maintain possession and easily move the ball to the free player** (RCB).

The pages to follow show how the ball is progressed.

The Tempo and Rhythm of Bayer Leverkusen's Possession Play

Controlling the Rhythm of Play

Xabi Alonso's Bayer Leverkusen team are experts at controlling the tempo of a game. This allows the team to mix measured and calculated build up play with sudden, explosive bursts of speed. This **keeps opponents on the back foot and enables Leverkusen to dictate the rhythm/flow of the game** with precision. Their possession based strategy is designed to craft the most effective attacking opportunities, whether it's advancing systematically up the pitch or quickly exploiting open spaces on the opposite flank. By carefully orchestrating when to slow down the play and when to speed up, **Leverkusen maximise their chances to break through defensive lines** and create scoring opportunities.

Overloads and Controlling the Tempo

Central to Xabi Alonso's tactics is the **clever use of overloads around the ball area**, where players concentrate near the ball to disrupt the opposition's defensive positioning and organisation. This approach is not just about moving the ball forward, it is about methodically creating space for an attack. By keeping possession and drawing opponents out of their positions/shape, Leverkusen patiently wait for the ideal moment to increase the tempo and launch an attack.

Creating and Exploiting Space

Xabi Alonso's strategy of overloads around the ball area is highly effective in forcing opponents to commit more defenders to a concentrated area, thereby disrupting their defensive balance. By **drawing multiple defenders into a single zone**, Leverkusen create opportunities to **exploit the gaps that inevitably form elsewhere on the pitch**. This tactic is especially effective when combined with their precise, high-tempo passing, which allows them to quickly transition from congested areas into open spaces. As they disrupt their opponent's structure, the team can then quickly progress the ball and launch effective attacks.

Tactical Security

Leverkusen's effectiveness comes from their disciplined execution Xabi Alonso's tactics. Each player is aware of their role in both the build up, possession, and attacking phases of the game. By controlling the tempo and rhythm and drawing opponents outside of their shape, they can quickly progress controlled possession into potent attacks.

Xabi Alonso's Bayer Leverkusen: Possession and Midfield Control Tactics

Xabi Alonso's Bayer Leverkusen Midfield Control (3-2-5)

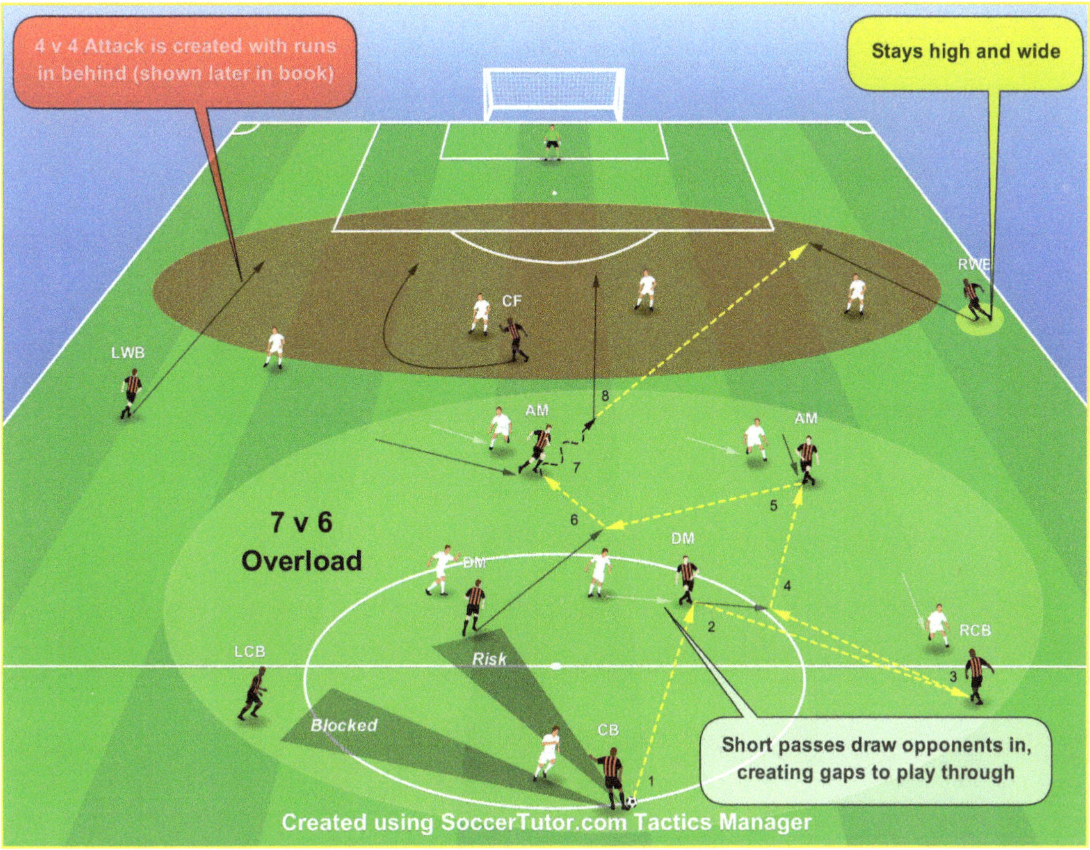

In this example, **Bayer Leverkusen create a 7 v 6 overload in the central area** against a 4-2-3-1 formation. They use short passes to draw opponents in and open gaps for advancing the play.

The right wing back (**RWB**) remains high and wide to help pin back the opposition's defence and leave space in the centre.

Central areas are key for Xabi Alonso's possession phase tactics, **focusing on quick passes that draw the opposition into pressing**. As defenders commit, gaps are created which enable Bayer Leverkusen to thread passes to **progress the ball and create advantageous attacking situations**, like this 4 v 4 attack situation created here.

This possession strategy is about quick, short passes that draw the opposition in, which open up spaces to exploit.

Note: Use of correct body shape ensures safer passes and encourages further pressing from opponents, creating more opportunities to exploit.

Xabi Alonso's Bayer Leverkusen: Possession and Midfield Control Tactics

Body Shape and Spatial Awareness in Bayer Leverkusen's Possession (3-2-5)

1. Body Shape and Positioning to Play "Bounce" Passes

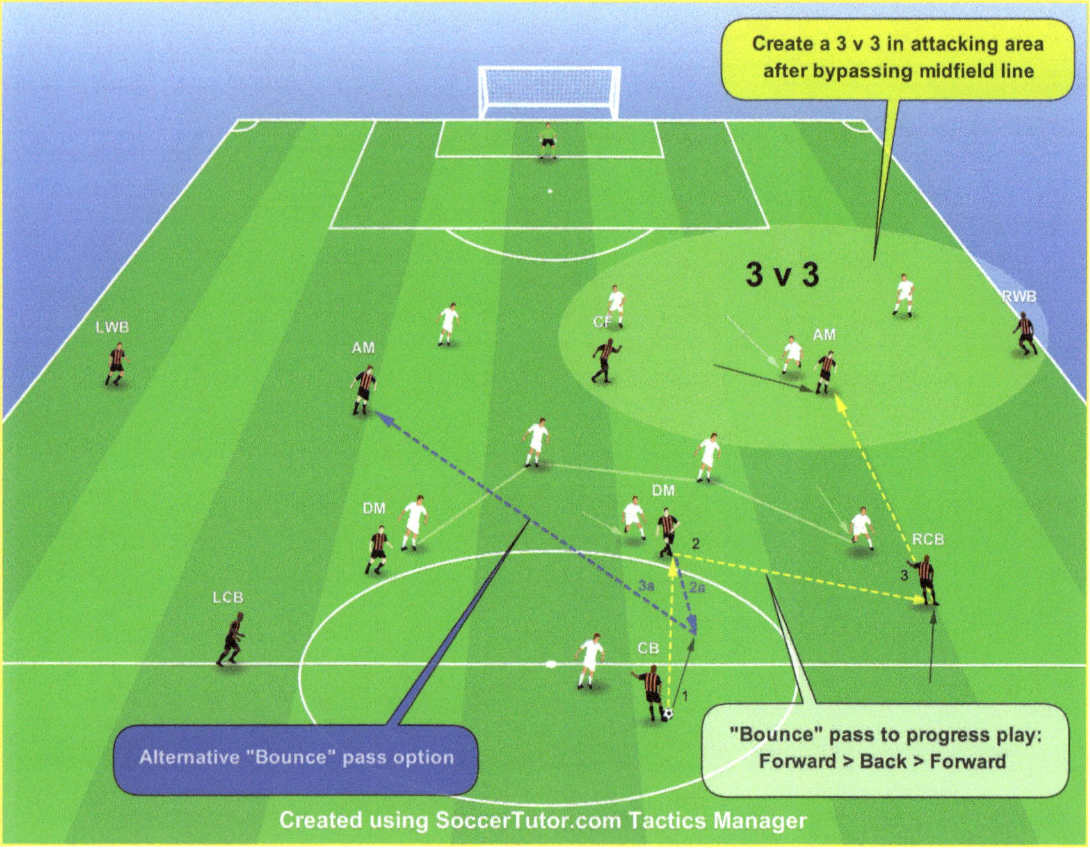

A key aspect of Bayer Leverkusen's possession play is their players' body shape, ensuring they face the ball for quick and effective passes.

In addition, they **often use "bounce" passes to progress the play**, as shown in the diagram: Forward → Back → Forward.

The defender (**CB** in diagram example) passes to a defensive midfielder (**DM**), who then plays it back to a defender.

This **creates new angles to advance the ball to an attacking player**, exploiting gaps left by defenders who are drawn in to follow their direct opponents.

It disrupts the opposition's balance and enables a **smooth transition from the defensive line into attack**. In this example, a 3v3 is created on the right flank after bypassing the midfield. An alternative is also shown with the blue arrow line.

XABI ALONSO: PRACTICES DIRECT FROM SESSIONS

Xabi Alonso's Bayer Leverkusen: Possession and Midfield Control Tactics

2. Body Shape and Awareness to Break Midfield Line

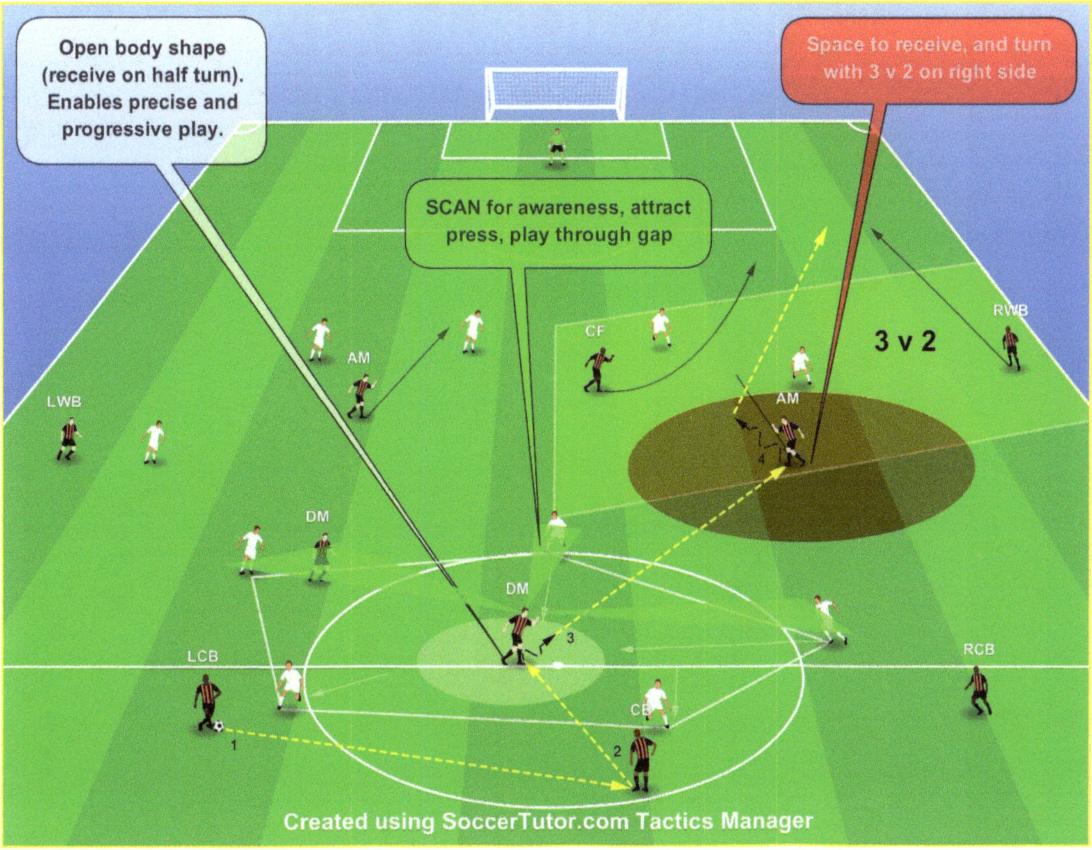

The diagram example shows how Xabi Alonso's Bayer Leverkusen players maintain an **open body shape**, receiving on the half-turn to enable precise, progressive play. They **scan the pitch and player positions before receiving the ball**, which helps them **attract the press and then exploit gaps by playing through their opponent's lines**. This approach highlights the crucial link between body shape, spatial awareness, and breaking lines.

Under pressure, the Bayer Leverkusen players are able to **turn and play forward**. They first always make sure to at least keep possession, and secondly look to progress the team forward.

The midfielders' **composure and ability to play in pockets of space is key** to success. In this example, the defensive midfielder (**DM**) is able to receive and turn while drawing in his opponents' pressing.

From there, the **DM** breaks the midfield line of pressure to pass to the attacking midfielder (**AM**) between the midfield and defensive lines. The **AM has space to receive (red highlighted area)** and Bayer have a **3 v 2 overload on the right flank**, which is an advantageous attacking situation to exploit. The right wing back (**RWB**) is always looking to make runs in behind the defensive line.

XABI ALONSO: PRACTICES DIRECT FROM SESSIONS

Xabi Alonso's Bayer Leverkusen: Possession and Midfield Control Tactics

Creating Overload on Right Side of Pitch and then Switching Play (4-2-4)

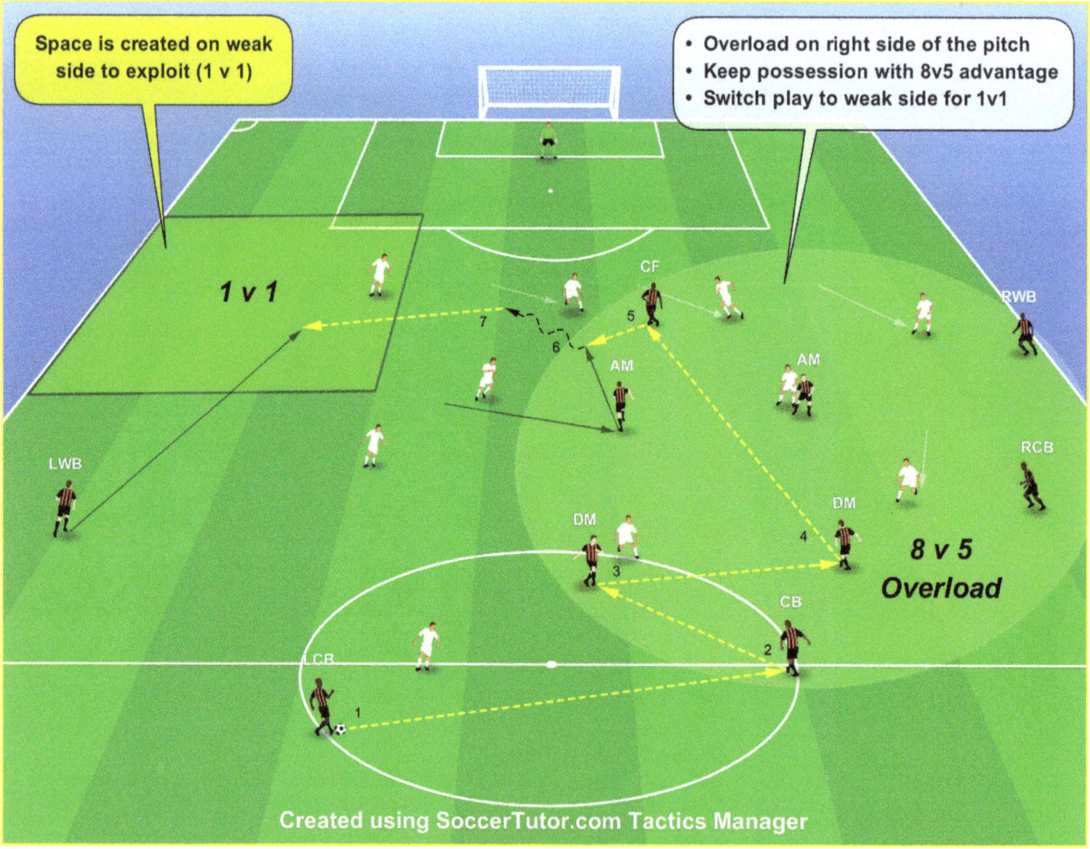

![tactics diagram]

- Space is created on weak side to exploit (1 v 1)
- Overload on right side of the pitch
- Keep possession with 8v5 advantage
- Switch play to weak side for 1v1

Creating an overload on the right side of the pitch is a key element of Xabi Alonso and Bayer Leverkusen's possession phase tactics.

In this example, Bayer are in a 4-2-4 shape vs the 4-2-3-1. Space is created between opposing midfielders as they are drawn to one side of the pitch where Bayer have an 8v5 overload to progress the ball through open gaps. By **overloading one side, they free up space on the opposite flank (weak side)** for a potential 1v1 situation.

In this situation where the **opponents are forced out of their defensive shape**, forward passing lanes begin to appear.

In this example, the defensive midfielder (**DM**) is able to play a long ground pass into the feet of the centre forward (**CF**). From there, the team effectively move the ball to the left wing back (**RWB**) in a 1v1 situation, via the forward run of the attacking midfielder (**AM**).

Xabi Alonso's Bayer Leverkusen Progression from Possession to Attack

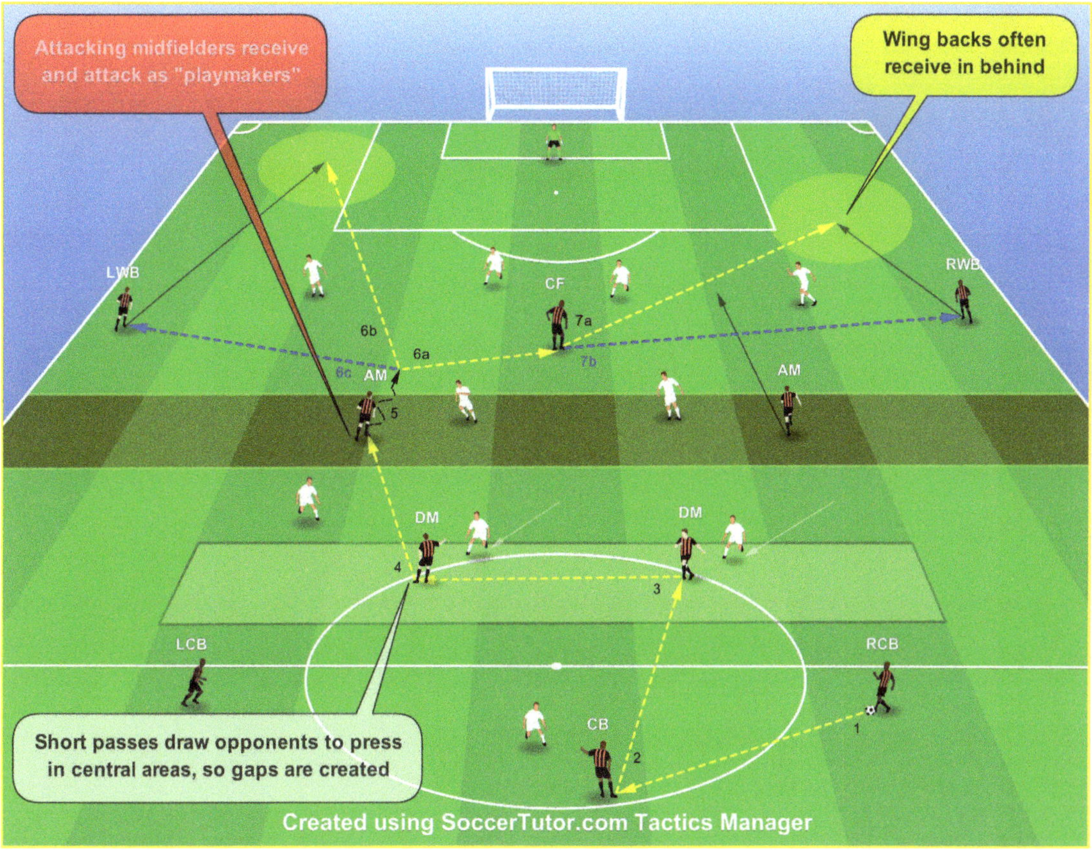

Bayer Leverkusen use short quick passes in central areas to draw opponents into pressing, creating gaps which can then be exploited to progress the play forward.

As these gaps open, the defensive midfielders (**DM**) pass to the attacking players.

In this example, Bayer are in a 3-2-5 shape vs the 4-2-3-1. **After bypassing the line of 3, the attacking midfielders (AM) act as playmakers**, either driving forward with the ball, or passing to their teammates.

In this example, we show the different options **AM** has when he receives. These include passing to the left wing back's (**LWB**) feet or in behind and passing short for the centre forward (**CF**) to carry on the attack.

In addition, it is also possible for the **CF** to make a run in behind to receive a through pass from **AM**.

Positional Possession Games

**Direct from
Xabi Alonso's
Training Sessions**

Xabi Alonso Practices: Positional Possession Games

Possession

"Possession football is not about keeping the ball for the sake of it. It's about patience, precision, and creating the right opportunities to break down the opposition."

Xabi Alonso

Xabi Alonso Practices: Positional Possession Games

1. Pass Through Central Gate 4v4 (+3) Positional Possession Game

Diagram annotations:
- **3** If Blues win the ball, switch roles with Reds
- **2** Aim is to keep possession and play the ball through the 2 white cones (gate)
- All players 1-2 touches
- **1** 3 Jokers play with team in possession (1 at each end + 1 in middle)
- 4v4+3

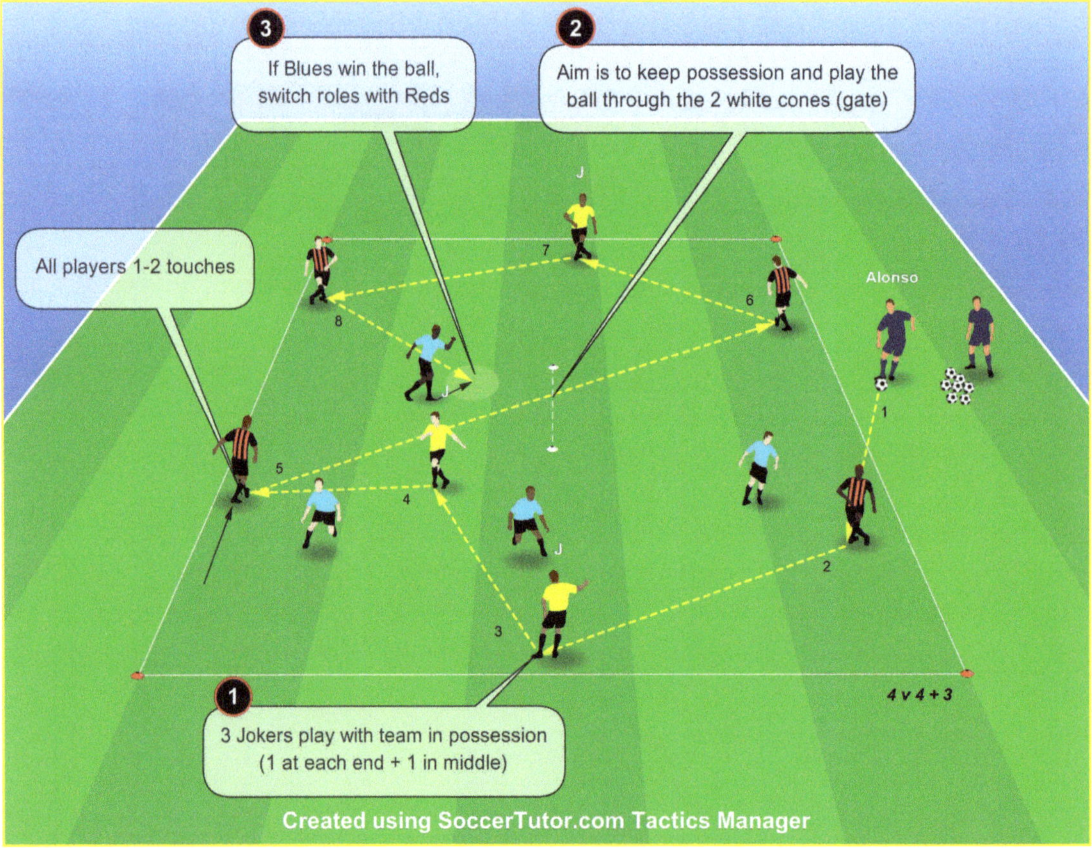

Practice Description

- There are 4 reds vs 4 blues + 3 yellow Jokers (1 at each end + 1 in middle).
- **Alonso** passes to one team (reds) to start the possession game. There are 2 reds positioned on each side, as shown.
- The aim is to keep possession using a maximum of 2 touches with help from 3 Jokers, which creates a **7v3 advantage**. They also try to pass through the white central cone gate.
- The 4 blue players (defending team) are all positioned inside and work together to press and close off the angles, trying to win the ball.
- If the blues win the ball, they switch roles with the reds and move towards the sides of the area to keep possession with the Jokers.
- The reds must react quickly and collectively to press and try to win the ball back as soon as possible.

Source: Xabi Alonso's Bayer Leverkusen training session at Bayer 04 Leverkusen Training Ground - 3rd Jan 2023

Xabi Alonso Practices: Positional Possession Games

2. Build Up in 3-2 Shape and Progress Play Through the Centre 5v5 (+3) Positional Possession Game

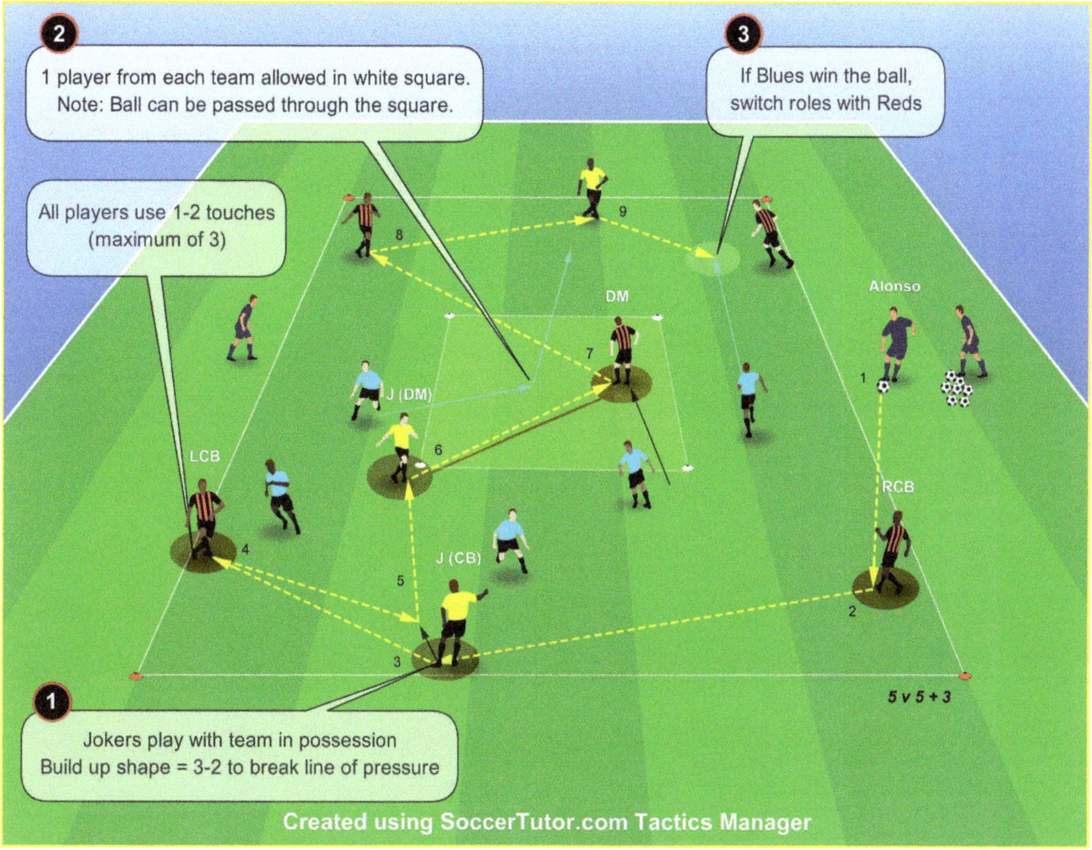

Practice Description

- **Alonso** passes to the reds to start the game and they have an **8v5 advantage** with the 3 Jokers. The aim is to play through the blue team's pressing and the central square, utilising the **DMs** to play to the other side, and back again.
- Only 1 player from each team is allowed in the white central square at any time.
- If the blues win the ball, they switch roles with the reds.

Positional Play

- The 3 centre backs (**LCB**, **CB**, & **RCB**) and 2 defensive midfielders (**DM**) form the 3-2 from Bayer Leverkusen's 3-2-5 build up play shape *(see pages 60-62)*.
- The centre backs deliberately draw in pressure from their direct opponents (often by pausing) to create space behind the first line of pressure for a **DM** to receive, and then progress the play forward to the other side.

Source: Xabi Alonso's Bayer Leverkusen training session at Bayer 04 Leverkusen Training Ground - 3rd Jan 2024

Xabi Alonso Practices: Positional Possession Games

3. Three Team High Speed of Play End to End 4v4 (+4) Positional Possession Game

"2 interceptions and we change, ok. Passes, tact-tac-tac, ok. 2 touches. Get into positions."

Positional practice: Quick passes (tac-tac-tac), to break through defending team's pressing ①

Aim = Switch to other side (to Reds) ②

2 touches maximum

4 v 4 + 4

Alonso's Key Points
1. Positional play
2. Quick passes
3. Switch the play

③ 2 interceptions and switch roles with team that lost the ball

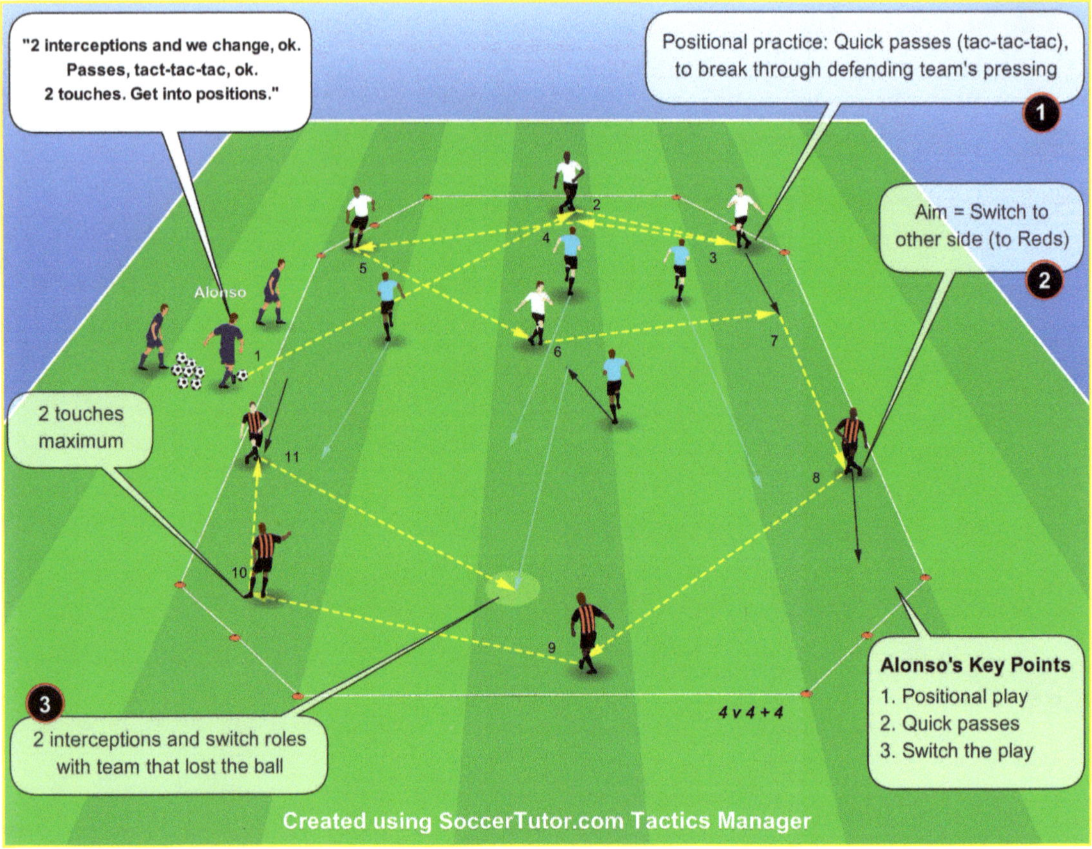

Practice Description

- There are 3 teams of 4 players (whites, reds, and blues). The whites and reds start with 3 players at each end + 1 in the middle, and the blues start as the defending team.

- **Alonso** passes to the white team who must play through the blue team's pressing with quick passes. Their aim is to use their middle player to help switch the play to the opposite end (to reds).

- If the reds receive successfully, they then have the same aim in the opposite direction (switch to whites through pressure of blues). The players are restricted to 2 touches throughout.

- The 4 blue players (defending team) work together to press and close off the angles, trying to win the ball. After they make 2 interceptions, they switch roles with the team that lost the ball, and the game continues with the same aims.

Source: Xabi Alonso's Bayer Leverkusen training session at Bayer 04 Leverkusen Training Ground - 22nd Feb 2023

Xabi Alonso Practices: Positional Possession Games

4. Support Play in the Centre End to End 5v5 (+3) Positional Possession Game

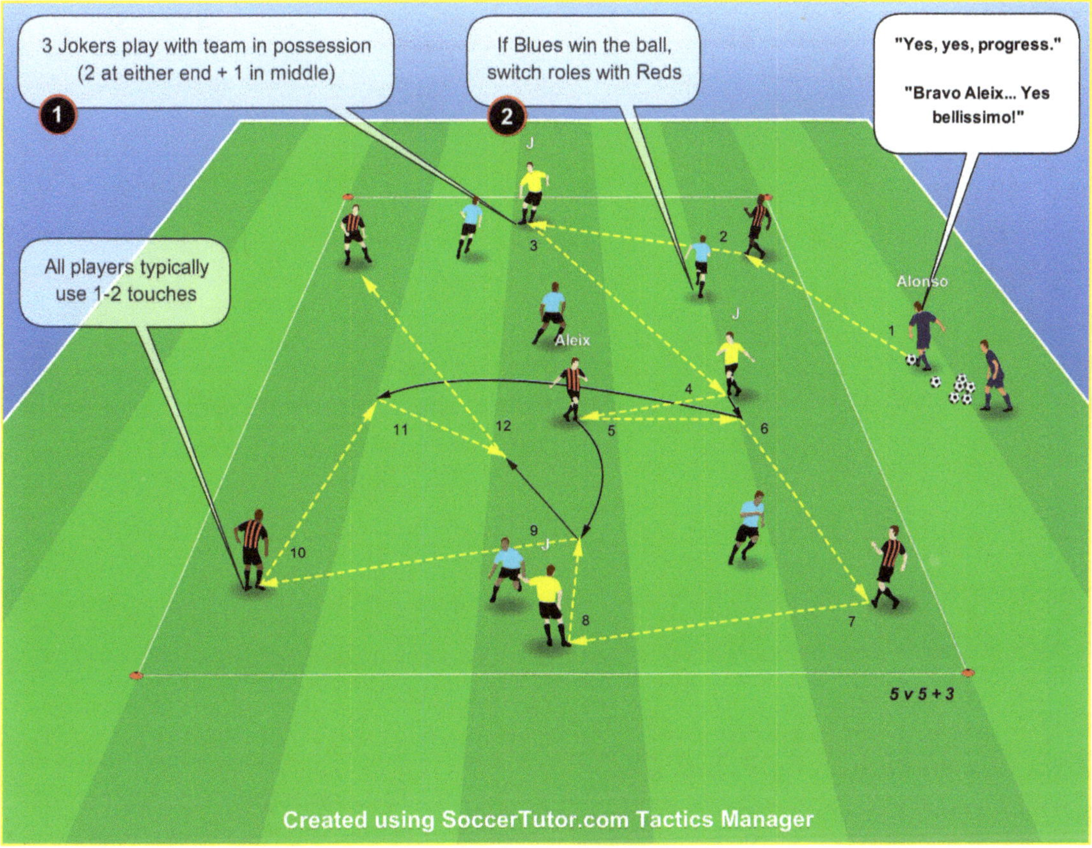

Practice Description

- **Alonso** passes to the reds to start the game and they have an **8v5 advantage** with the 3 Jokers vs the blues.
- The aim is to play through the blue team's pressing and use the 2 central players (**Aleix García** + Joker) to progress the play from end to end.
- All players use a maximum of 2 touches throughout.
- If the blues win the ball, they switch roles with the reds.
- The blues then try to keep possession with the same 8v5 advantage, trying to move the ball from end to end.

Coaching Points

- During this practice, **Xabi Alonso** shared many positional and support play coaching points which are outlined on the following pages.

Source: Xabi Alonso's Bayer Leverkusen preseason training session in Donaueschingen, Germany - 29th July 2024

Xabi Alonso Practices: Positional Possession Games

4.1. Alonso's Positional Coaching During Practice Setup

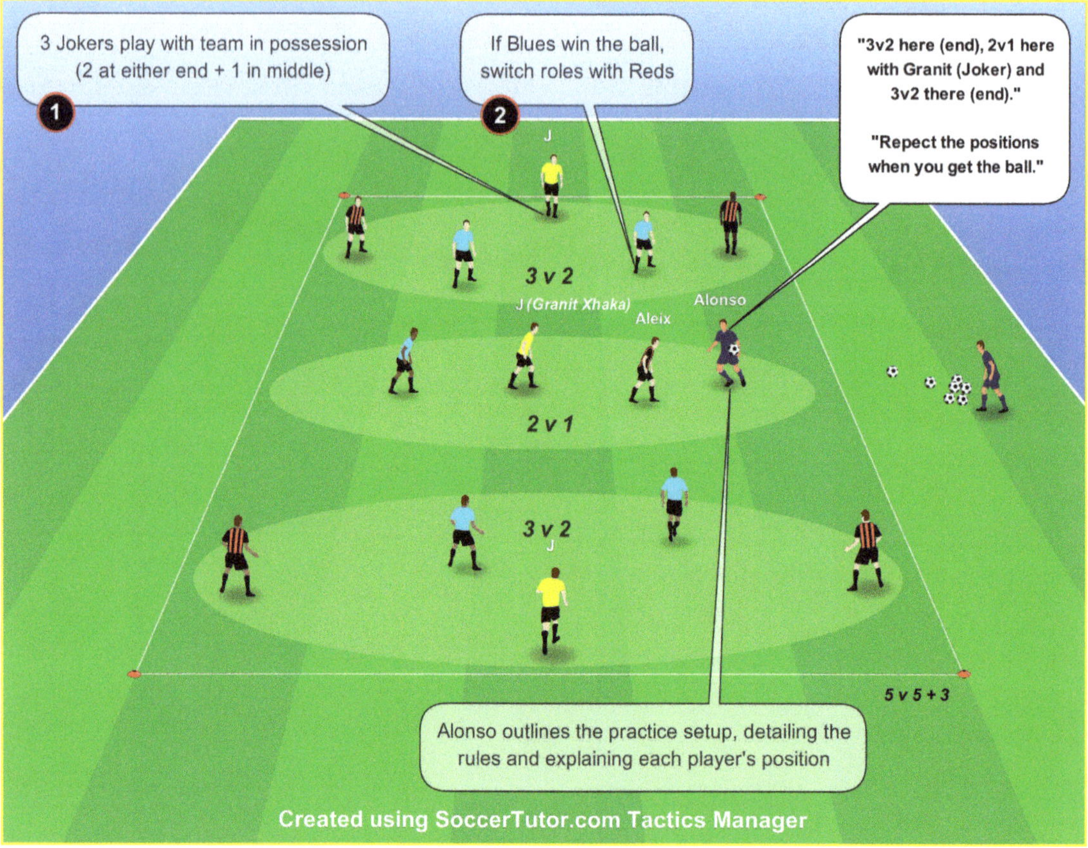

Diagram annotations:

1. 3 Jokers play with team in possession (2 at either end + 1 in middle)
2. If Blues win the ball, switch roles with Reds

"3v2 here (end), 2v1 here with Granit (Joker) and 3v2 there (end)."

"Repect the positions when you get the ball."

Alonso outlines the practice setup, detailing the rules and explaining each player's position

Labels on pitch: 3 v 2, J (Granit Xhaka), Aleix, Alonso, 2 v 1, 3 v 2, 5 v 5 + 3

Created using SoccerTutor.com Tactics Manager

Xabi Alonso Coaching Points (4.1)

- This diagram follows on from the practice on the previous page: **Support Play in the Centre End to End 5v5 (+3) Positional Possession Game**.
- Here we show what happened when **Xabi Alonso** was setting up the practice and explaining the positional roles to his Bayer Leverkusen players.
- The players are told to stay in their positions when in possession.
- Alonso also explains how there is an initial **3v2 advantage when playing out from one end**, and a **2v1 advantage in the central area** which is used to progress the play to the other end.
- The aim is to draw in opponents to press, move the ball to a free central player, who then passes to a player at the opposite end, and the game continues.

Source: Xabi Alonso's Bayer Leverkusen preseason training session in Donaueschingen, Germany - 29th July 2024

©SOCCERTUTOR.COM   XABI ALONSO: PRACTICES DIRECT FROM SESSIONS

Xabi Alonso Practices: Positional Possession Games

4.2. Alonso's Coaching Points for Support Play Movements

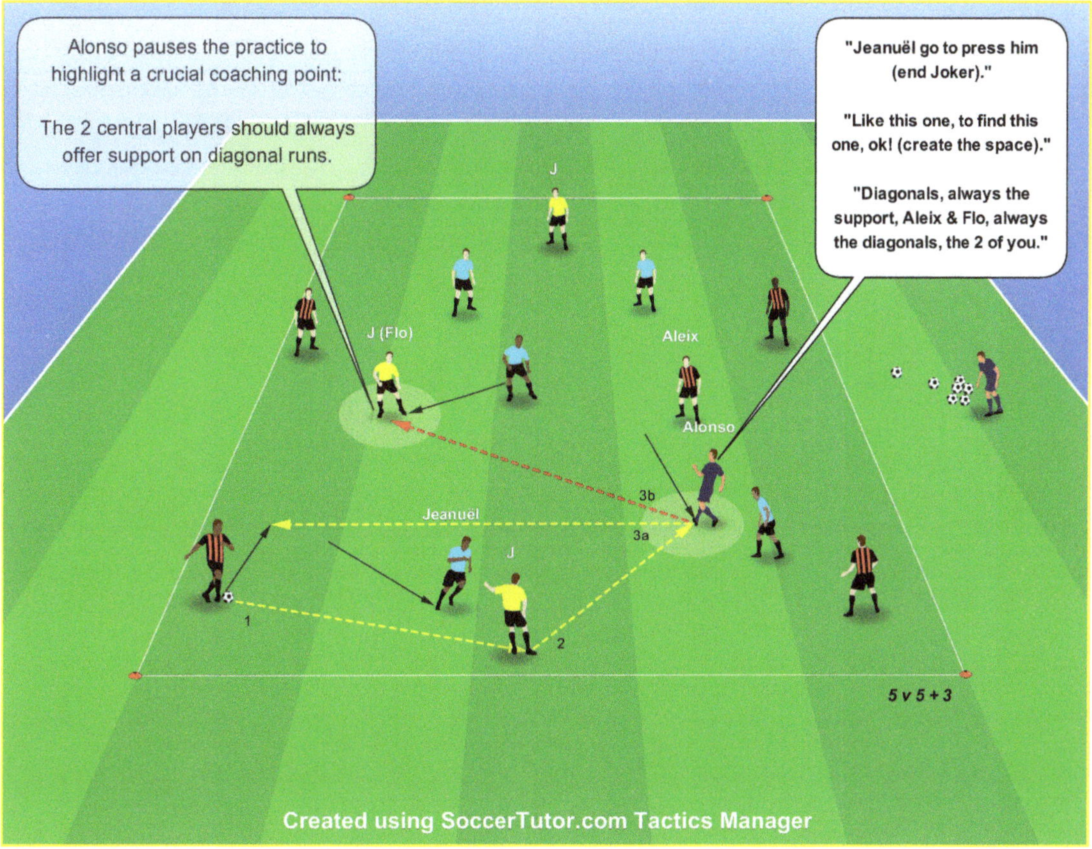

Alonso pauses the practice to highlight a crucial coaching point:

The 2 central players should always offer support on diagonal runs.

"Jeanuël go to press him (end Joker)."

"Like this one, to find this one, ok! (create the space)."

"Diagonals, always the support, Aleix & Flo, always the diagonals, the 2 of you."

5v5 +3

Xabi Alonso Coaching Points (4.2)

- This diagram follows on from the practice fully described on page 97: **Support Play in the Centre End to End 5v5 (+3) Positional Possession Game**.

- Here we show what happened when **Xabi Alonso** paused the practice and explained the correct positioning and movement for the support play of the 2 central players.

- **Alonso** emphasises the need for the central red player (**Aleix Garcia**) and the central Joker (**Florian Wirtz**) to always move in diagonal lines.

- By doing this, the central support players create the correct angles for their teammates to find them with a pass.

- This achieves one of two things. The first, they can **create an angle to receive in space (away from opponent)** and then progress the ball, or second they can **draw an opponent away to press them, then play a first time pass** to the other central player free in space because there is a 2v1 advantage in the centre.

Source: Xabi Alonso's Bayer Leverkusen preseason training session in Donaueschingen, Germany - 29th July 2024

Xabi Alonso Practices: Positional Possession Games

4.3. Alonso's Coaching Points for Wide Players

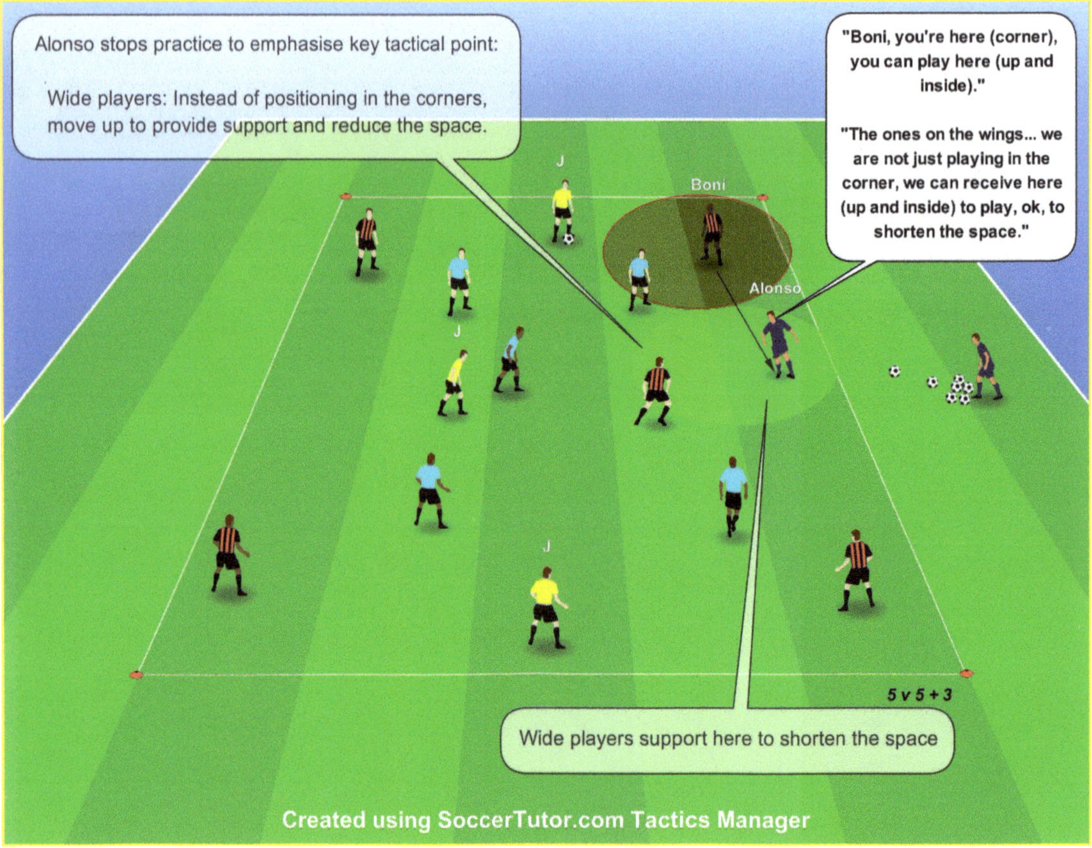

Alonso stops practice to emphasise key tactical point:

Wide players: Instead of positioning in the corners, move up to provide support and reduce the space.

"Boni, you're here (corner), you can play here (up and inside)."

"The ones on the wings... we are not just playing in the corner, we can receive here (up and inside) to play, ok, to shorten the space."

Wide players support here to shorten the space

5 v 5 +3

Created using SoccerTutor.com Tactics Manager

Xabi Alonso Coaching Points (4.3)

- This diagram follows on from the practice fully described on page 97: **Support Play in the Centre End to End 5v5 (+3) Positional Possession Game**.

- Here we show what happened when **Xabi Alonso** paused the practice and explained how the wide end players can operate in different positions to provide support to their teammates.

- **Alonso** emphasises that the 4 wide red players should not simply play in the corners when in possession. They can also move up and inside to play.

- The diagram example shows **Alonso** explaining that the wide players can move forward into the centre to receive (to shorten the space) and help progress the play to the other side.

- <u>Note</u>: *Please review the practice description on page 97 and the following 3 pages including this one for the key coaching points outlined by Xabi Alonso to his players.*

Source: Xabi Alonso's Bayer Leverkusen preseason training session in Donaueschingen, Germany - 29th July 2024

Xabi Alonso Practices: Positional Possession Games

5. Open Up and Spread Out to Maximise Space and Play Through Pressure
7 v 7 (+3) Positional Possession Game

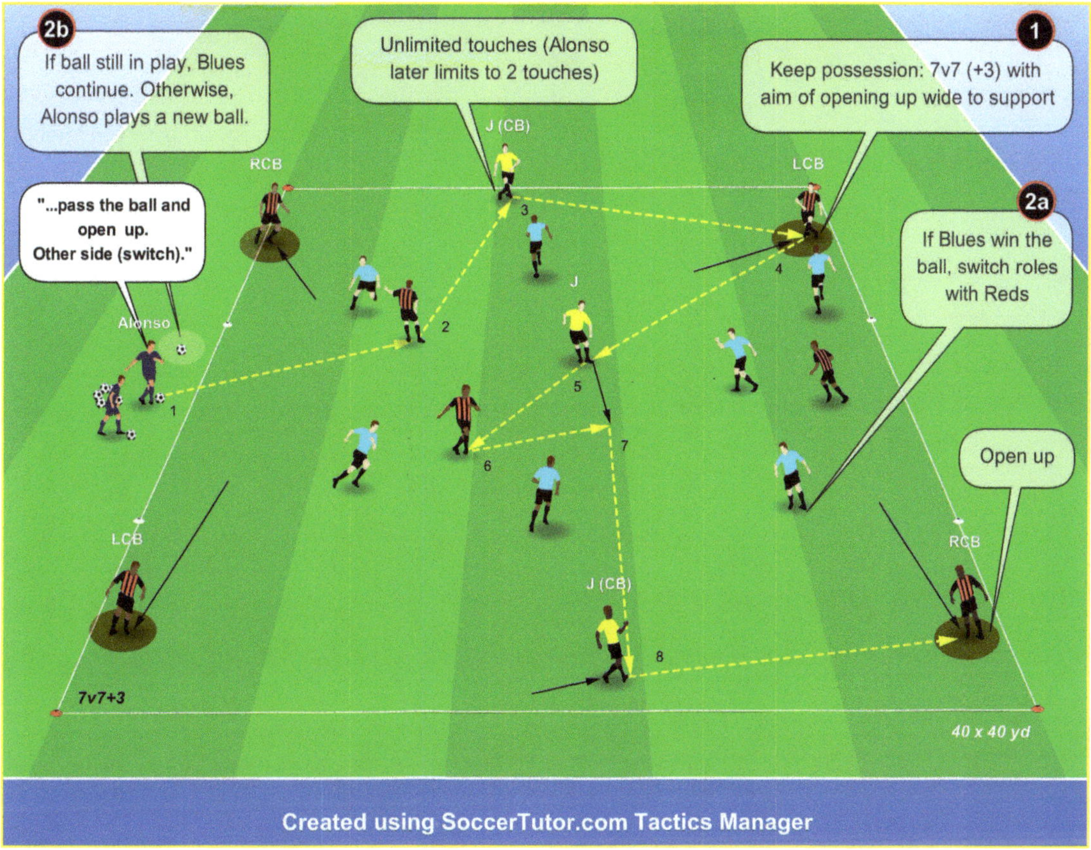

Practice Description

- **Alonso** passes to the reds who have a **10 v 7 advantage** with the 3 Jokers. The aim is to keep possession with the wide centre backs (**LCB** & **RCB**) opening up into wide positions to provide support, and then quickly play to other side.

- If the blues win the ball, they switch roles with the reds. If the ball is still in play, they continue with the same ball. If not, Alonso passes a new ball to a blue player.

- The players start with unlimited touches but Alonso later progresses to a maximum of 2 touches allowed.

Positional Play

- The players at the ends best represent the 3 centre backs (**LCB**, **CB**, & **RCB**) from Bayer Leverkusen's 3-4-2-1 formation.

- The emphasis is on **LCB** and **RCB** who open up to receive in the corners, then play into the centre to progress play.

Source: Xabi Alonso's Bayer Leverkusen training session at Bayer 04 Leverkusen Training Ground - 2nd Dec 2022

Xabi Alonso Practices: Positional Possession Games

6. Build Up with Different Positional Structures 8v8 (+4) Possession Game

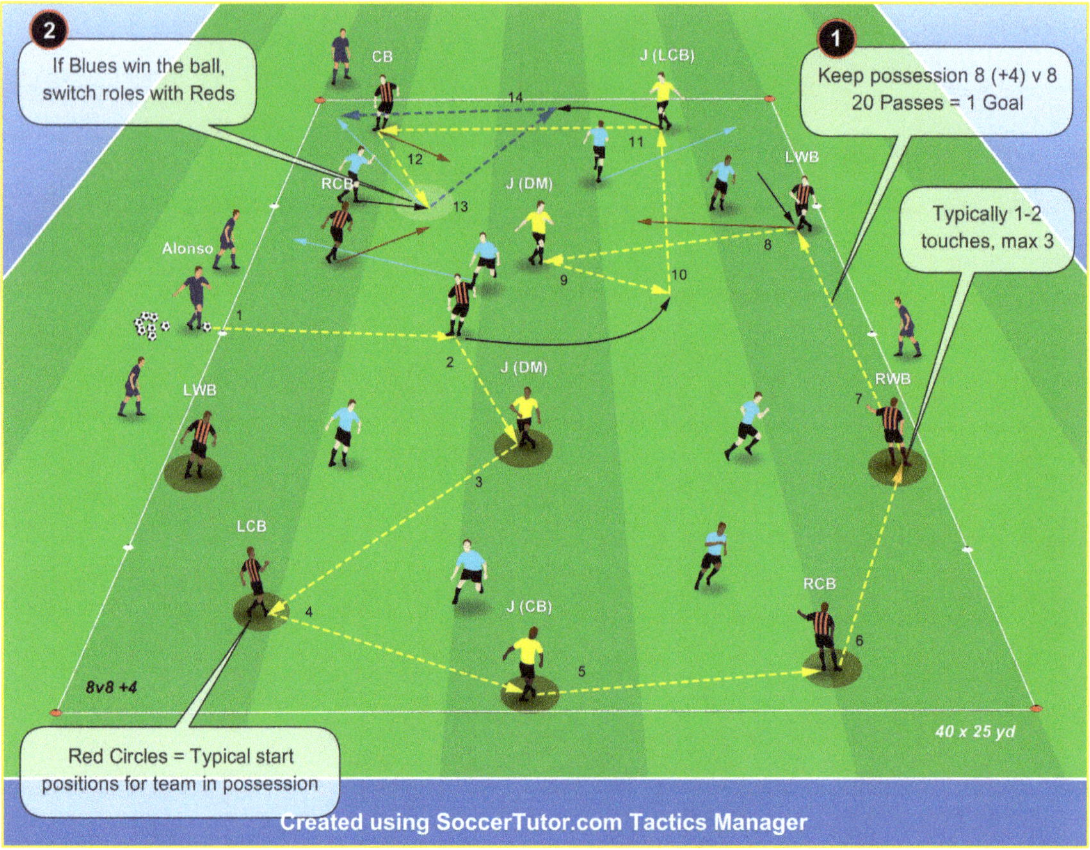

Practice Description

- There are 8 reds vs 8 blues + 4 yellow Jokers (1 at each end + 2 in middle). **Alonso** passes to start and the reds have a **12v8 advantage** with the 4 Jokers.

- The aim is to play through the blue's pressing within their positional shape and keep possession. 20 Passes = 1 Goal.

- The blue players (defending) work together to press and win the ball. If they do, they switch roles with the reds.

Positional Play

- The red circles show starting positions of 3 centre backs (**LCB**, **CB**, & **RCB**), 1 defensive midfielder (**DM**), and 2 wing backs (**LWB** & **RWB**) from Bayer Leverkusen's 3-4-2-1 formation.

- The players were also observed to play out from the end of the area in a 4-1, forming part of Bayer's Leverkusen's 4-2-4 build up play shape *(as shown at the top of diagram + see pages 64-65)*.

Source: Xabi Alonso's Bayer Leverkusen training session at Bayer 04 Leverkusen Training Ground - 2024

Xabi Alonso Practices: Positional Possession Games

7. 8v8 (+5) Positional Possession Game with Jokers in Plus (+) Shape

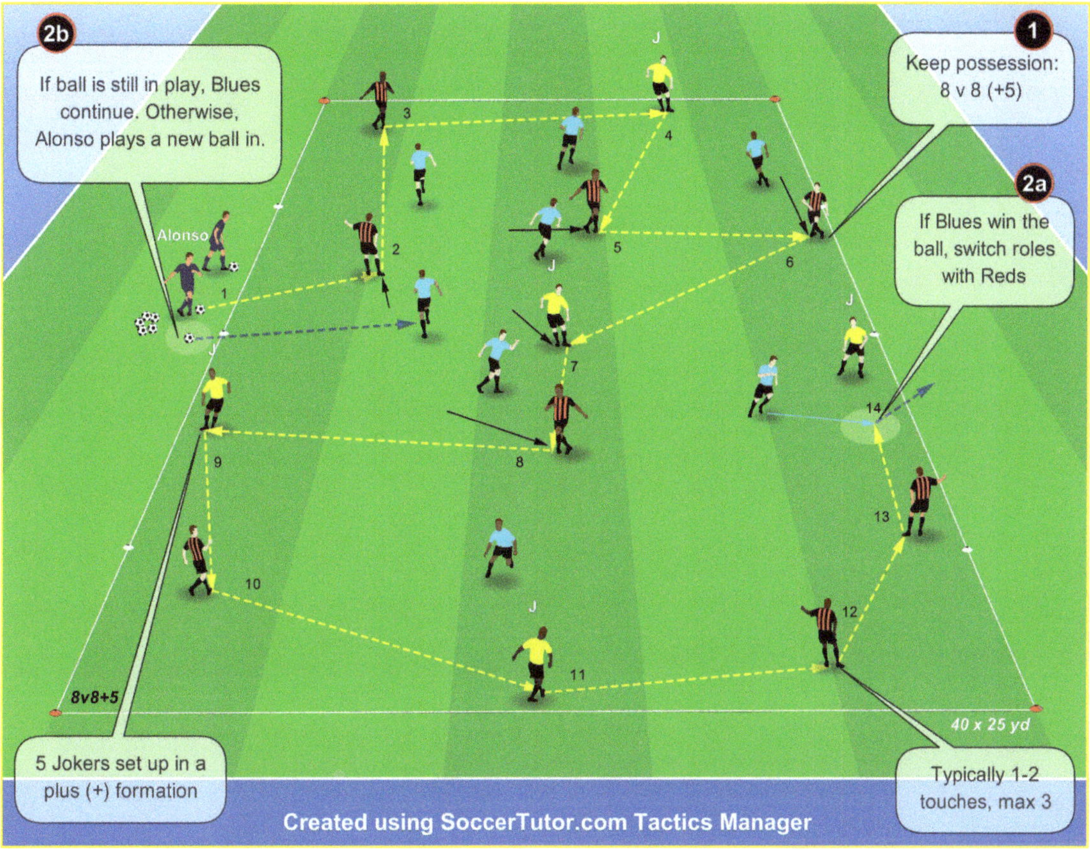

Practice Description

- There are 8 reds vs 8 blues + 5 yellow Jokers, with 1 at each end, 1 on each side, and 1 in the middle to create a plus (+) shape.
- **Alonso** passes to start and the reds have a **13 v 8 advantage** with the 5 Jokers.
- The aim is to play through the blue's pressing and keep possession using the full width and length of the area.
- The blue players (defending) work together to press and win the ball. If they do, they switch roles with the reds.
- If the ball is still in play, the blues continue and the reds must make a fast transition to try and win the ball back as quickly as possible.
- If the ball goes out of play, **Alonso** quickly passes a new ball in.

Source: Xabi Alonso's Bayer Leverkusen training session at Bayer 04 Leverkusen Training Ground - 12th April 2023

Xabi Alonso Practices: Positional Possession Games

8. Progress Play with 3-5 (from 2-3-5) Attacking Shape 8v8 (+6) Positional Possession Game

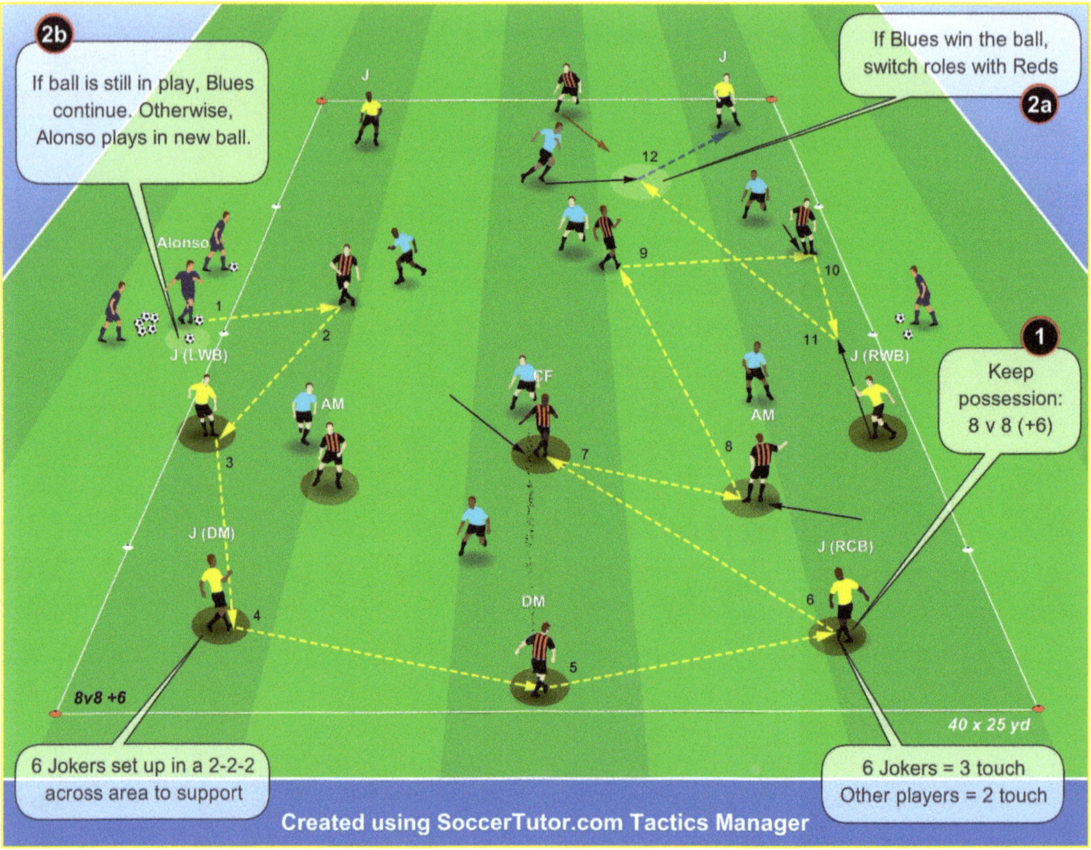

Practice Description

- There are 8 reds vs 8 blues + 6 yellow Jokers (2 low, 2 middle, 2 high). **Alonso** passes to the reds and they keep possession with a **14 v 8 advantage**. The team in possession (reds) are restricted to 2 touches, and the Jokers have 3.

- The blue players (defending) work together to press and win the ball. If they do, they switch roles with the reds. If the ball is still in play, the blues continue with the same ball. If not, Alonso passes a new ball to a blue player.

Positional Play

- The positional roles in this practice are focused on the front 2 lines.

- The centre back (**RCB**), 2 defensive midfielders (**DM**), 2 wing backs (**LWB** & **RWB**), 2 attacking midfielders, and centre forward (**CF**) form the 3-5 from Bayer Leverkusen's 2-3-5 attacking phase shape *(see page 118)*.

Source: Xabi Alonso's Bayer Leverkusen training session at Bayer 04 Leverkusen Training Ground - 15th Feb 2023

Xabi Alonso Practices: Positional Possession Games

9. Build Up in 2-3 Shape and Play Through the Lines 6v6 (+6) Positional Possession Game

(Diagram: 40 x 35 yd, 6v6 +6)

- **3**: If Blues win ball, switch roles with Reds. If ball goes out, Alonso plays a new ball in.
- **2**: 2 Yellows remain in middle zone but can be pressed.
- **1**: Keep possession + play to opposite end.
- 3 v 2 Advantage around ball area to play out.
- Players observed in 2-3 shape at this end, 3-2 at the other end.

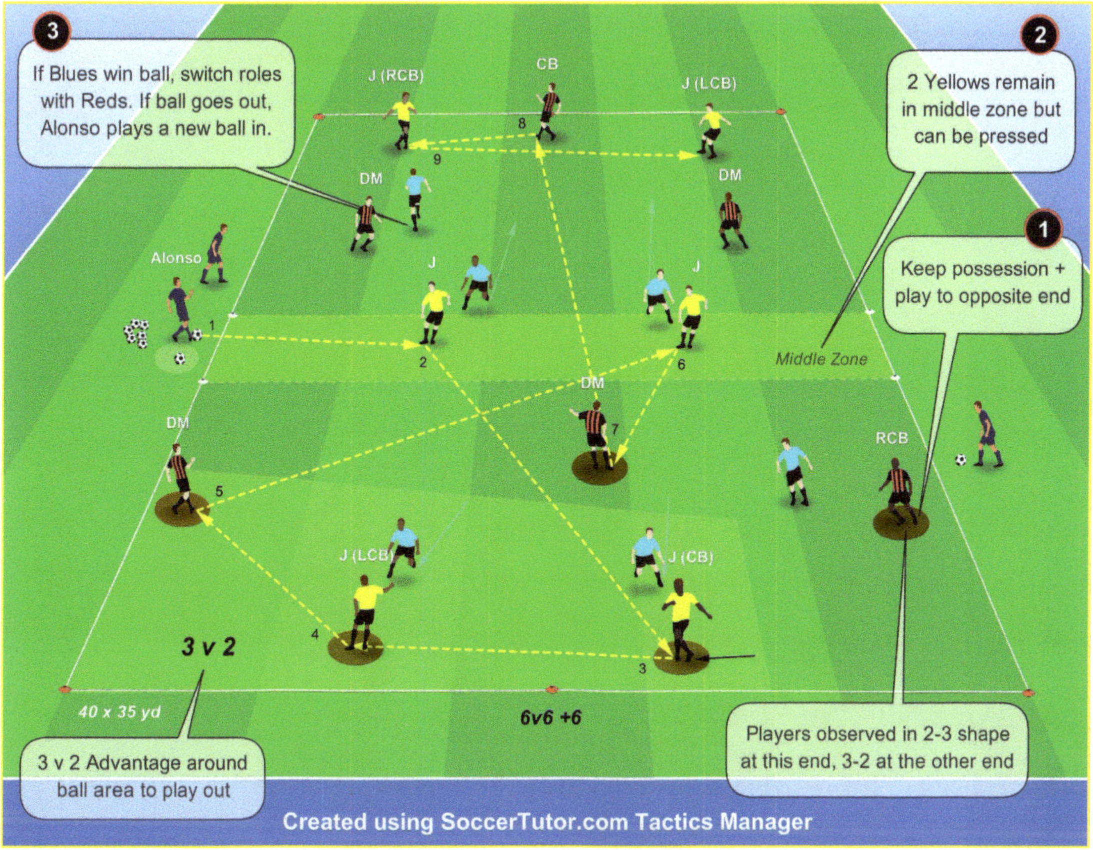

Practice Description

- There are 6 reds vs 6 blues + 6 yellow Jokers (2 low zone, 2 middle, 2 high).
- **Alonso** passes into play and the reds keep possession on one side with help from the 2 low zone and 2 middle zone Jokers (**7v3 advantage**).
- The aim is to **create a 3v2 advantage around the ball area to build up through the first line of pressure**, and then move the ball to the opposite end.
- Players use 1-2 touches (3 maximum). The 2 middle Jokers stay within their zone but can be pressed. If the blues win the ball, they switch roles with the reds.

Positional Play

- The 3 centre backs (**RCB**, **CB** & **LCB**) and 2 defensive midfielders (**DM**) form the 3-2 back and middle line structure at the top and the 2-3 structure at the bottom from Bayer Leverkusen's 3-2-5 and 2-3-5 build up shapes *(see pages 60-63)*.

Source: Xabi Alonso's Bayer Leverkusen training session at Bayer 04 Leverkusen Training Ground - 8th Nov 2023

Xabi Alonso Practices: Positional Possession Games

10. Build Up in 3-2 Shape and Play Through the Lines 8v8 (+4) Positional Possession Game

(Diagram: 40 x 25 yd pitch, 8v8+4 positional game)

Annotations on diagram:
- **3** If Blues win the ball, switch roles with Reds
- **2** 2 Yellows remain in middle zone but can be pressed
- **1** Positional game (3-2-2) to quickly move ball to other end
- In 3-2 Build Up Shape, Bayer DMs aim to receive behind first line of pressure
- "Open up!"
- Middle Zone

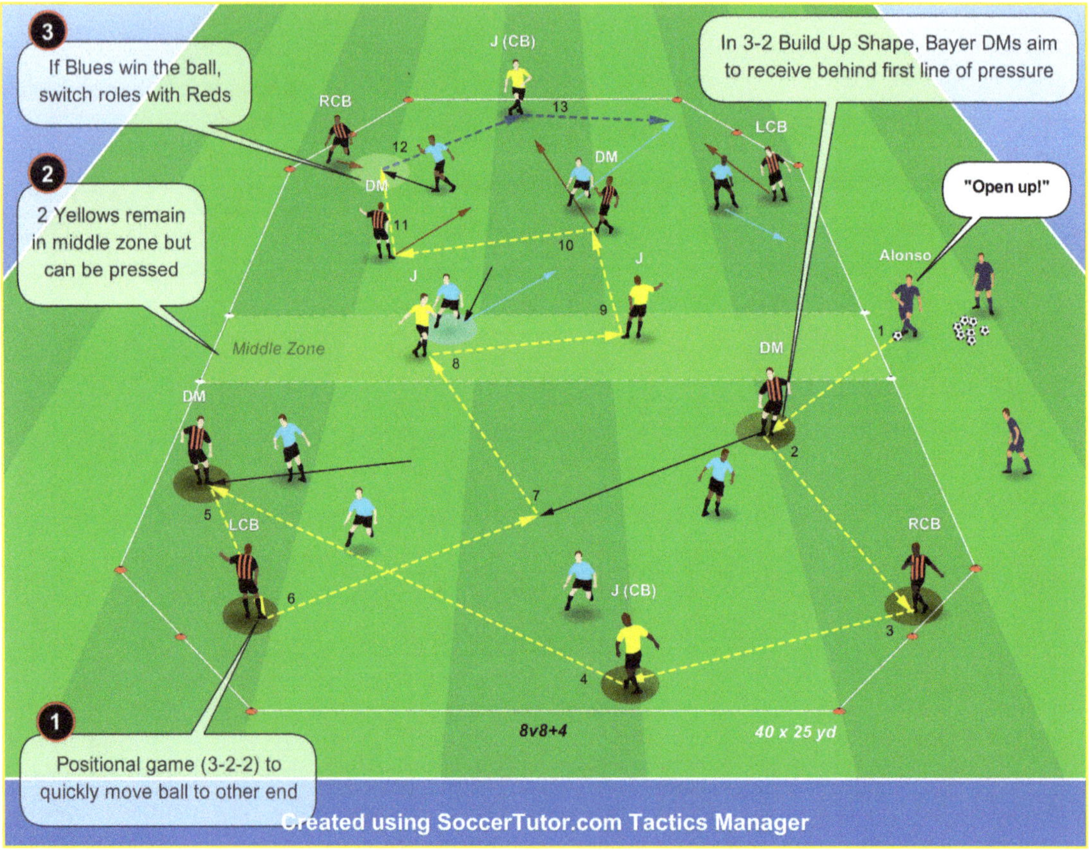

Practice Description

- There are 8 reds vs 8 blues + 4 yellow Jokers (1 at each end + 2 in middle zone). **Alonso** passes a ball in to start.
- The reds aim to keep possession at one end, build up through pressure for either of the **DMs** to receive, progress the ball to the middle zone Jokers, and then play to the opposite end.
- Most of the players are limited to 2 touches, but the end Jokers (**CB**) have 3.
- The 2 middle Jokers stay within their zone but can be pressed.
- If the blues win the ball, they switch roles with the reds.

Positional Play

- The 3 centre backs (**RCB**, **CB** & **LCB**) and 2 defensive midfielders (**DM**) form the 3-2 back and middle line structure from Bayer Leverkusen's 3-2-5 build up shape *(see pages 60-62)*.

Source: Xabi Alonso's Bayer Leverkusen training session at Bayer 04 Leverkusen Training Ground - 2024

Xabi Alonso Practices: Positional Possession Games

10.1. Xabi Alonso Coaching Points for Opening Up Wide

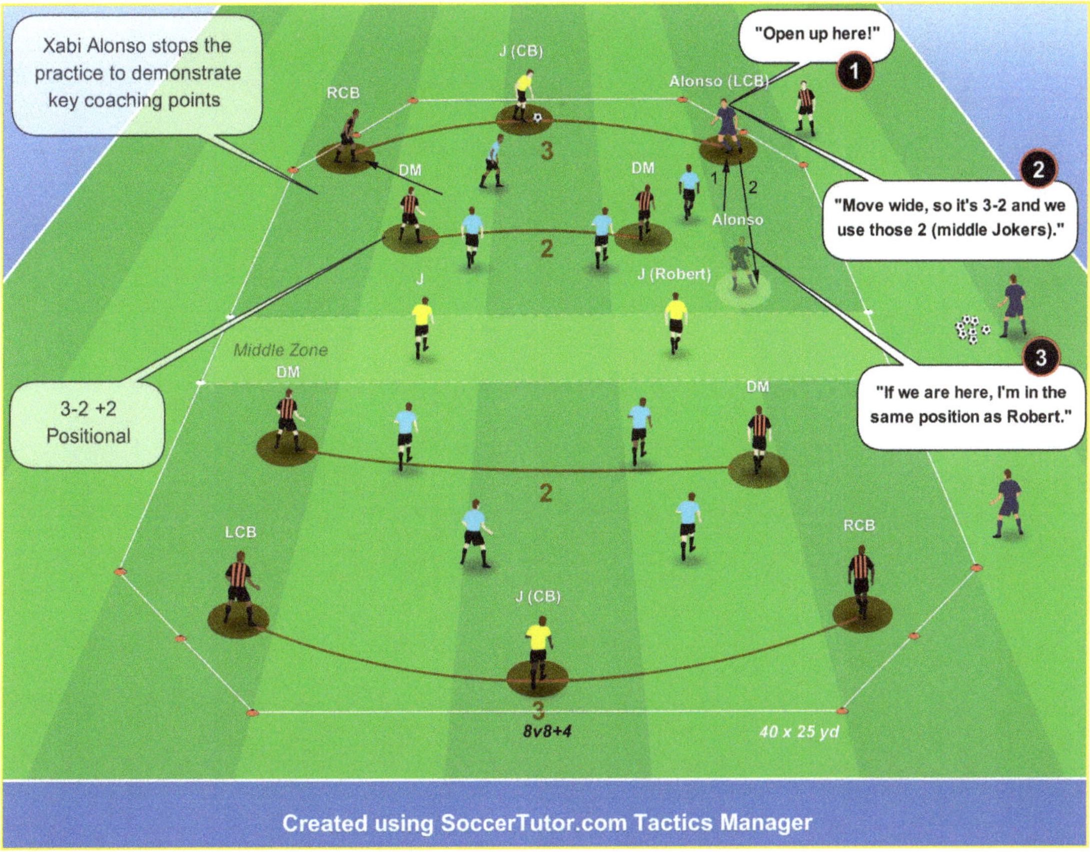

[Diagram: 3-2 +2 Positional, 8v8+4, 40 x 25 yd. Xabi Alonso stops the practice to demonstrate key coaching points.

1. "Open up here!"
2. "Move wide, so it's 3-2 and we use those 2 (middle Jokers)."
3. "If we are here, I'm in the same position as Robert."]

Xabi Alonso Coaching Points (9.1)

- This diagram follows on from the practice on the previous page: **Build Up in 3-2 Shape and Play Through the Lines 8v8 (+4) Positional Possession Game**.

- Here we show what happened when **Xabi Alonso** paused his training session to explain some key points to his players.

- He describes the positional roles within the 3-2-5 build up shape, in which we have the 3-2-2 here with the 3 centre backs (**LCB**, **CB** & **RCB**), 2 defensive midfielders (**DM**), and 2 middle zone Jokers.

- Alonso stresses the importance of the **LCB** and **RCB** to open up in the corner of the area to maximise the width to provide support and create space to then play through pressure.

- This is also the focus of the practice on page 101: **Open Up and Spread Out to Maximise Space and Play Through Pressure 7v7 (+3) Positional Possession Game**.

- The aim is to draw in opponents to press, move the ball to the **DMs** behind the first line of pressure, then play to the middle zone Jokers to progress the play to the other side.

Source: Xabi Alonso's Bayer Leverkusen training session at Bayer 04 Leverkusen Training Ground - 2024

Xabi Alonso Practices: Positional Possession Games

10.2. Xabi Alonso Coaching Points for Decision Making

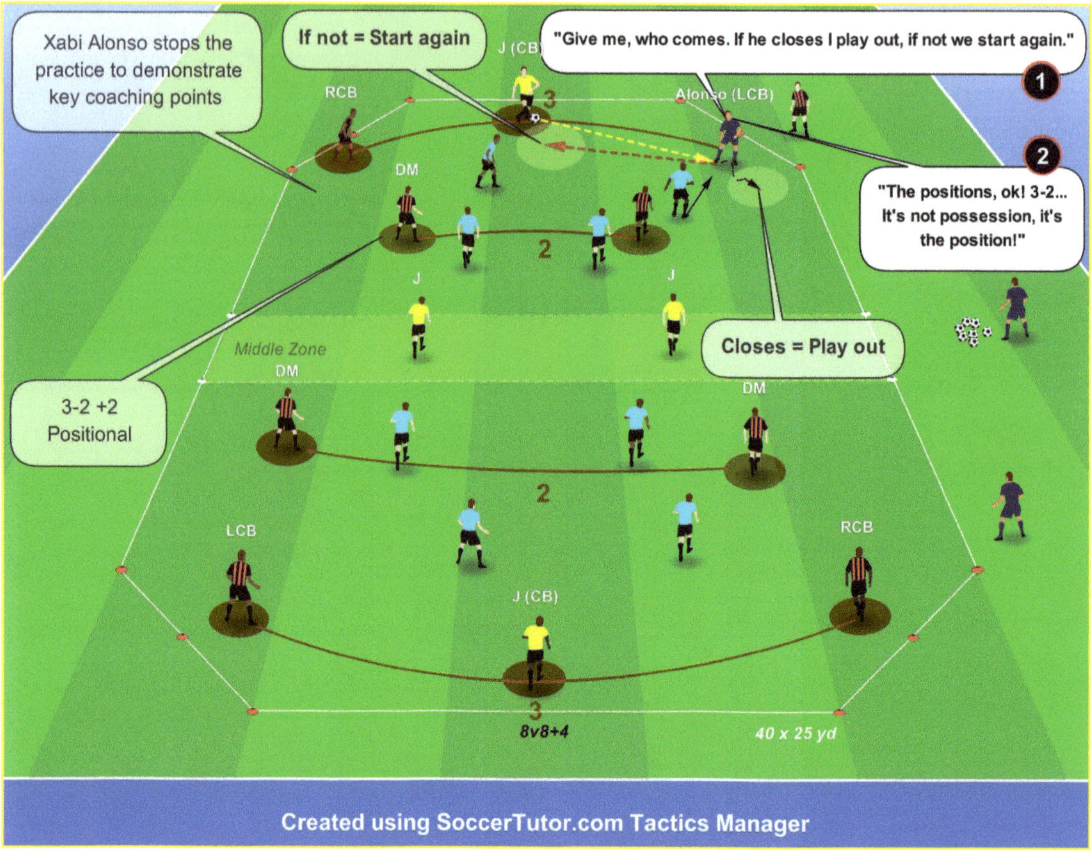

[Diagram: 8v8+4 positional possession game on a 40 x 25 yd pitch with Middle Zone. Annotations include:]
- Xabi Alonso stops the practice to demonstrate key coaching points
- If not = Start again
- "Give me, who comes. If he closes I play out, if not we start again."
- "The positions, ok! 3-2... It's not possession, it's the position!"
- Closes = Play out
- 3-2 +2 Positional

Created using SoccerTutor.com Tactics Manager

Xabi Alonso Coaching Points (9.2)

- This diagram follows on from the positional possession game described on the previous 2 pages: **Build Up in 3-2 Shape and Play Through the Lines 8v8 (+4) Positional Possession Game**.
- Here we show what happened when **Xabi Alonso** paused his training session to explain some key points to his players.
- Alonso speaks to his players about their decision making when playing in their 3-2 shape, which forms part of Bayer Leverkusen's **3-2-5 build up shape shown on pages 60-62**.

- Alonso stresses the **importance of the LCB and RCB to provide support and receive in an open wide position** and try to attract an opponent to press.
- **If an opponent is drawn in to press, then the defender should play out**. If not, they can simply recycle possession of the ball (to reset).
- In addition, **Alonso stresses the importance of positional discipline**. This is not a normal possession game; it is a **positional possession game** with the focus on progressing the play in a structured shape.

Source: Xabi Alonso's Bayer Leverkusen training session at Bayer 04 Leverkusen Training Ground - 2024

Xabi Alonso Practices: Positional Possession Games

10.3. Xabi Alonso Coaching Points for Quickly Breaking Lines

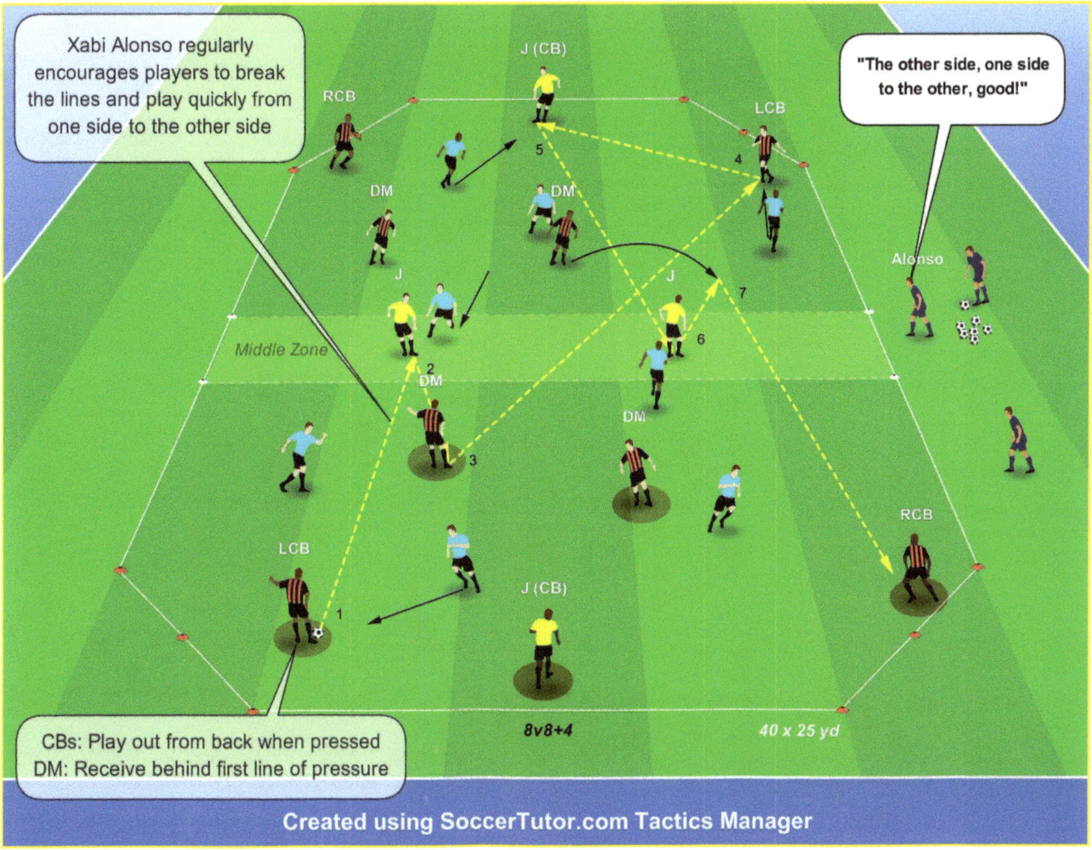

(Diagram: 8v8+4, 40 x 25 yd)

- Xabi Alonso regularly encourages players to break the lines and play quickly from one side to the other side
- "The other side, one side to the other, good!"
- CBs: Play out from back when pressed
- DM: Receive behind first line of pressure

Xabi Alonso Coaching Points (9.3)

- This diagram follows on from the positional possession game described on the previous 3 pages: **Build Up in 3-2 Shape and Play Through the Lines 8v8 (+4) Positional Possession Game**.
- Here we illustrate the encouragement and coaching points **Xabi Alonso** shared with his players during the practice.
- The players were heavily encouraged to move the ball with a high speed of play and intensity, so that they could quickly break the lines and play to the other side, as shown in the diagram example.

- The key components are in place within this positional possession game; **playing out from the back within the 3-2 structure** from Bayer Leverkusen's 3-2-5 build up shape, **moving the ball to DMs behind the first line of pressure**, and moving the **ball to the AMs to progress the attack**.
- This way the players are **constantly practicing their positional roles within the team shape**, enabling them to progress the ball up the pitch quickly and decisively to play through their opponents.

Source: Xabi Alonso's Bayer Leverkusen training session at Bayer 04 Leverkusen Training Ground - 2024

Xabi Alonso Practices: Positional Possession Games

11. Build Up in 4-2 Shape and Play Through the Lines 8v8 (+6) Positional Possession Game

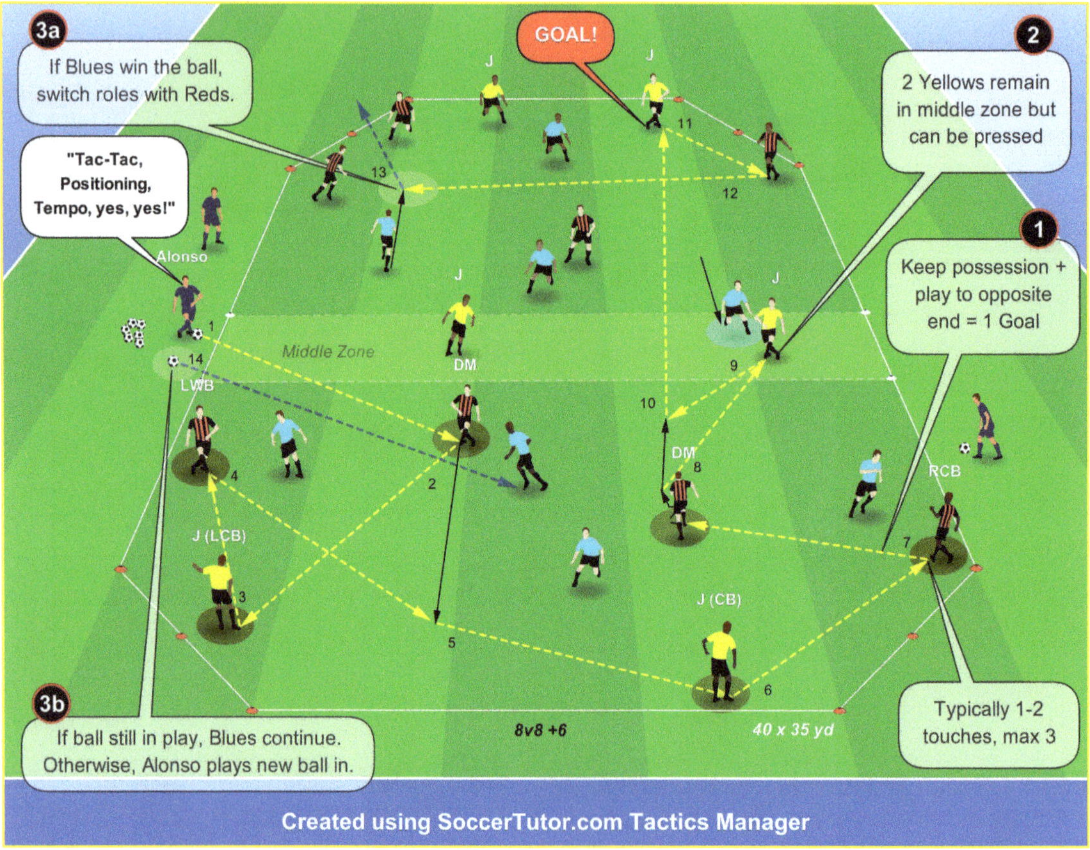

Practice Description

- There are 8 reds vs 8 blues + 6 yellow Jokers (2 at each end + 2 in middle zone). **Alonso** passes a ball in to start.
- The reds aim to keep possession, build up through pressure, and combine with the middle zone Jokers to play to the opposite end (1 Goal scored).
- Players use 1-2 touches (3 maximum). The 2 middle Jokers stay within their zone but can be pressed, as shown.
- If the blues win the ball, they switch roles with the reds. If the ball is still in play, the blues continue. If not, Alonso passes a new ball in to the blues.

Positional Play

- The 3 centre backs (**RCB**, **CB** & **LCB**), left wing back (**LWB**), and 2 defensive midfielders (**DM**) form the 4-2 back and middle line structure from Bayer's 4-2-4 build up shape *(see pages 64-65)*.

Source: Xabi Alonso's Bayer Leverkusen training session at Bayer 04 Leverkusen Training Ground - 13th March 2024

Xabi Alonso's Coaching During Positional Possession Games

1. **Xabi Alonso actively leads Bayer Leverkusen's training**, especially during the positional possession games in this section.

2. Alonso often pauses the session to highlight key points, ensuring a **high attention to detail**.

3. The coaching staff and players maintain a strong focus, with **Alonso consistently praising and encouraging the players**, creating a positive atmosphere.

4. Prepared with his notes, **Alonso's training is highly structured**, with every detail preplanned for maximum effectiveness.

5. In positional possession practices, **players are assigned specific positions for targeted coaching, refining their understanding and execution of tactical roles**. He ensures each player's positioning and decision making align with the team's tactical plan.

Xabi Alonso's Bayer Leverkusen: Attacking in the Final Third Tactics

Xabi Alonso's Bayer Leverkusen: Attacking in the Final Third Tactics

Attacking Through the Centre

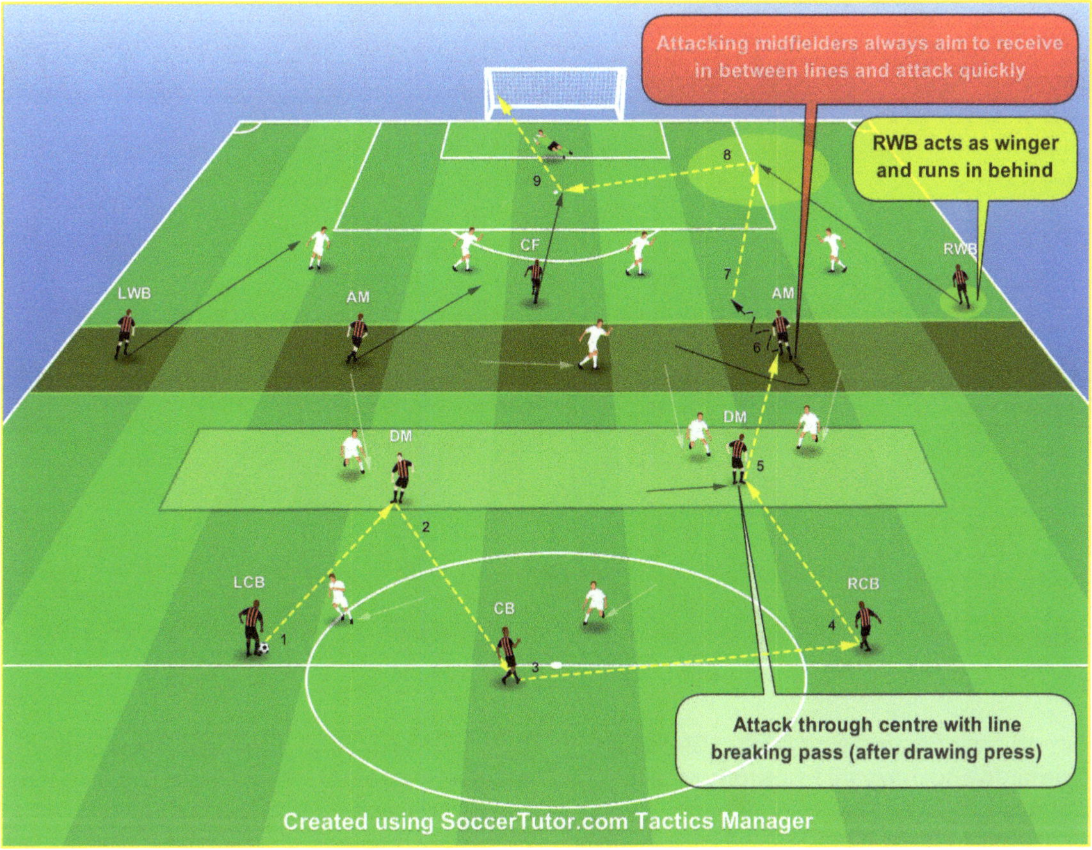

Attacking midfielders always aim to receive in between lines and attack quickly

RWB acts as winger and runs in behind

Attack through centre with line breaking pass (after drawing press)

Created using SoccerTutor.com Tactics Manager

Bayer Leverkusen's central attack under Xabi Alonso focuses on two main options within this 3-2-5 shape, which are **line breaking passes through the centre or "bounce passes" to draw opponents in** before progressing.

The **double pivot of defensive midfielders (DM) is key and they are positioned to receive passes in front of the defenders**, offering very reliable support play.

Alonso emphasises aggressive forward passes if there is sufficient space.

If passing lanes are blocked, players drop back for bounce passes, drawing in opposing players and creating space for progression. As the ball advances, **Leverkusen look to move the ball to an attacking midfielder (AM) in between the lines** (red highlighted area).

From there, they look to attack quickly. In the diagram example, **AM** carries the ball forward and plays a through pass for the advanced right wing back (**RWB**) in behind, who cuts the ball back for **CF** to score.

XABI ALONSO: PRACTICES DIRECT FROM SESSIONS

The Wing Backs as Key Attacking Players

Bayer Leverkusen's wing backs, **Alejandro Grimaldo** and **Jeremie Frimpong**, are key players in Xabi Alonso's 4-2-4 and 3-2-5 attacking shapes (from 3-4-2-1 formation).

The left wing back **Grimaldo** excels at build up play, precision passes and crossing skills, whilst also being able to easily switch positions and play comfortably as an attacking midfielder in the attacking phase. **Frimpong's** high positioning and speed creates a big threat on the right side. He creates constant problems on the flank.

The duo were vital to Bayer Leverkusen's incredible success during the 2023/24 season, **combining for 54 goals and assists across all competitions**.

Grimaldo scored 12 goals and provided 18 assists (30 goal contributions). He also led the Bundesliga with 13 assists.

Frimpong scored 14 goals and provided 10 assists (24 goal contributions).

Under Xabi Alonso, Leverkusen's wing backs have become crucial to the team's attacking tactics, and we look at how on the following pages.

Note: Their defensive efforts also helped Leverkusen concede the fewest goals in the Bundesliga.

Xabi Alonso's Bayer Leverkusen: Attacking in the Final Third Tactics

Tactical and Positional Fluidity in Attack: Left Wing Back Grimaldo

1. High and Wide Position in Attacking Phase (3-2-5)

Grimaldo (LWB) advances into attacking half later, often as a free player on the outside

Grimaldo (LWB) had significant attacking output with assists and goals

The left wing back Grimaldo's presence on the left wing poses a constant challenge for opponents, even when he's off the ball. His mere potential as a threat forces defenders to stay close, creating valuable space in the centre for Bayer Leverkusen's other players to exploit.

During Bayer record-breaking 2023/2024 season, **Grimaldo (LWB) made significant contributions with both assists and goals**.

This example shows Bayer's 3-2-5 attacking formation, where **Grimaldo (LWB)** typically starts in a deeper position compared to **Frimpong (RWB)** on the opposite side. As the play progresses, **Grimaldo (LWB)** moves into a more advanced position later in the phase, often receiving the ball as a free player from an attacking midfielder (**AM**). From there, he advances forward, and **creates opportunities to either cross or shoot**.

Xabi Alonso's Bayer Leverkusen: Attacking in the Final Third Tactics

2. Moving into Attacking Midfield "Playmaker" Position

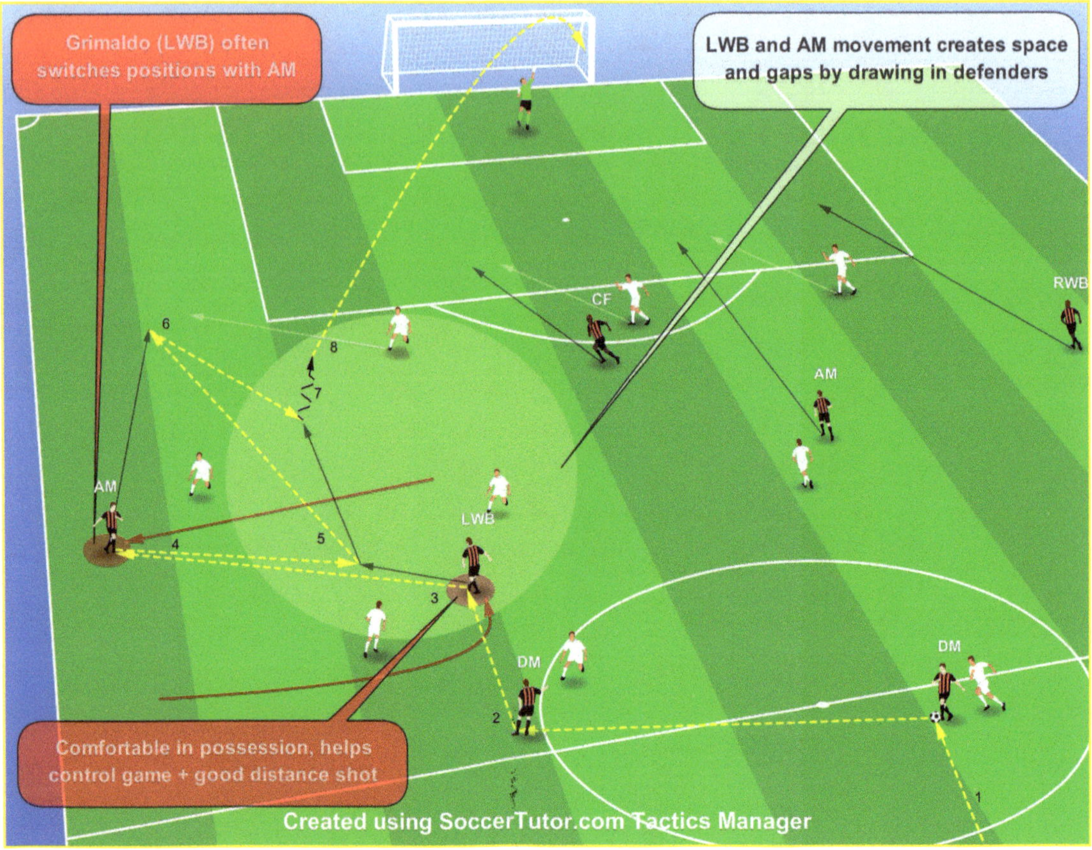

![Tactical diagram showing Grimaldo (LWB) switching positions with AM, with annotations: "Grimaldo (LWB) often switches positions with AM", "LWB and AM movement creates space and gaps by drawing in defenders", and "Comfortable in possession, helps control game + good distance shot"]

The **left wing back (LWB) Grimaldo's ability to invert into midfield provides a numerical security**, helping Bayer Leverkusen in possession to control the tempo of the game. He is comfortable in possession, has a strong shot from distance, and frequently switches positions with the attacking midfielder, drawing opponents in and creating exploitable gaps, showcasing his **versatility in both the left wing back and attacking midfielder roles**.

As Bayer Leverkusen move into the attacking phase, **Grimaldo (LWB) often shifts centrally where he is adept at playing the attacking midfielder role**.

As explained, in central positions, **Grimaldo (LWB)** moves the ball quickly and draws defenders to create space for others. This can open up space to play in and **Grimaldo (LWB)** will try to attack towards goal, as in this example where he plays a quick combination, and then shoots from distance.

Grimaldo's ability to keep possession and maintain control, as well as provide an attacking threat again helps Bayer Leverkusen with their unpredictable attacking style which makes them such a big threat to their opponents.

Xabi Alonso's Bayer Leverkusen: Attacking in the Final Third Tactics

Right Wing Back Frimpong Used as a "High Flying Winger"

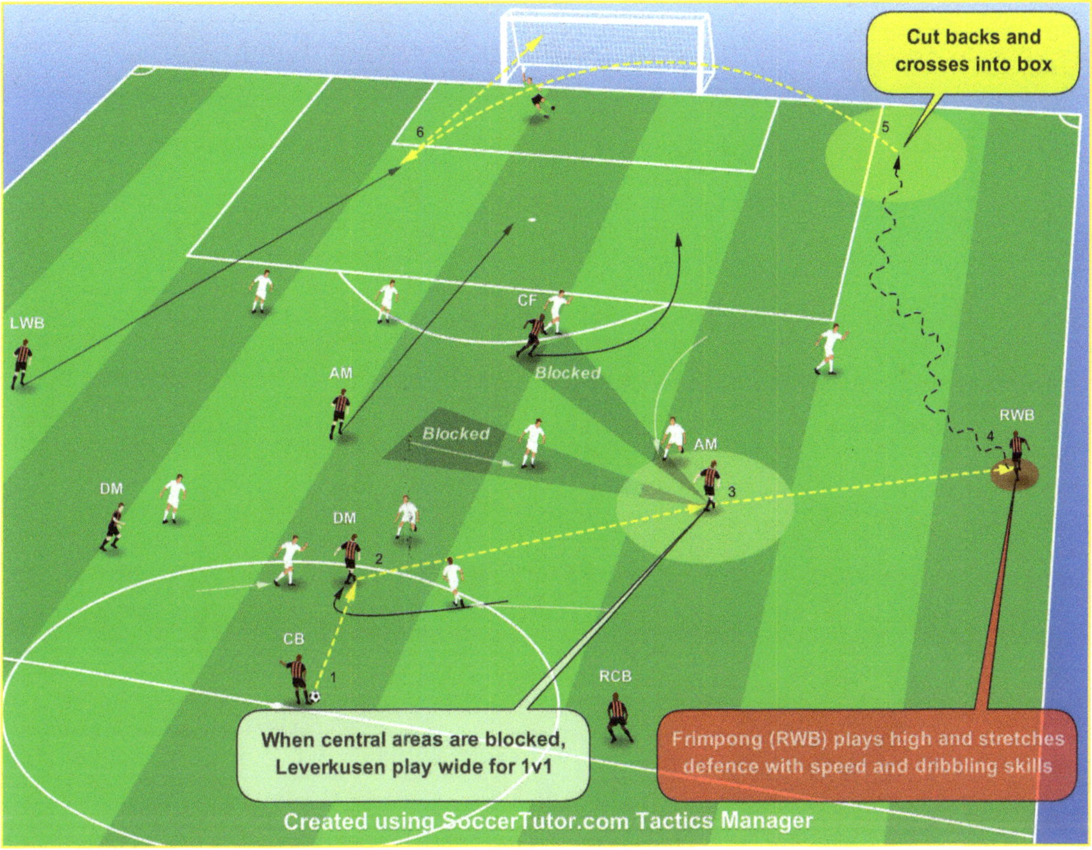

Bayer Leverkusen's **right wing back Frimpong plays a dynamic, attack focused "winger" role on the right**, making him a key attacking player in Xabi Alonso's team.

Frimpong's speed, ball control, and agility are of a high level and consistently stretch defences.

His crosses and cut backs are crucial to Leverkusen's wing play, which form part of a vital strategy for breaking their opponent's defensive structure and providing a constant threat in behind.

When central areas are blocked, Leverkusen look to play the ball wide for 1v1 situations, especially where Frimpong is strong on he right flank.

In this example, **Frimpong** (**RWB**) is able to win his 1v1 with high speed and dribbling skills on display. He is then able to deliver a cross for the opposite wing back **Grimaldo** (**LWB**) to score at the back post.

Xabi Alonso's Bayer Leverkusen: Attacking in the Final Third Tactics

Bayer Leverkusen's Overloading Final Zone of Pitch to Finish Attacks

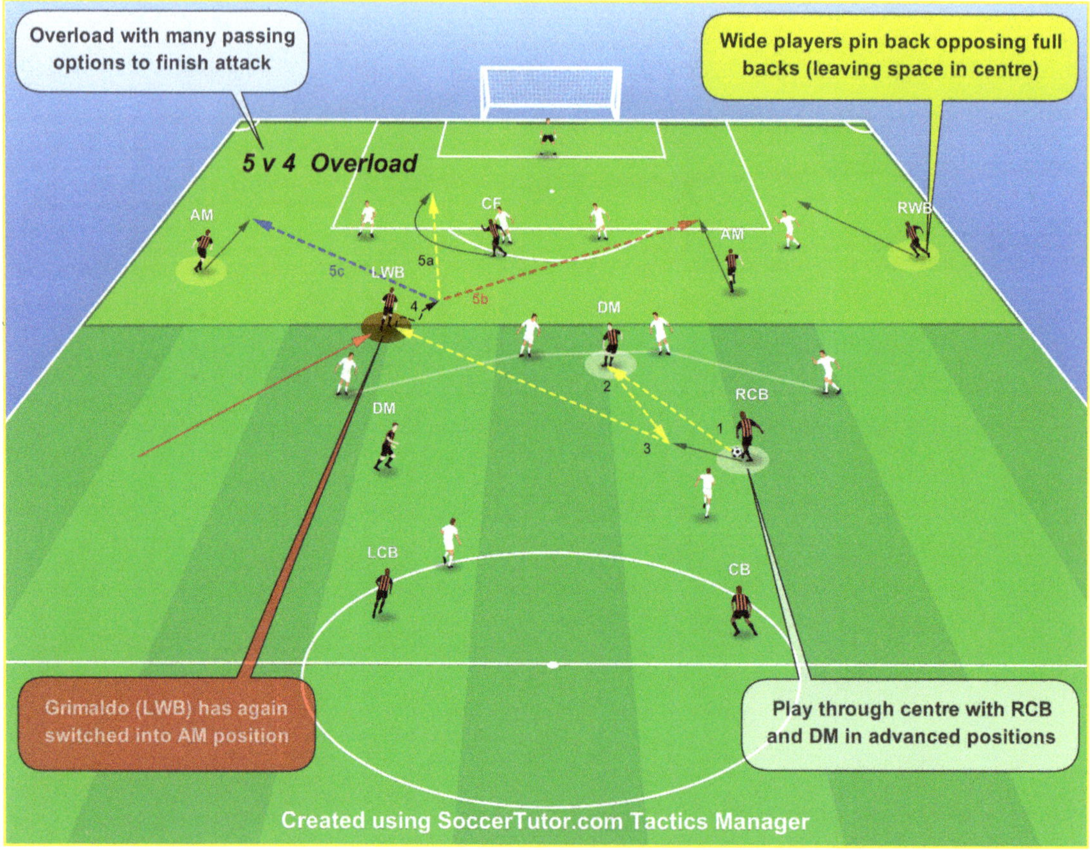

Overload with many passing options to finish attack

Wide players pin back opposing full backs (leaving space in centre)

5 v 4 Overload

Grimaldo (LWB) has again switched into AM position

Play through centre with RCB and DM in advanced positions

Created using SoccerTutor.com Tactics Manager

Xabi Alonso's attacking approach in the final third is direct and highly effective, focused on creating scoring opportunities through dribbling, cut backs, and through passes, with a preference for central channels over wide crosses if possible.

They **use 2 players to stretch the opposition's back-line, opening space for central players to make forward runs**. This often results in a front 5 shape that can overwhelm opposing defences with 5v5 situations or even 5v4 overloads, as shown.

In this example, **Grimaldo (LWB)** is again in an attacking midfielder position and receives from **RCB** (who is in an advanced position) after a "bounce" pass from the defensive midfielder (**DM**).

From there, the favoured pass for **Grimaldo (LWB)** is for the run of the centre forward (**CF**), but there are also other options.

Bayer Leverkusen's adaptability and varied attack routes keep opponents under constant pressure, making them a very efficient attacking team.

Attacking Positional Patterns of Play

Direct from
Xabi Alonso's
Training Sessions

Xabi Alonso Practices: Attacking Positional Patterns of Play

Coaching Style of Play

"The team has to know how we want to play. Dominant, intense, controlled, with a winning mentality and that should be from the first kick-off until the final whistle. I will try to give the players clear instructions and ideas."

Xabi Alonso

Xabi Alonso Practices: Attacking Positional Patterns of Play

Xabi Alonso's Bayer Leverkusen 3-4-2-1 Formation

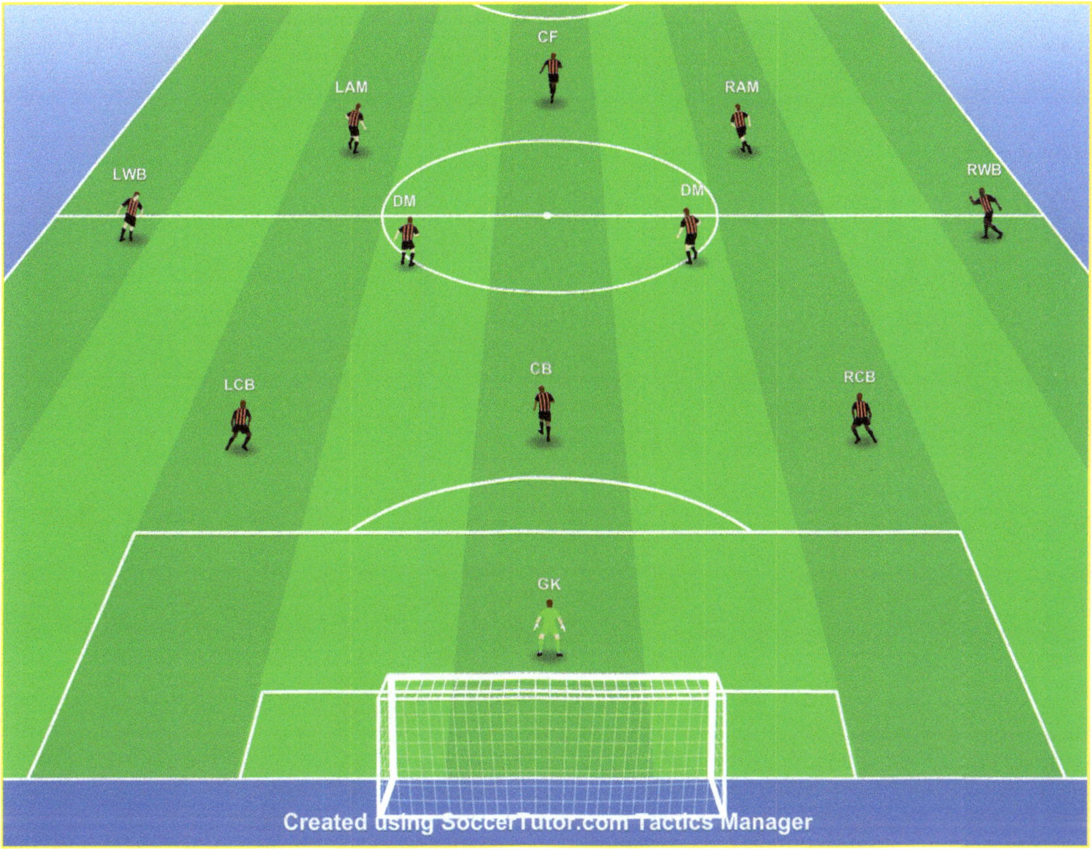

- **GK:** Goalkeeper

- **LCB:** Left Centre Back

- **CB:** Middle Centre Back

- **RCB:** Right Centre Back

- **DM:** Defensive Midfielder (x 2)

- **LWB:** Left Wing Back

- **RWB:** Right Wing Back

- **LAM:** Attacking Midfielder

- **RAM:** Right Attacking Midfielder

- **CF:** Centre Forward

Source: Xabi Alonso's Bayer Leverkusen training session at Bayer 04 Leverkusen Training Ground - 2024

Xabi Alonso Practices: Attacking Positional Patterns of Play

Positional Patterns Training Setup with 3-1-5 Shape (from 3-2-5)

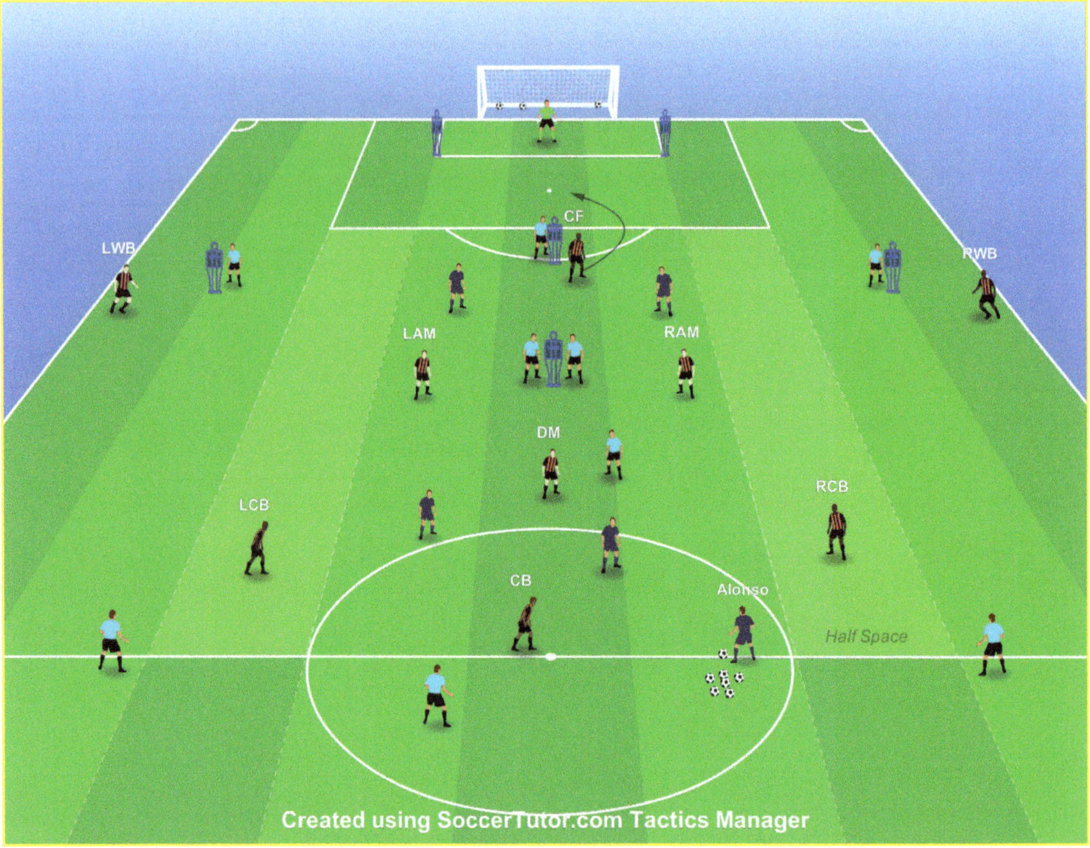

- This diagram shows **Alonso's setup** for practicing **attacking positional patterns of play with Bayer Leverkusen** using 9 players (one DM missing from the 3-2-5 build up shape - *see pages 60-62*).

- There are coaches in different positions. **Xabi Alonso** passes new balls in and the other coaches close down players, apply pressure to block passing lanes at certain points, and help make the positional patterns of play more game realistic, with some defensive resistance.

- There are 4 blue mannequins which help the players with opposition's likely positioning in central midfield, central defence, and full/wing back positions.

- In each position, there are 2 players (extras in blue bibs), who form 2 teams of 9 outfield players to practice patterns.

- The 2 teams **run the patterns outlined by Xabi Alonso** alternately. As soon as one team finishes, they jog back to their positions and the next team goes.

Source: Xabi Alonso's Bayer Leverkusen training session at Bayer 04 Leverkusen Training Ground - 2024

Xabi Alonso Practices: Attacking Positional Patterns of Play

1. Draw in Press to Play Out, Switch, and Attacking Midfielder's Through Pass to Wing Back from the Half Space

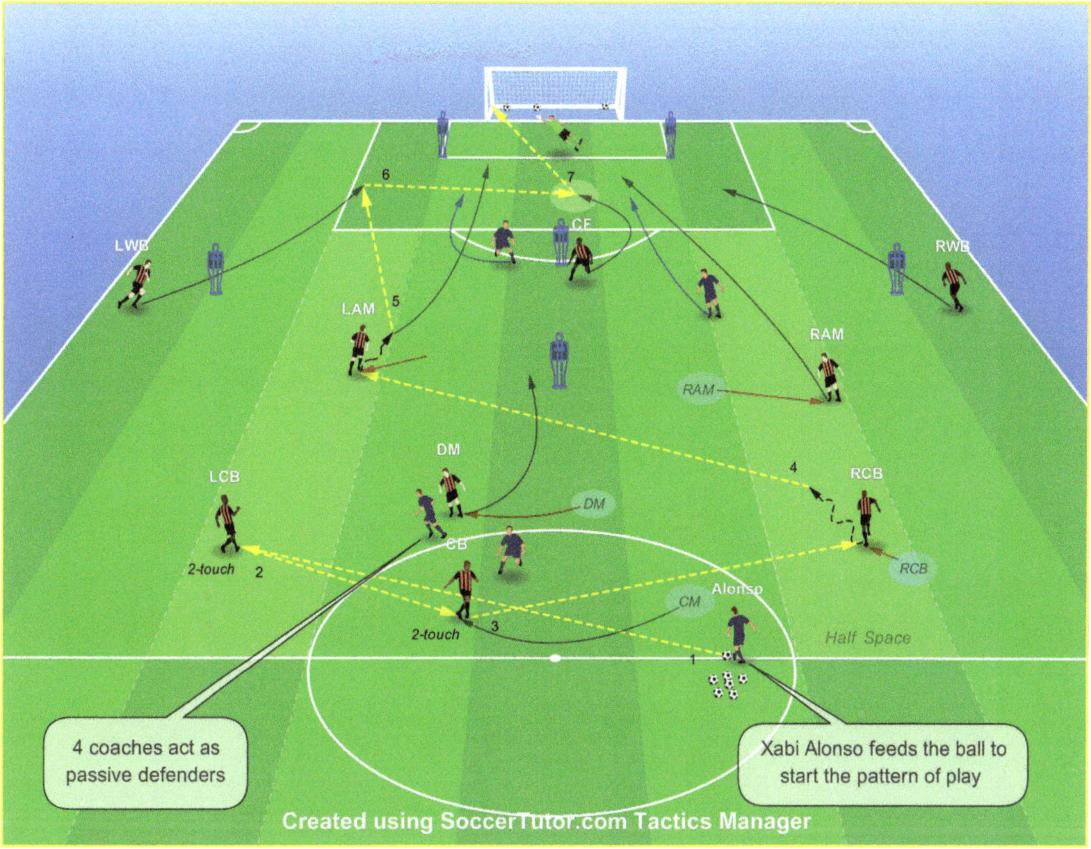

2 coaches use passive pressing for the build up and the other 2 use passive defending in the box. Blue circles = starting positions.

Practice Description

1-2. Alonso passes wide to the left centre back (**LCB**), who passes back to the centre back (**CB**).

3. Their 4v2 advantage enables **CB** to pass to the right centre back (**RCB**), who can move forward to progress the play.

4. RCB receives and moves forward with the ball and plays a switch pass to the left attacking midfielder (**LAM**) high up the pitch within the half space.

5. LAM plays a through pass for the left wing back's (**LWB**) inside run off the flank in behind and into the box.

6-7. LWB passes the ball across the box for the centre forward (**CF**) to score. **LAM**, **RAM**, and **RWB** also make runs into the box to provide options.

Source: Xabi Alonso's Bayer Leverkusen training session at Bayer 04 Leverkusen Training Ground - 2024

Xabi Alonso Practices: Attacking Positional Patterns of Play

2. Centre Back Runs Out with Ball, Switch, and Through Pass to Wing Back for Cross with Supporting Runs into Box

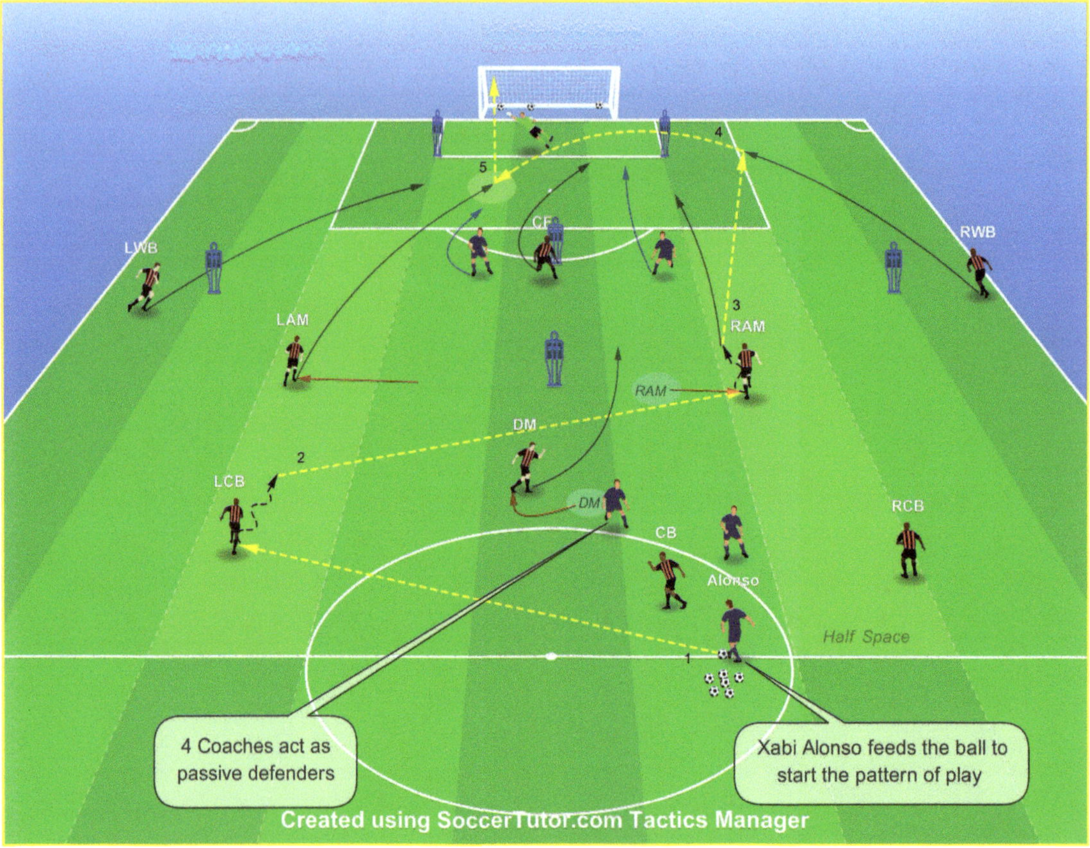

2 coaches use passive pressing for the build up and the other 2 use passive defending in the box. Blue circles = starting positions.

Practice Description

1. **Alonso** passes wide to the left centre back (**LCB**), who moves forward with the ball.

2. **LCB** plays a switch pass to the right attacking midfielder (**RAM**) high up the pitch within the half space.

3. **RAM** receives, moves forward with the ball, and plays a through pass for the wing back's (**RWB**) advanced run in behind towards the by-line.

4-5. **RWB** crosses the ball (stands it up) timed well for the deep run of **LAM** to score in the centre of the box. **RAM**, **CF**, and **LWB** also make runs into the box to provide support for the attack.

Source: Xabi Alonso's Bayer Leverkusen training session at Bayer 04 Leverkusen Training Ground - 2024

Xabi Alonso Practices: Attacking Positional Patterns of Play

3. Support to Play Out, Switch, Through Pass to Wing Back, and Cut Back for Attacking Midfielder's Run into Box

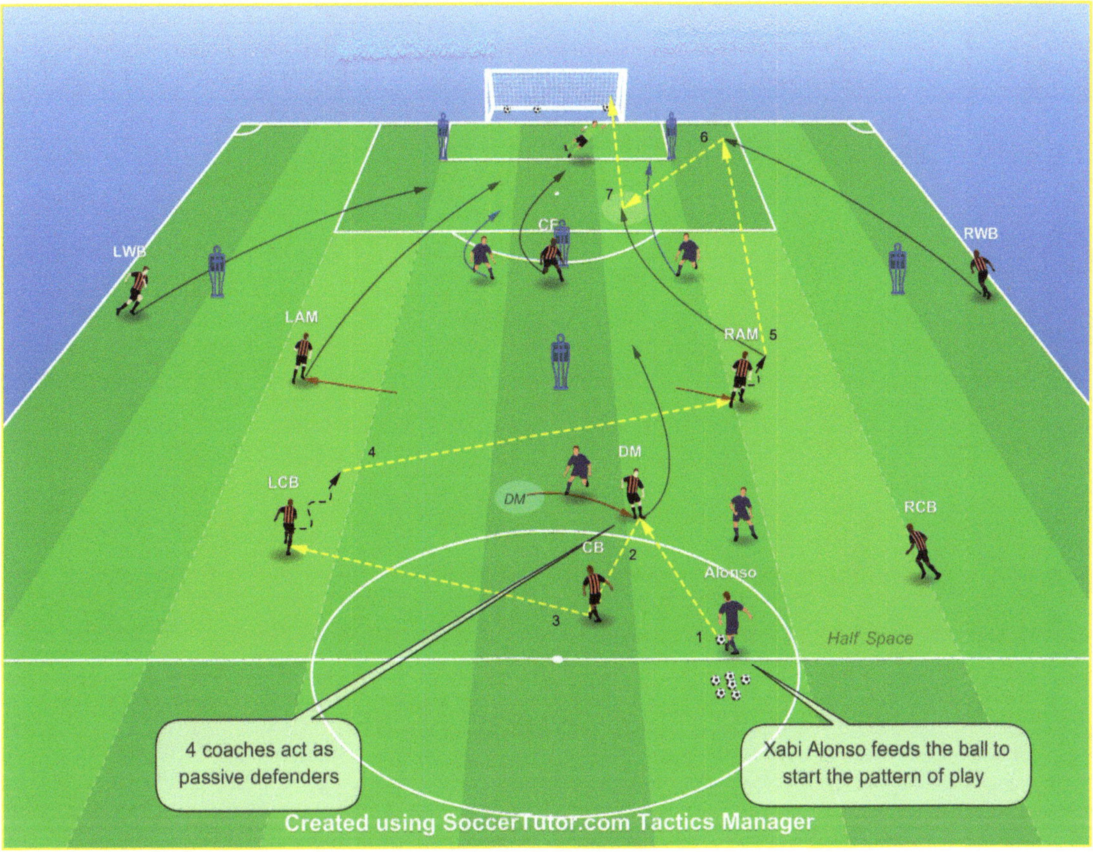

2 coaches use passive pressing for the build up and the other 2 use passive defending in the box. Blue circles = starting positions.

Practice Description

1-2. Alonso passes to the defensive midfielder (**DM**), who is pressed from behind, so he passes back to the middle centre back (**CB**).

3. The 4v2 advantage enables **CB** to pass to the left centre back (**LCB**) in space.

4. LCB receives, moves forward with the ball, and plays a switch pass to the right attacking midfielder (**RAM**).

5. RAM turns forward and plays a through pass for the wing back's (**RWB**) high run towards the by-line and into the box.

6-7. RWB cuts the ball back for **RAM's** incisive run to score. **CF**, **LAM**, and **LWB** also make runs into the box to provide support for the attack.

Source: Xabi Alonso's Bayer Leverkusen training session at Bayer 04 Leverkusen Training Ground - 2024

Xabi Alonso Practices: Attacking Positional Patterns of Play

4. Switch to Play Out, Switch Again, Attacking Midfielder's Through Pass to Wing Back, and Supporting Runs into Box

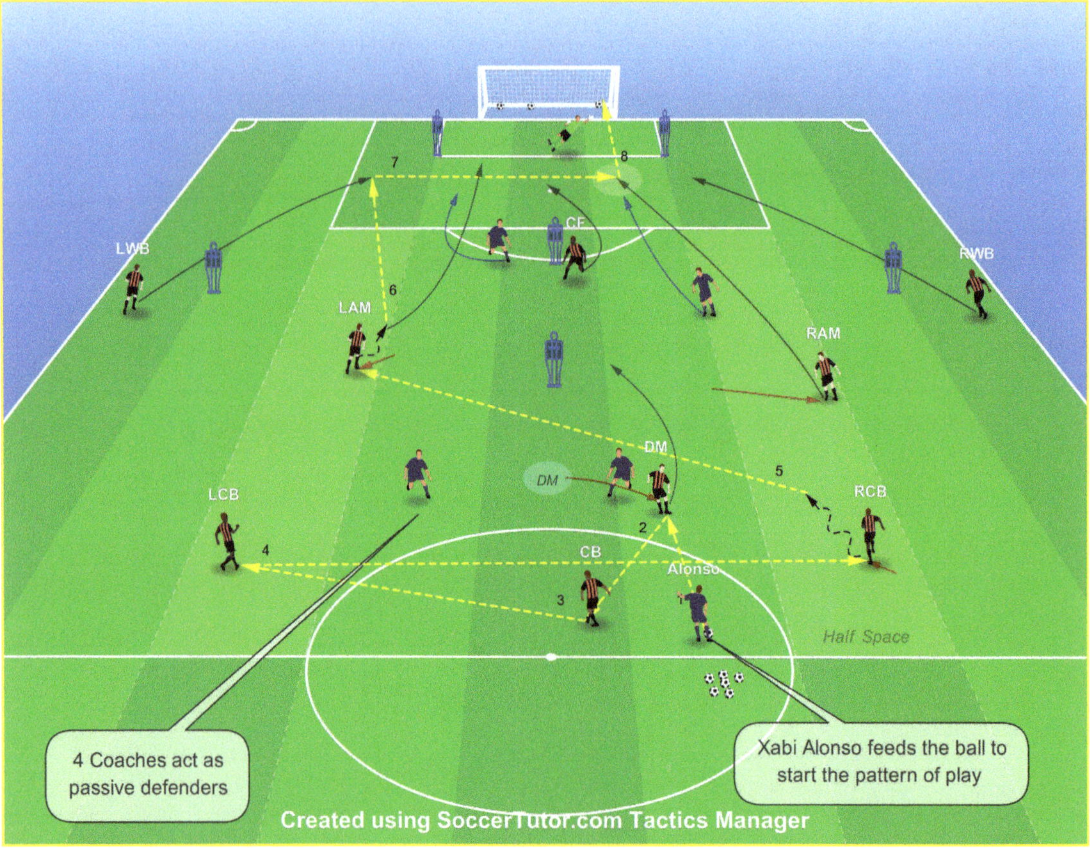

4 Coaches act as passive defenders

Xabi Alonso feeds the ball to start the pattern of play

2 coaches use passive pressing for the build up and the other 2 use passive defending in the box. Blue circles = starting positions.

Practice Description

1-2. Alonso passes to the defensive midfielder (**DM**), who is pressed from behind, so he passes back to the middle centre back (**CB**).

3-4. CB to passes to the left centre back (**LCB**), who switches play to **RCB**.

5. The right centre back (**RCB**) receives and can move forward with the ball to progress the play. He then plays a switch pass to the left attacking midfielder (**LAM**) high up the pitch (in half space).

6. LAM plays a through pass for the left wing back's (**LWB**) inside run off the flank in behind and into the box.

7-8. LWB delivers a low cross for **RAM** to score at the back post. **CF**, **LAM**, and **RWB** also make runs into the box.

Source: Xabi Alonso's Bayer Leverkusen training session at Bayer 04 Leverkusen Training Ground - 2024

Xabi Alonso Practices: Attacking Positional Patterns of Play

5. Short Passing Build Up, Play Out, Forward's Support Play, and Attacking Midfielder's Third Man Run in Behind

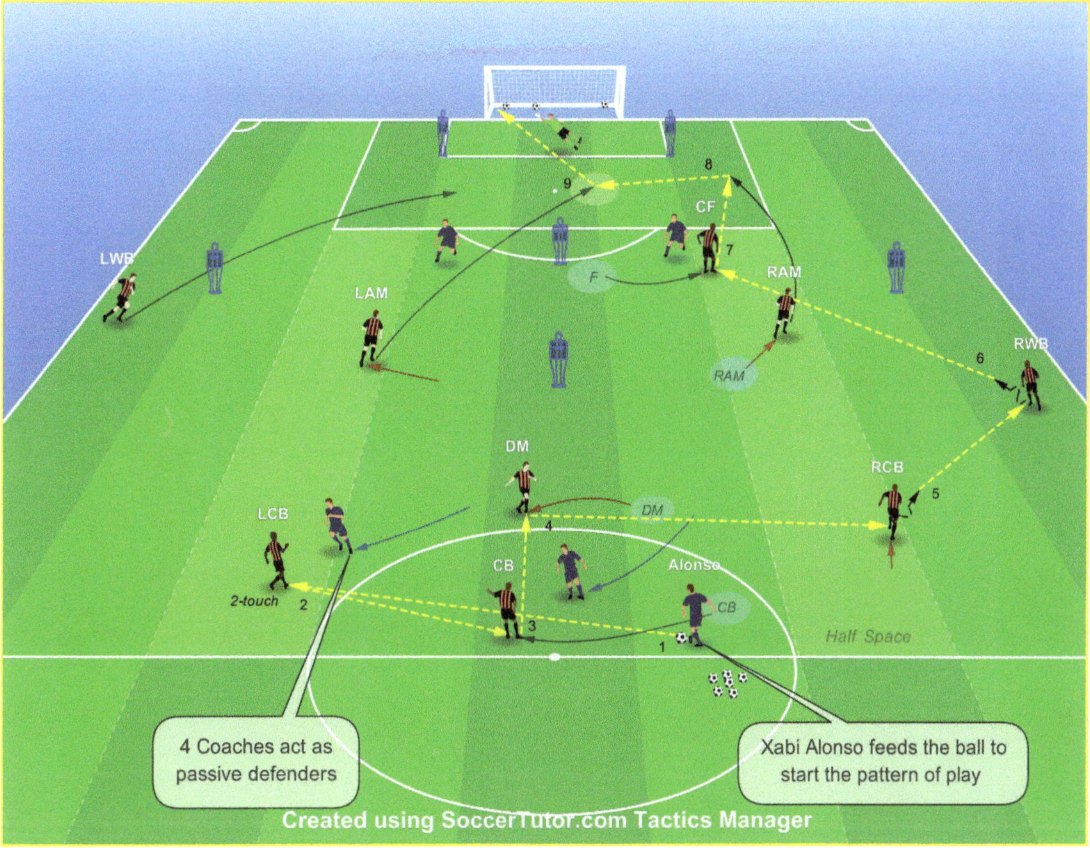

2 coaches use passive pressing for the build up and the other 2 use passive defending in the box. Blue circles = starting positions.

Practice Description

1-2. **Alonso** passes wide to the left centre back (**LCB**), who is pressed, so passes back to the middle centre back (**CB**).

3. **CB** is pressed but is able to break the first line of pressure with a short forward pass to the defensive midfielder (**DM**).

4-5. **DM** passes to the right centre back (**RCB**), who plays wide to the right wing back (**RWB**).

6-7. The centre forward (**CF**) moves across to that side so **RWB** can pass to his feet. As the ball is travelling, the attacking midfielder (**RAM**) on that side makes a third man run to receive **CF's** first time pass in behind and into the box.

8-9. **RAM** cuts the ball back for **LAM** to score after a well timed forward run.

Source: Xabi Alonso's Bayer Leverkusen training session at Bayer 04 Leverkusen Training Ground - 2024

Xabi Alonso Practices: Attacking Positional Patterns of Play

6. Short Passing Build Up Play in Centre, Play Out, and Attack with Right Wing Back Moving Inside to Dribble into Box

4 Coaches act as passive defenders

Xabi Alonso feeds the ball to start the pattern of play

2 coaches use passive pressing for the build up and the other 2 use passive defending in the box. Blue circles = starting positions.

Practice Description

1-2. Alonso passes wide to the left centre back (**LCB**), who is pressed, so passes back to the middle centre back (**CB**).

3. CB is pressed but is able to break the first line of pressure with a short forward pass to the defensive midfielder (**DM**).

4-5. DM passes to the right centre back (**RCB**), as the attacking midfielder (**RAM**) drops back and wide to receive the next pass.

6-7. RAM passes forward to **RWB**, who receives high in the half space after inside movement, then dribbles past the coach and into the box.

8-9. RWB passes into the centre of the box for **LAM** to score. **CF** and **LWB** also make runs into the box to support the attack.

Source: Xabi Alonso's Bayer Leverkusen training session at Bayer 04 Leverkusen Training Ground - 2024

Xabi Alonso Practices: Attacking Positional Patterns of Play

7. Long Aerial Switch of Play to Left Wing Back, Attacking Midfielder's Third Man Run in Behind, Cut Back, and Finish

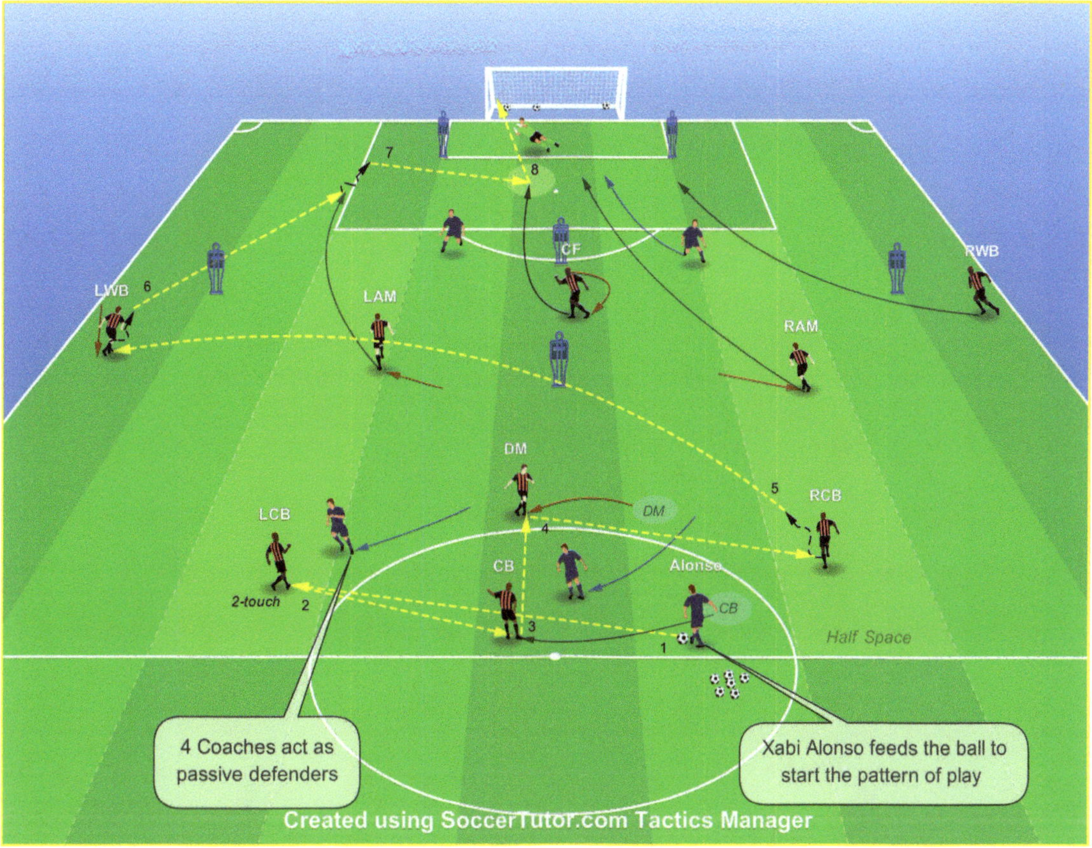

2 coaches use passive pressing for the build up and the other 2 use passive defending in the box. Blue circles = starting positions.

Practice Description

1-2. **Alonso** passes wide to the left centre back (**LCB**), who is pressed, so passes back to the middle centre back (**CB**).

3. **CB** is pressed but is able to break the first line of pressure with a short forward pass to the defensive midfielder (**DM**).

4-5. **DM** passes to the right centre back (**RCB**), who plays a long aerial switch of play to the left wing back (**LWB**).

6. **LWB** passes outside the full back mannequin, well timed for the run of the attacking midfielder (**LAM**) in behind.

7-8. **LAM** receives, enters the box, and cuts the ball back into the centre for the centre forward (**CF**) to score. **RAM** and **RWB** also make runs into the box to support the attack.

Source: Xabi Alonso's Bayer Leverkusen training session at Bayer 04 Leverkusen Training Ground - 2024

Xabi Alonso Practices: Attacking Positional Patterns of Play

8. Long Aerial Switch of Play to Right Wing Back, Attacking Midfielder's Third Man Run in Behind, Cross, and Finish

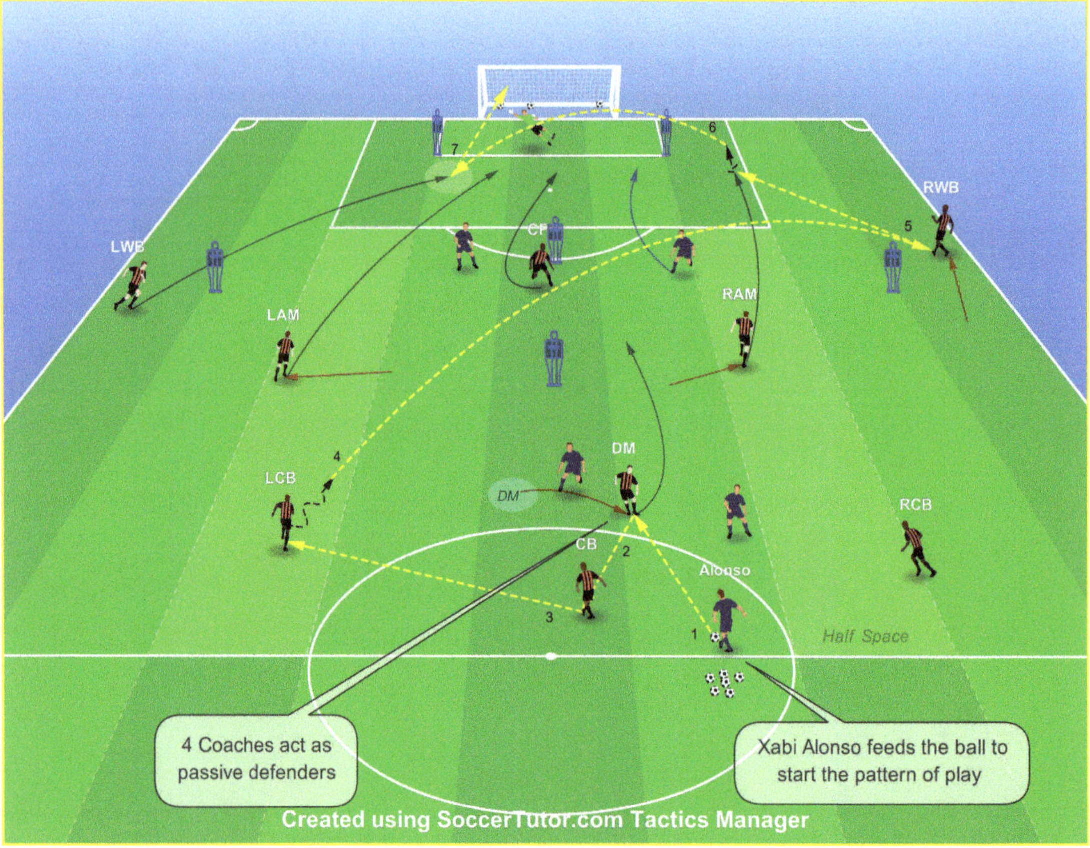

2 coaches use passive pressing for the build up and the other 2 use passive defending in the box. Blue circles = starting positions.

Practice Description

1-2. Alonso passes to the defensive midfielder (**DM**), who is pressed from behind, so he passes back to the middle centre back (**CB**).

3. CB passes to the left centre back (**LCB**), who receives and moves forward.

4. DM plays a long aerial switch of play to the right wing back (**RWB**), who makes a forward run to receive beyond the mannequin.

5. The attacking midfielder (**RAM**) had already shifted across, and then makes an incisive run in behind to receive from **RWB** in the box.

6-7. RWB receives and crosses for **LWB** to score at the back post. **CF** and **LAM** also make runs into the box.

Source: Xabi Alonso's Bayer Leverkusen training session at Bayer 04 Leverkusen Training Ground - 2024

Xabi Alonso Practices: Attacking Positional Patterns of Play

Positional Patterns Training Setup with 2-5 Shape (from 3-2-5)

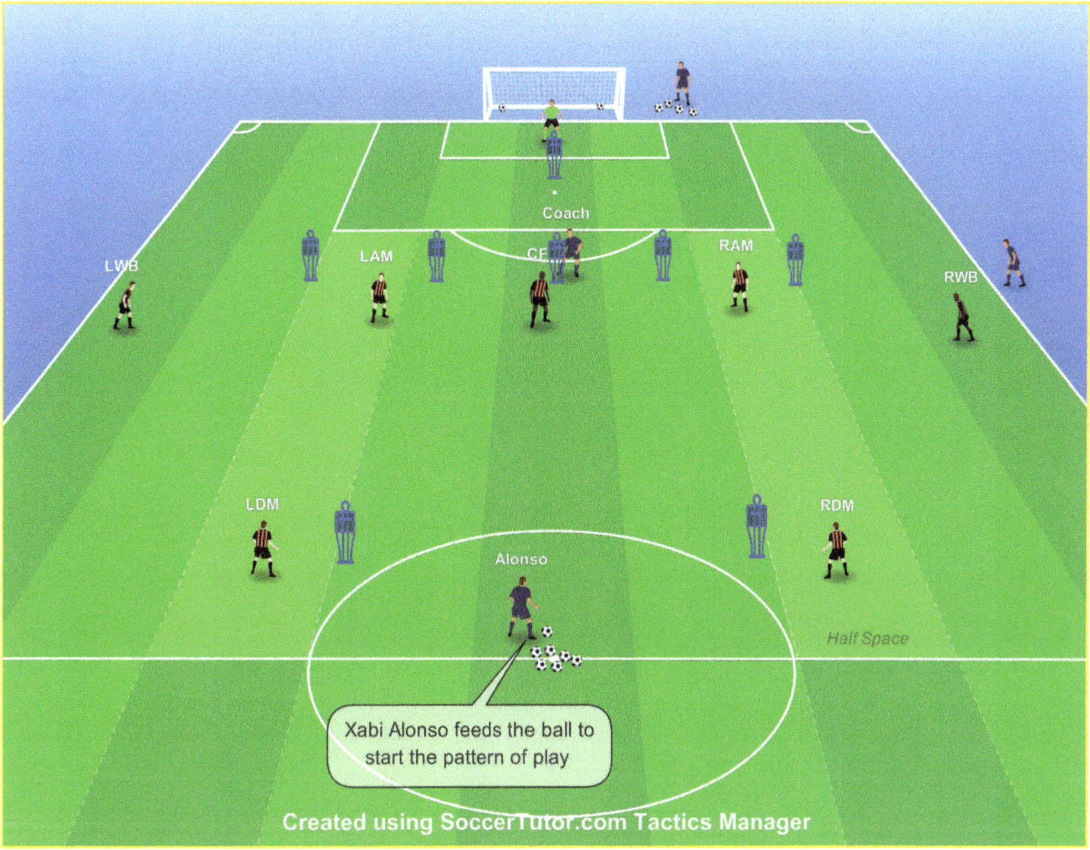

- This diagram shows **Alonso's setup** for practicing **attacking positional patterns of play with Bayer Leverkusen** using 7 players (midfield and forward lines from 3-2-5 build up shape - *see pages 60-62*).

- There are 2 defensive midfielders (**LDM** & **RDM**), 2 wing backs (**LWB** & **RWB**), 2 attacking midfielders (**LAM** & **RAM**), and the centre forward (**CF**).

- There are 7 blue mannequins which help the players with the opposition's likely positioning in central midfield and the defensive line. There is also another mannequin in the box and a coach who can apply passive defence - this is to make finishing the attack a little more match realistic.

- *Note: There were extra players in the DM, AM, and CF positions at times (waiting for their turn), but they are not shown in this diagram or those to follow.*

Source: Xabi Alonso's Bayer Leverkusen session, Aviva Stadium, Dublin (UEFA Europa League Final) - 21st May 2024

Xabi Alonso Practices: Attacking Positional Patterns of Play

1. Long Aerial Switch of Play to Left Wing Back, Defensive Midfielder's Supporting Run, Through Pass, and Cut Back

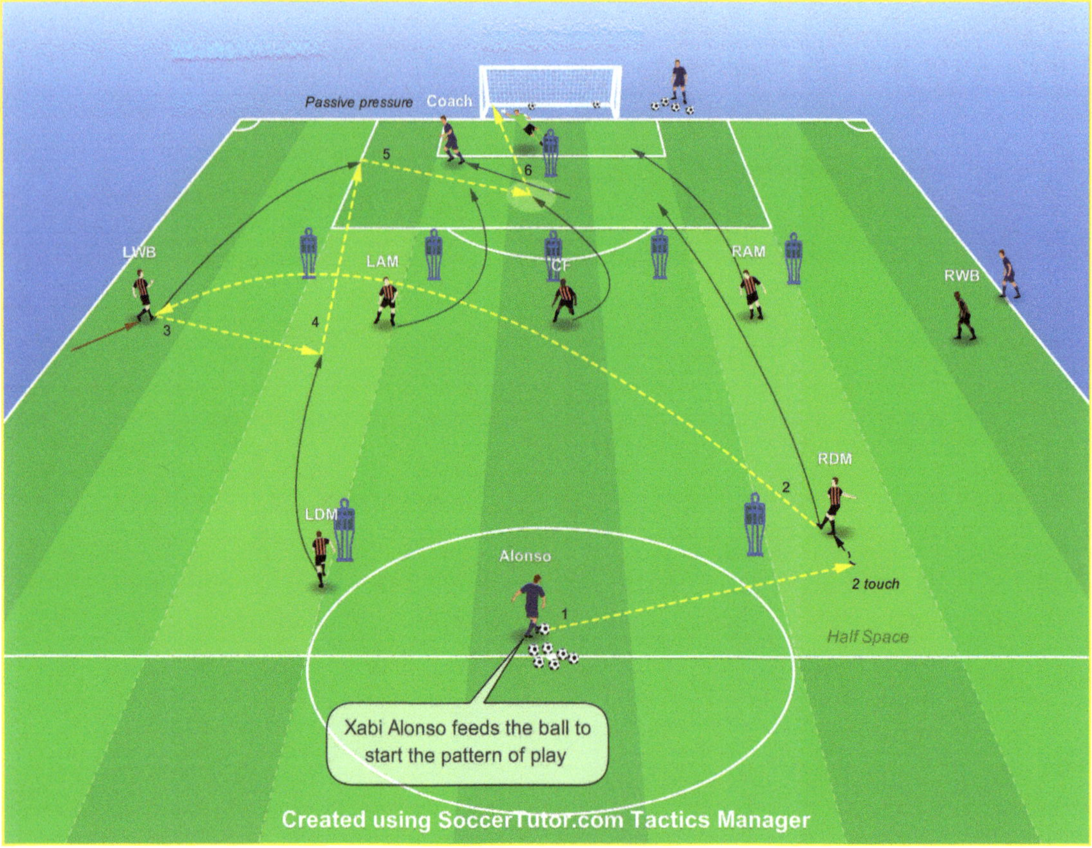

Practice Description

1. Xabi Alonso passes to the right defensive midfielder (**RDM**) to the right of the mannequin in the half space.

2. RDM plays a long aerial switch of play to the left wing back (**LWB**), as the left defensive midfielder (**LDM**) makes a forward run.

3-4. LWB plays a give & go with **LDM** to receive in behind.

5-6. The coach applies passive pressure and **LWB** cuts the ball back for the run of the centre forward (**CF**) to score.

→ The 2 attacking midfielders (**LAM** & **RAM**) also make runs into the box to provide support for the attack.

Source: Xabi Alonso's Bayer Leverkusen session, Aviva Stadium, Dublin (UEFA Europa League Final) - 21st May 2024

©SOCCERTUTOR.COM — XABI ALONSO: PRACTICES DIRECT FROM SESSIONS

2. Diagonal Pass to Attacking Midfielder, Give & Go with Centre Forward to Receive in the Box, and Shoot

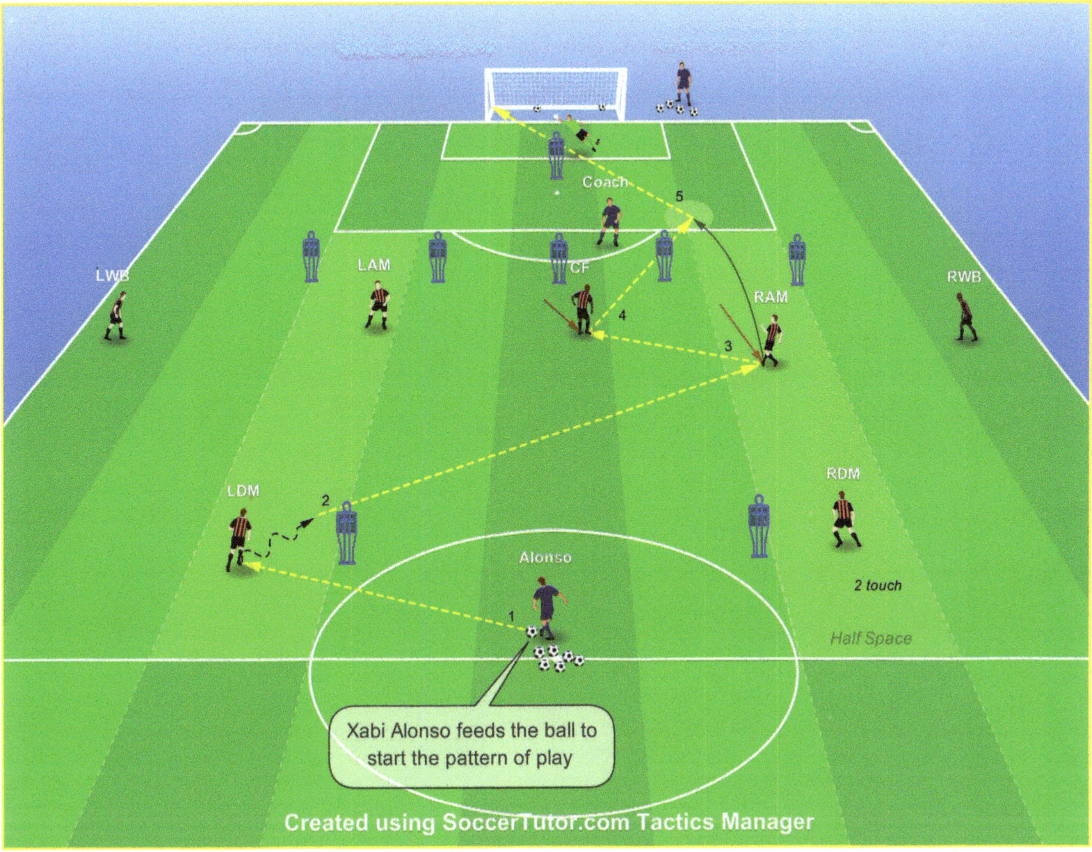

Xabi Alonso Practices: Attacking Positional Patterns of Play

Practice Description

1. **Xabi Alonso** passes to the left defensive midfielder (**LDM**) to the left of the mannequin in the half space.

2. **LDM** passes diagonally to the right attacking midfielder (**RAM**), who drops back to receive within the half space.

3-4. **RAM** plays a give & go with the centre forward (**CF**), who drops back to play a through pass in behind.

5. **RAM** times his run well to meet the correctly weighted pass with a first time shot.

Source: Xabi Alonso's Bayer Leverkusen session, Aviva Stadium, Dublin (UEFA Europa League Final) - 21st May 2024

Xabi Alonso Practices: Attacking Positional Patterns of Play

3. Diagonal Pass to Attacking Midfielder, Centre Forward Drops Off to Receive, and Shoot from Distance

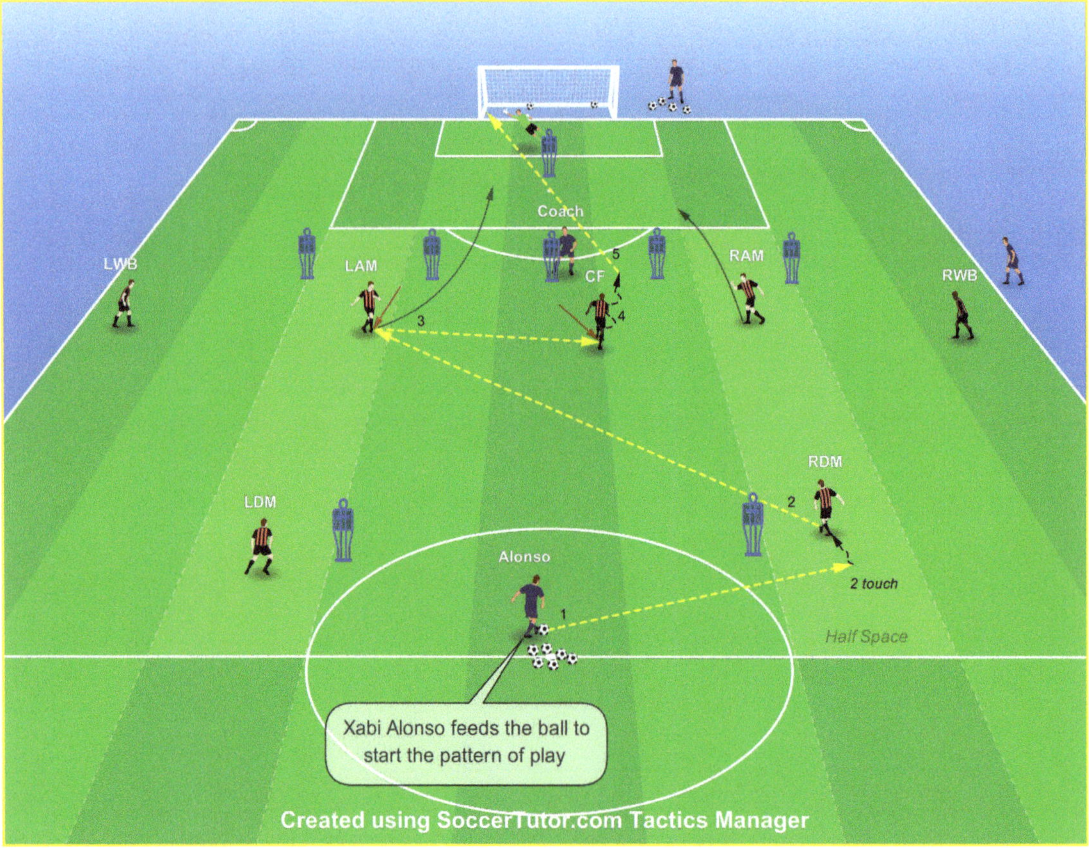

Practice Description

1. **Xabi Alonso** passes to the right defensive midfielder (**RDM**) to the right of the mannequin in the half space.

2. **RDM** passes diagonally to the left attacking midfielder (**LAM**), who drops back to receive within the half space.

3. **RAM** passes inside to the centre forward (**CF**), who also drops back to provide support.

4-5. **CF** moves forward with the ball and creates an angle to shoot from outside the box.

→ The 2 attacking midfielders (**LAM** & **RAM**) make runs into the box to provide support and alternative options.

Source: Xabi Alonso's Bayer Leverkusen session, Aviva Stadium, Dublin (UEFA Europa League Final) - 21st May 2024

©SOCCERTUTOR.COM   XABI ALONSO: PRACTICES DIRECT FROM SESSIONS

Xabi Alonso Practices: Attacking Positional Patterns of Play

4. Forward Pass to Centre Forward with Back to Goal, Lay-off, Deep Third Man Run, and Shot from Distance

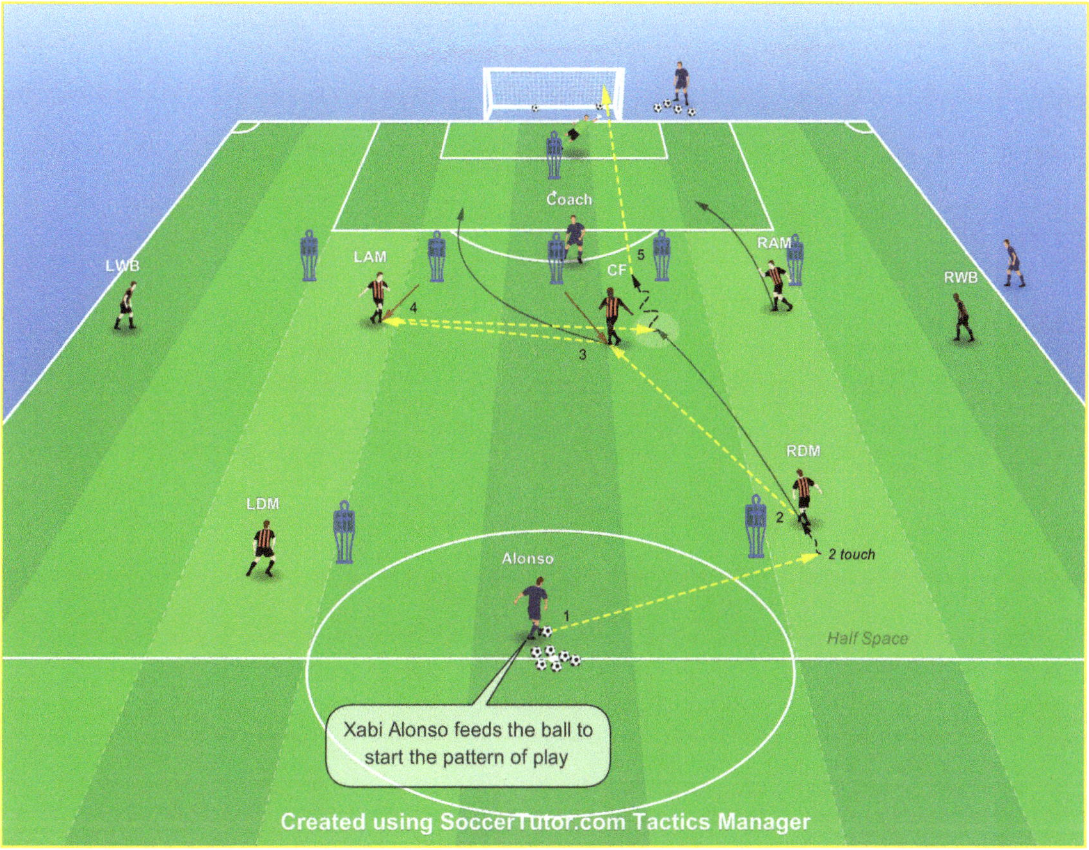

Practice Description

1. **Xabi Alonso** passes to the right defensive midfielder (**RDM**) to the right of the mannequin in the half space.

2. **RDM** passes forward and follows his pass. The centre forward (**CF**) drops back to receive.

3. **CF** passes across to the left attacking midfielder (**LAM**), who also drops back to receive.

4. **LAM** passes back across the pitch, timed for the oncoming run of **RDM**.

5. **RDM** moves forward with the ball in between 2 mannequins and shoots from outside the box.

→ **CF** and **RAM** make runs into the box to provide support and alternative options.

Source: Xabi Alonso's Bayer Leverkusen session, Aviva Stadium, Dublin (UEFA Europa League Final) - 21st May 2024

Xabi Alonso Practices: Attacking Positional Patterns of Play

5. Defensive Midfielder's Deep Through Pass in Behind and into Box for the Run of the Centre Forward

Practice Description

1. **Xabi Alonso** dribbles forward with the ball.

2. **Alonso** passes back for the left defensive midfielder (**LDM**), who has first checked to the left of the mannequin before moving forward at an angle to receive. At the same time, the left attacking midfielder (**LAM**) and centre forward (**CF**) check away from the mannequins, ready to make a run in behind.

3. **LDM** plays a long (ground) through pass for the run of **CF** in behind.

4. **CF** receives in the box, moves towards goal with the ball, and tries to score past the goalkeeper.

Source: Xabi Alonso's Bayer Leverkusen session, Aviva Stadium, Dublin (UEFA Europa League Final) - 21st May 2024

Attacking Positional Patterns of Play + 2nd Ball Finishing

Direct from Xabi Alonso's Training Sessions

Xabi Alonso Practices: Attacking Positional Patterns + 2nd Ball Finishing

Xabi Alonso's Positional Patterns + 2nd Ball Finishing Training Setup

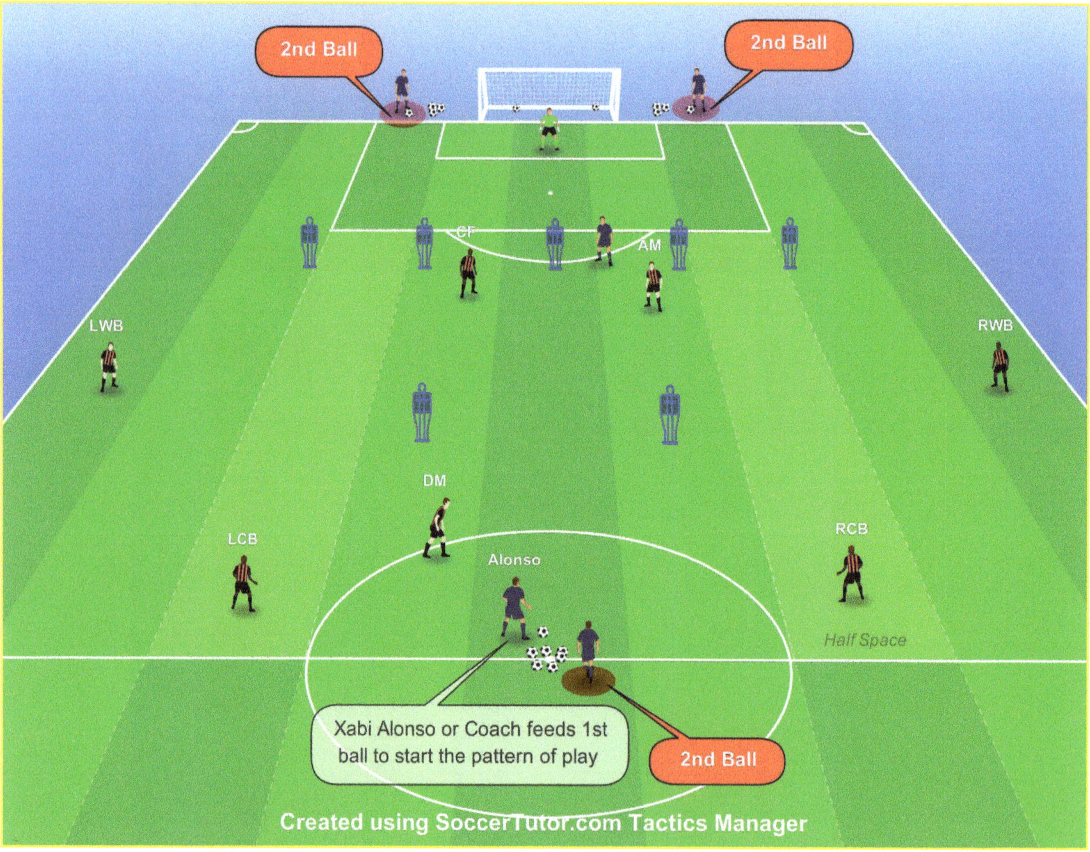

Xabi Alonso or Coach feeds 1st ball to start the pattern of play

- This diagram shows **Xabi Alonso's setup** for practicing **attacking positional patterns of play + 2nd ball finishing with Bayer Leverkusen** using 7 players.

- There are 2 centre backs (**LCB** & **RCB**), 1 defensive midfielder (**DM**), 2 wing backs (**LWB** & **RWB**), 1 attacking midfielder (**AM**) and the centre forward (**CF**).

- There is a **CB**, **DM** and **AM** missing from the 3-2-5 build up shape used by Bayer *(see pages 60-62 for details)*.

- There are 7 blue mannequins which help the players with the opposition's likely positioning in central midfield and the defensive line.

- **Alonso** feeds the 1st ball in. The 2nd ball (finishing) can be fed from any of the 3 coaches highlighted in red.

- *Note: There were extra players in some positions at times (waiting for their turn), but they are not shown in this diagram or those to follow.*

Source: Xabi Alonso's Bayer Leverkusen session, Aviva Stadium, Dublin (UEFA Europa League Final) - 21st May 2024

Xabi Alonso Practices: Attacking Positional Patterns + 2nd Ball Finishing

1. Switch Play Combinations, Wide Through Pass for Cut Back Finish + 2nd Ball Finish for Deep Run

The blue circles highlight starting positions.

Practice Description

1-3. **Xabi Alonso** passes to the right centre back (**RCB**) in the half space. He receives and passes to the attacking midfielder (**AM**), who drops back in between the 2 mannequins and sets the ball back for the defensive midfielder (**DM**).

4-5. **DM** completes the switch of play with a pass to the left wing back (**LWB**), who plays a forward pass for the curved run of the centre forward (**CF**) in behind.

6-7. **CF** cuts the ball back for the run of **AM** to score. The right wing back (**RWB**) also makes a run into the box.

2nd Ball (8-9). The coach next to the goal passes a new ball in for the oncoming advanced run of **RCB**, who takes a touch, and then shoots at goal from outside the box.

Source: Xabi Alonso's Bayer Leverkusen session, Aviva Stadium, Dublin (UEFA Europa League Final) - 21st May 2024

Xabi Alonso Practices: Attacking Positional Patterns + 2nd Ball Finishing

2. Switch Play Combinations, Give & Go in Behind for Cut Back Finish + 2nd Ball Shot

The blue circles highlight starting positions.

Practice Description

1-3. **Xabi Alonso** passes to the right centre back (**RCB**) in the half space. He receives and passes to the attacking midfielder (**AM**), who drops back in between the 2 mannequins and sets the ball back for the defensive midfielder (**DM**).

4-6. **DM** completes the switch of play with a pass to the left wing back (**LWB**), who plays a give & go with the centre forward (**CF**) to receive in behind.

7-8. **LWB** delivers a low cross for the run of **AM** to score (the coach provides passive defence). The right wing back (**RWB**) also makes a run into the box.

2nd Ball (9-11). The coach on the halfway line passes a new ball in for **CF**, who receives, moves forward with the ball, and then shoots from outside the box.

Source: Xabi Alonso's Bayer Leverkusen session, Aviva Stadium, Dublin (UEFA Europa League Final) - 21st May 2024

Xabi Alonso Practices: Attacking Positional Patterns + 2nd Ball Finishing

3. Long Switch of Play, Give & Go in Behind for Cut Back Finish + 2nd Ball Shot from Distance

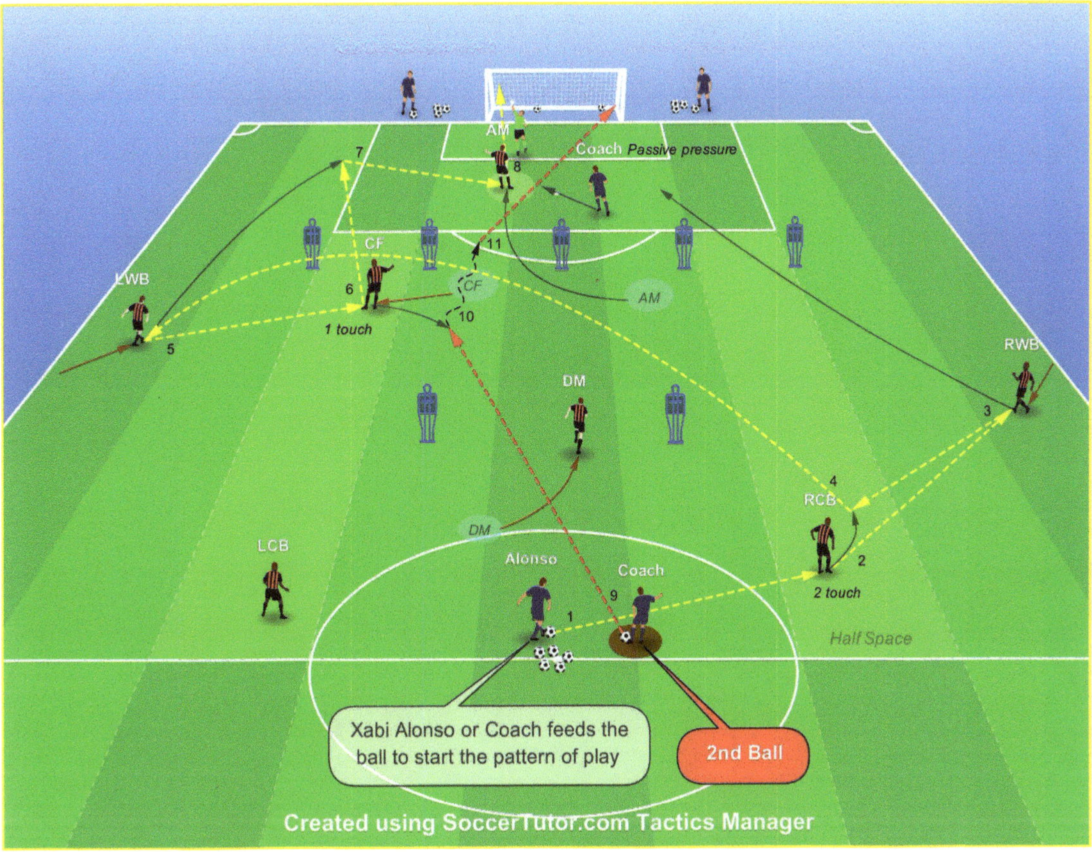

The blue circles highlight starting positions.

Practice Description

1-4. **Xabi Alonso** passes to the right centre back (**RCB**) in the half space. He plays a one-two with the right wing back (**RWB**), and then plays a long aerial switch of play to the left wing back (**LWB**).

5-6. **LWB** plays a give & go with the centre forward (**CF**), who moves across to support, to receive in behind.

7-8. **LWB** cuts the ball back for the attacking midfielder (**AM**), who makes a curved run towards the near post to score. The coach provides passive defence. **RWB** also makes a run into the box.

2nd Ball (9-11). The coach on the halfway line passes a new ball in for **CF**, who receives, moves forward with the ball, and then shoots from outside the box.

Source: Xabi Alonso's Bayer Leverkusen session, Aviva Stadium, Dublin (UEFA Europa League Final) - 21st May 2024

Xabi Alonso Practices: Attacking Positional Patterns + 2nd Ball Finishing

4. Long Aerial Switch of Play, Through Pass, Cut Back Finish + 2nd Ball Shot from Distance

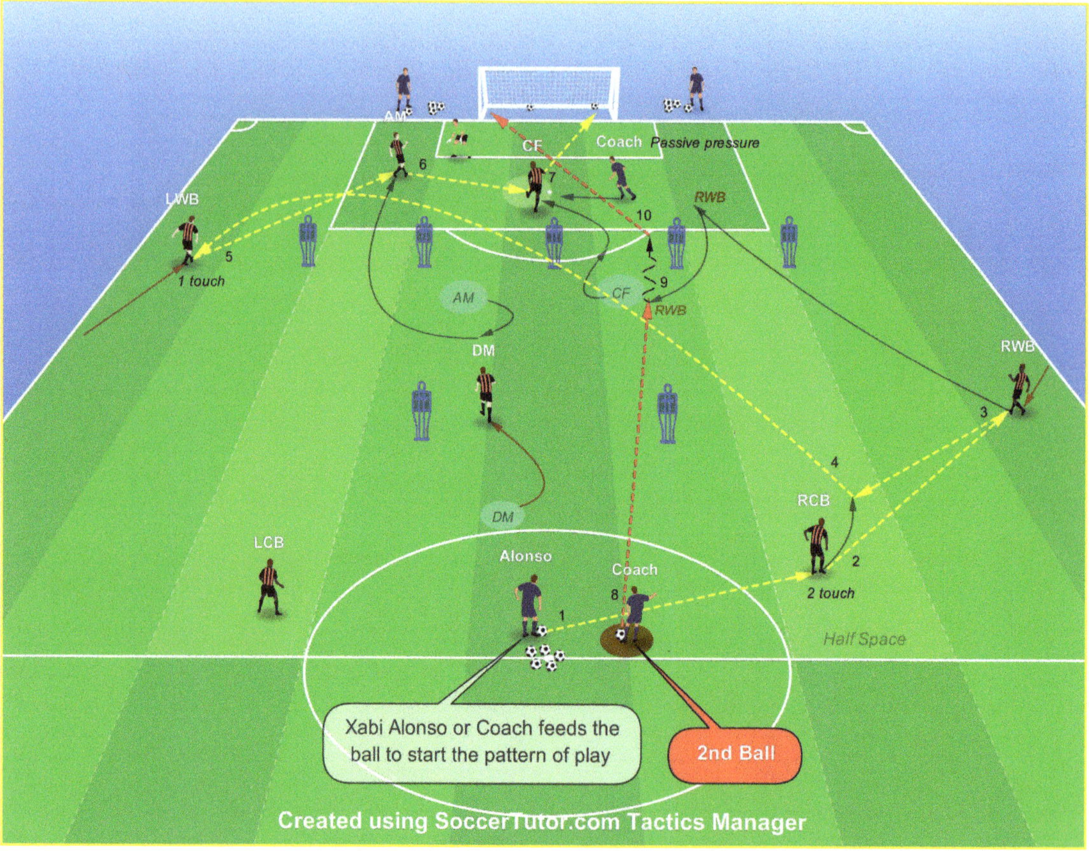

The blue circles highlight starting positions.

Practice Description

1-4. **Xabi Alonso** passes to the right centre back (**RCB**) in the half space. He plays a one-two with the right wing back (**RWB**), and then plays a long aerial switch of play to the left wing back (**LWB**).

5. **LWB** plays a first time pass in behind for the curved run of the attacking midfielder (**AM**) into the box.

6-7. **AM** cuts the ball back for the centre forward (**CF**), who makes a run towards the penalty spot to score. The coach provides passive defence. **RWB** also makes a run into the box.

2nd Ball (8-10). The coach on the halfway line passes a new ball in for **RWB**, who drops back, receives, moves forward with the ball towards the box, and shoots at goal.

Source: Xabi Alonso's Bayer Leverkusen session, Aviva Stadium, Dublin (UEFA Europa League Final) - 21st May 2024

Attacking and Finishing

Direct from
Xabi Alonso's
Training Sessions

Xabi Alonso Practices: Attacking and Finishing

1. Long Aerial Cross-Field Pass to Wide Player and Cross for Players Finishing in the Box vs Defender + GK

Target Zone

Xabi Alonso sends cross-field passes to the left wing back (LWB), who controls the ball and delivers both ground and aerial crosses for 3 players to finish

Practice Description

- **Xabi Alonso** takes up a deep position as shown, and another coach feeds him balls. He sends cross-field passes to the wide player (**Player A**) which all land within the highlighted target zone.

- **Player A** times his forward movement to control the pass within the target zone and then deliver a cross into the box where 1 coach provides passive resistance.

- 3 players make different runs into the box to try to score. In this example, **Player B** runs towards the near post, **Player D** runs towards the 6-yard line, and **Player C** makes a curved run towards the back post to score.

- Throughout the practice, the runs can vary and the wide players deliver both ground and aerial crosses.

- The practice can then be repeated on the right side.

Source: Xabi Alonso's Bayer Leverkusen training session at Bayer 04 Leverkusen Training Ground - 2024

Xabi Alonso Practices: Attacking and Finishing

2. Crossing and Finishing with Different Types of Delivery Team Scoring Competition

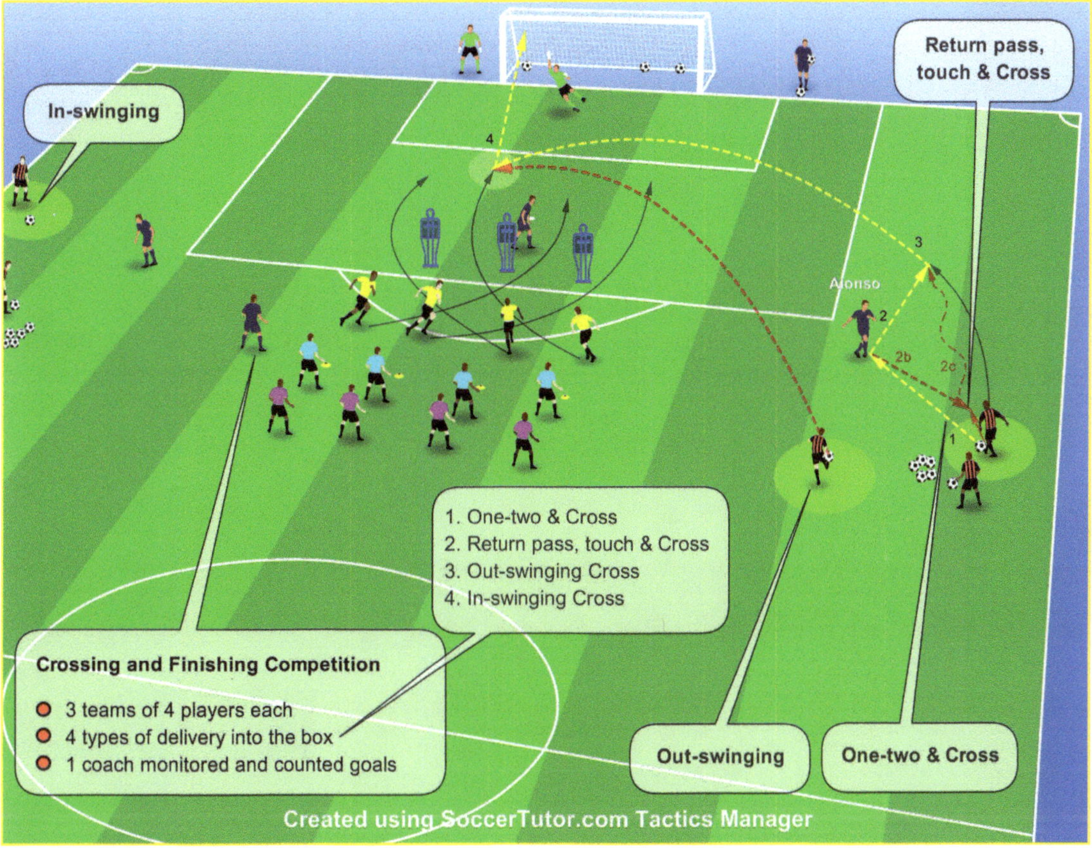

Practice Description

- There are 3 teams (yellow, blue and pink) for this finishing competition.
- The type of delivery is alternated from the red wide players:

  1) One two and cross with the coach.

  2) Return pass, touch, and cross.

  3) Out-swinging cross from deep.

  4) In-swinging cross from high position.

- Each team takes turns to make runs into the box and try to score from the cross that is delivered.
- As shown in the diagram example, the players need to coordinate to make runs into different areas of the box.
- One of the coaches monitors the scoring and counts the amount of goals throughout to determine which team is the winner.

Source: Xabi Alonso's Bayer Leverkusen session, Aviva Stadium, Dublin (UEFA Europa League Final) - 21st May 2024

Xabi Alonso Practices: Attacking and Finishing

3. Build Up, Attacking Combination on the Flank, Crossing and Finishing + 2nd Ball Transition Play

2nd Ball: Start transition with blues attacking opposite goal

3 v 3 In the box to finish the attack

Xabi Alonso starts the pattern of play by passing the ball and then pressing immediately

The blue circles highlight starting positions.

Practice Description

1. Xabi Alonso starts the practice by passing to the right centre back (**RCB**).

→ The ball is moved to the left wing back (**LWB**), who plays a give & go with the attacking midfielder (**AM**) to receive in behind.

→ **LWB** delivers a low cross into the box for a yellow player to score.

2. The 3 yellow attacking players make runs into the box to try to score (near post, centre, and far post). The 3 blue defenders track the runs and defend the goal.

2nd Ball (3). The coach in the box drops a ball for a blue player to start a transition from defence to attack (3v3) towards the opposite goal.

→ Once complete, **Alonso** starts again and the combination is on the right side.

Source: Xabi Alonso's Bayer Leverkusen preseason training session in Donaueschingen, Germany - 29th July 2024

Positional Training Games

Direct from
Xabi Alonso's
Training Sessions

Xabi Alonso Practices: Positional Training Games

Learning from Experience

"Every match, every training session, is a learning experience. The best coaches never stop learning and constantly seek ways to improve both themselves and their team."

Xabi Alonso

Xabi Alonso Practices: Positional Training Games

1. High Tempo Three Team 4v4 (+GKs) "Winner Stays On" Small Sided Game

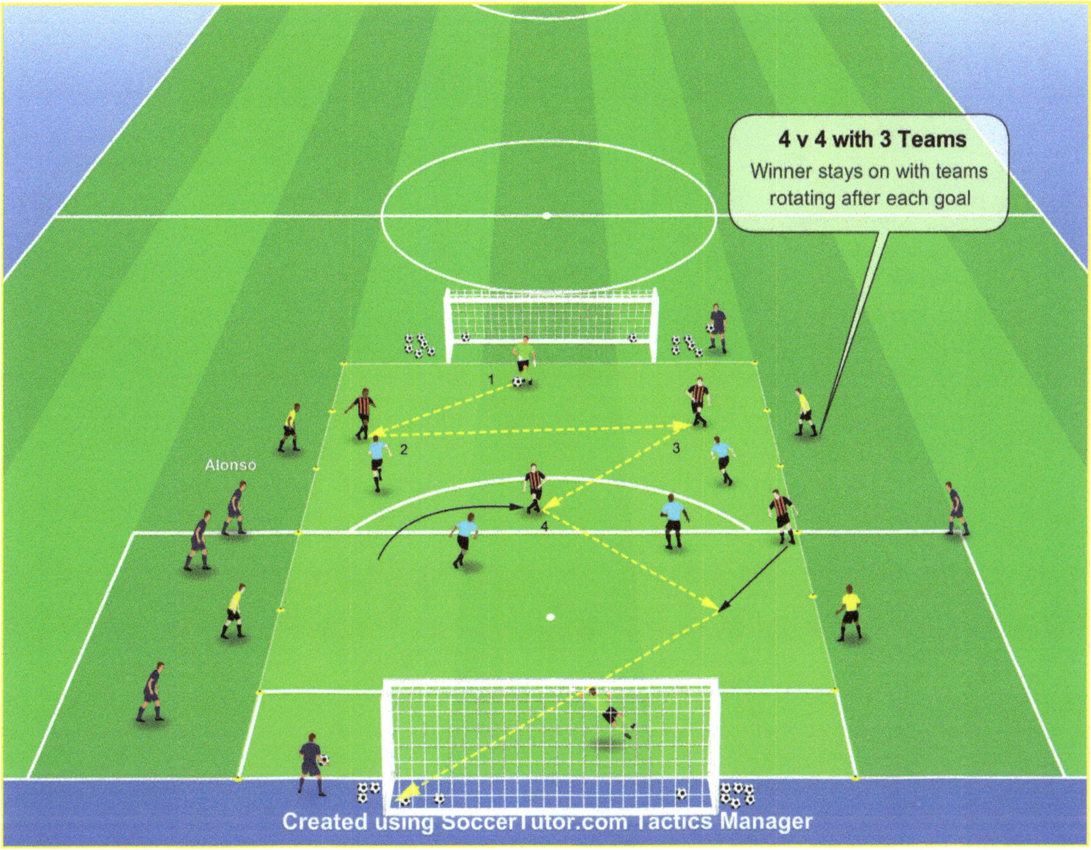

4 v 4 with 3 Teams — Winner stays on with teams rotating after each goal

Practice Description

- In the area shown, a normal 4v4 (+GKs) small sided game is played. The game starts with a GK who uses short distribution.
- The emphasis is on **high intensity and high speed of play (tempo)** games to try and score goals as quickly as possible.
- In this example, the reds start. If they score, they stay on and the blues rotate out with the yellows coming in.
- The game then restarts from the yellow team's GK.
- If a team wins the ball, they then quickly try to score themselves (early shots).
- The team that lost the ball reacts quickly to try and win the ball back as quickly as possible (fast transition).
- If the ball goes out of play, the other team's GK restarts with a new ball.
- The coaches keep count of the score.

Source: Xabi Alonso's Bayer Leverkusen training session at Bayer 04 Leverkusen Training Ground - 2024

Xabi Alonso Practices: Positional Training Games

2. Build Up Play vs Compact Middle Zone Pressing 6v7 (+GKs) Transition Game

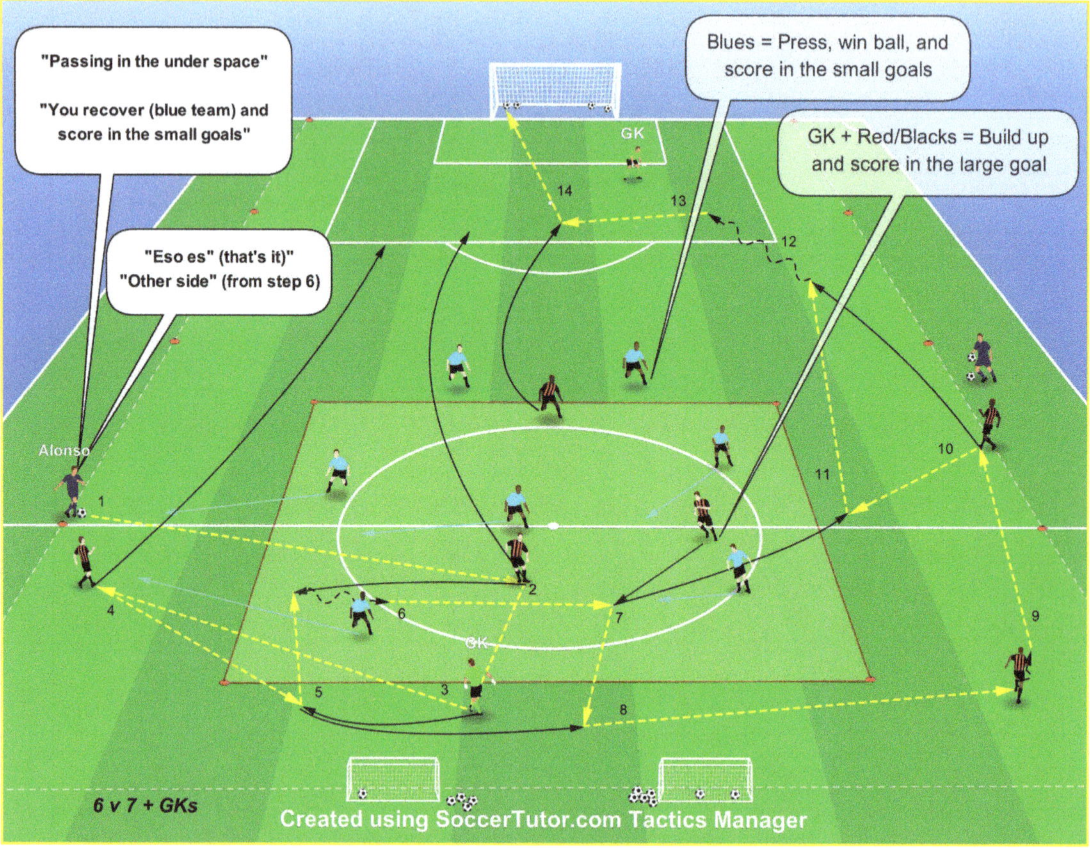

Practice Description

- In the area shown, there are 6 reds +GK vs 7 blues +GK. **Alonso** passes a ball in to start and the reds build up play with help from their GK. The focus during the build up is on **moving the ball from one side to the other to maximise the space, and then progress the play**.

- The build up passing pattern in the diagram is exactly as observed during Xabi Alonso's training session.

- The blues are in a compact central defensive organisation highlighted by the box in the diagram.

- As the reds aim to play around the blue team's pressure and score in the large goal past the GK, the blue team's aim is to win the ball and then score in the 2 small goals.

- Once the phase is complete, **Alonso** passes a new ball in and both teams have the same aims.

Source: Xabi Alonso's Bayer Leverkusen training session at Bayer 04 Leverkusen Training Ground - 13th Sep 2024

Xabi Alonso Practices: Positional Training Games

3. Combination Play from Defence to Attack Zonal 8v8 (+1) +GKs Conditioned Game

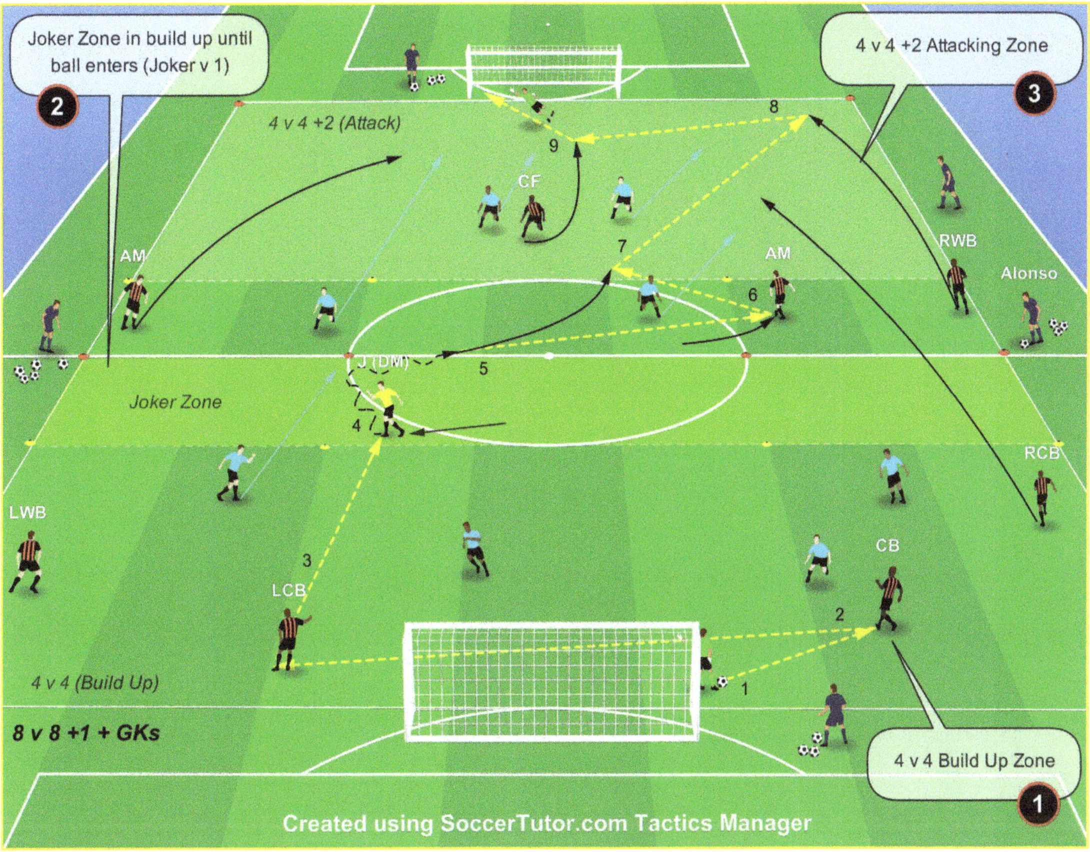

Practice Description

- There are 4 reds and 4 blue players in each half + 1 yellow Joker who takes the role of one of defensive midfielder for the team in possession.
- The GK starts and the reds build up play with an initial 4v4 situation (low zone).
- The aim is to **play through pressure and move the ball to the Joker (DM) in the Joker Zone**. Once that happens, 1 blue player can move back to press him.
- **J (DM)** starts an attack vs the 4 blue defenders. There are 4 red attackers + **J (DM)** + 1 more player (**RCB**) who moves forward to create a 4v4 (+2) attack
- If the blues win the ball or the ball goes out of play, the blue GK starts with the team roles reversed.

Positional Play

- Both teams use Bayer Leverkusen's 4-2-4 build up shape *(see pages 64-65)*.

Source: Xabi Alonso's Bayer Leverkusen preseason training session in Donaueschingen, Germany - 29th July 2024

Xabi Alonso Practices: Positional Training Games

4. Build Up Play and Playing in Behind to Score 9v9 (+1) 6-Goal Game with Offside Rule

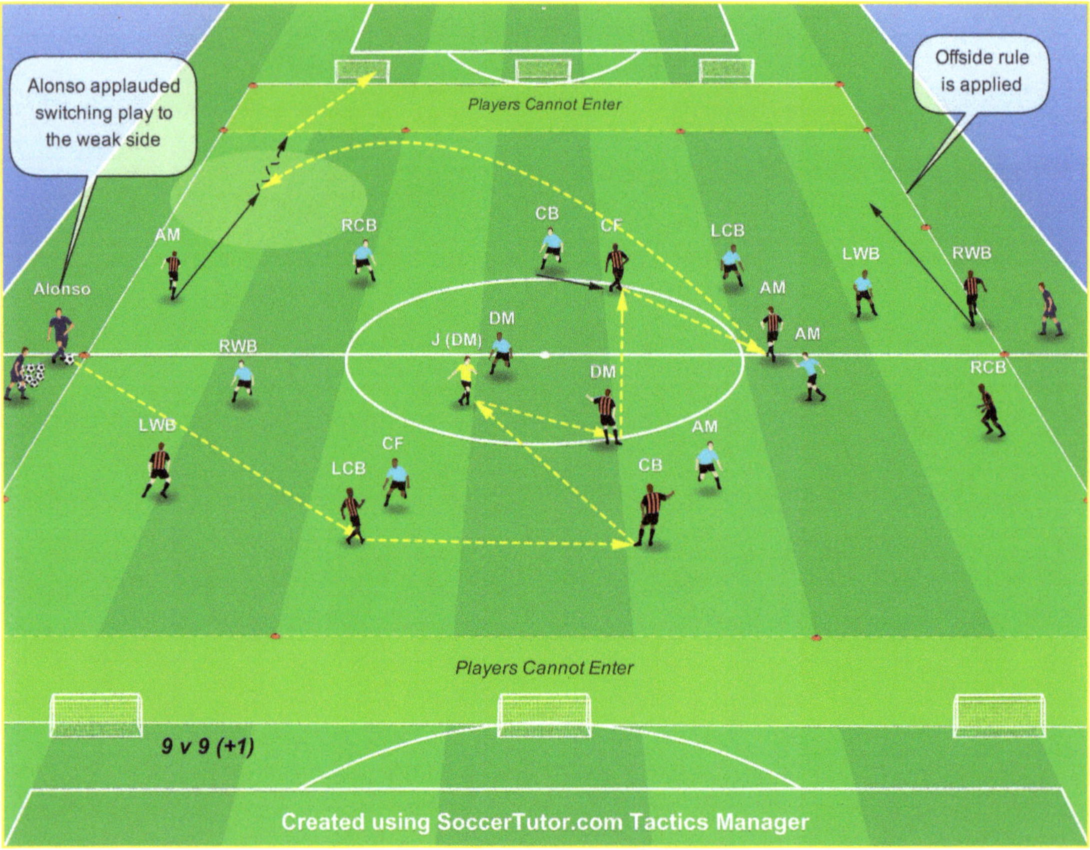

Practice Description
- There are 9 reds vs 9 blues + 1 yellow Joker who takes the role of one of the defensive midfielders for the team in possession.
- **Alonso** passes a ball in to start and the reds build up play trying to score.
- The aim is to **break the lines of pressure and create space to score a goal** via quick combination play, a through pass, or switch of play.
- The emphasis is on getting in behind (offside rule) and finishing before the end zones which can't be entered.
- If the blues win the ball, they try to score. If the ball goes out of play, Alonso plays a new ball in immediately.

Positional Play
- Both teams are using Bayer's 3-4-2-1 formation. When in possession, they use the 4-2-4 build up *(see pages 64-65)*.

Source: Xabi Alonso's Bayer Leverkusen training session at Bayer 04 Leverkusen Training Ground - 2024

Xabi Alonso Practices: Positional Training Games

5. Combination Play from Defence to Attack 9v9 (+GKs) Conditioned Zonal Game + 2nd Ball Transition

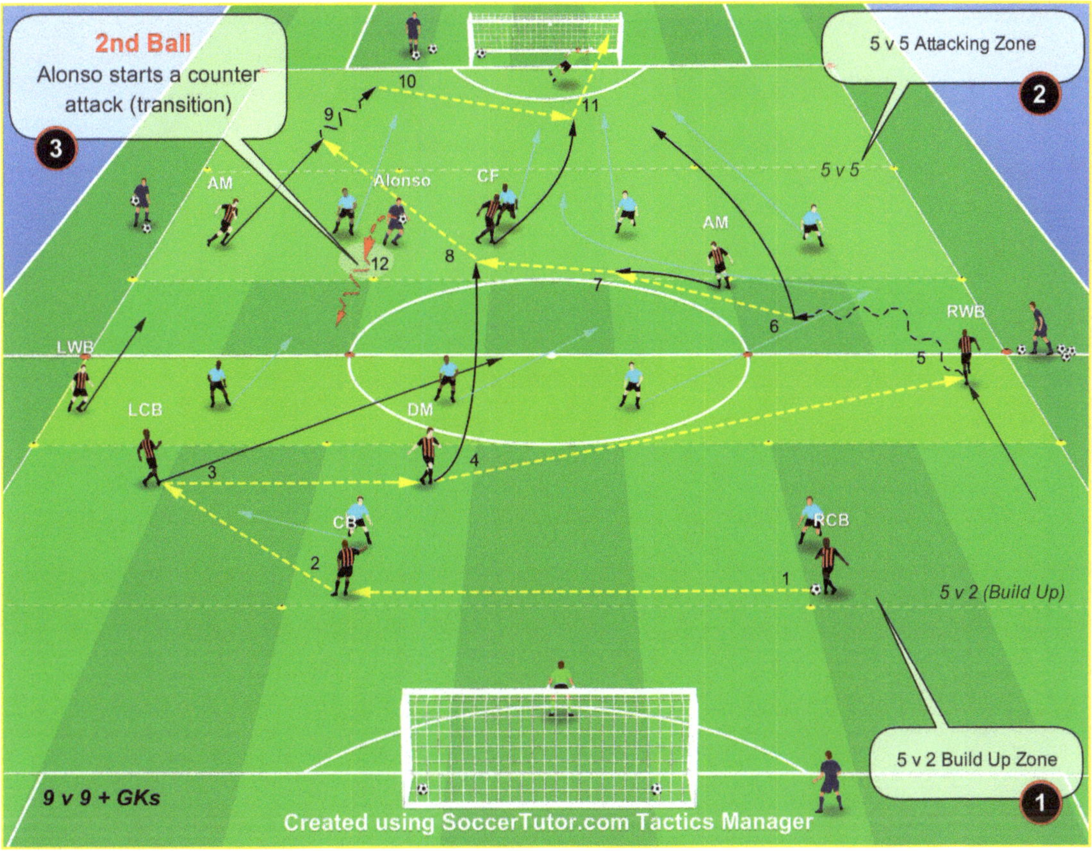

Practice Description

- One wing back (**RWB**) starts deep, and the other one (**LWB**) in the yellow zone.

- From the **5v2 Build Up Zone**, the reds aim to play through the pressure of 2 blue forwards, bypass the 3 blue midfielders, and score with a 5v5 attack.

- When playing out, the reds must avoid interceptions from the 3 blue midfielders. In this example, the **DM** passes wide for the forward run of **RWB**.

- From there, the reds move the ball into the Attacking Zone where there are 3 red attackers + 4 blue defenders. 2 red players (**RWB** & **DM**) + 1 blue midfielder move in there to create a 5v5 situation.

- If the blues win the ball or the ball goes out of play, the teams switch roles.

Source: Xabi Alonso's Bayer Leverkusen preseason training session in Donaueschingen, Germany - 29th July 2024

Xabi Alonso Practices: Positional Training Games

6. Build Up and Creating Opportunities to Score 9v9 (+2) 6-Goal Game with Changing Conditions

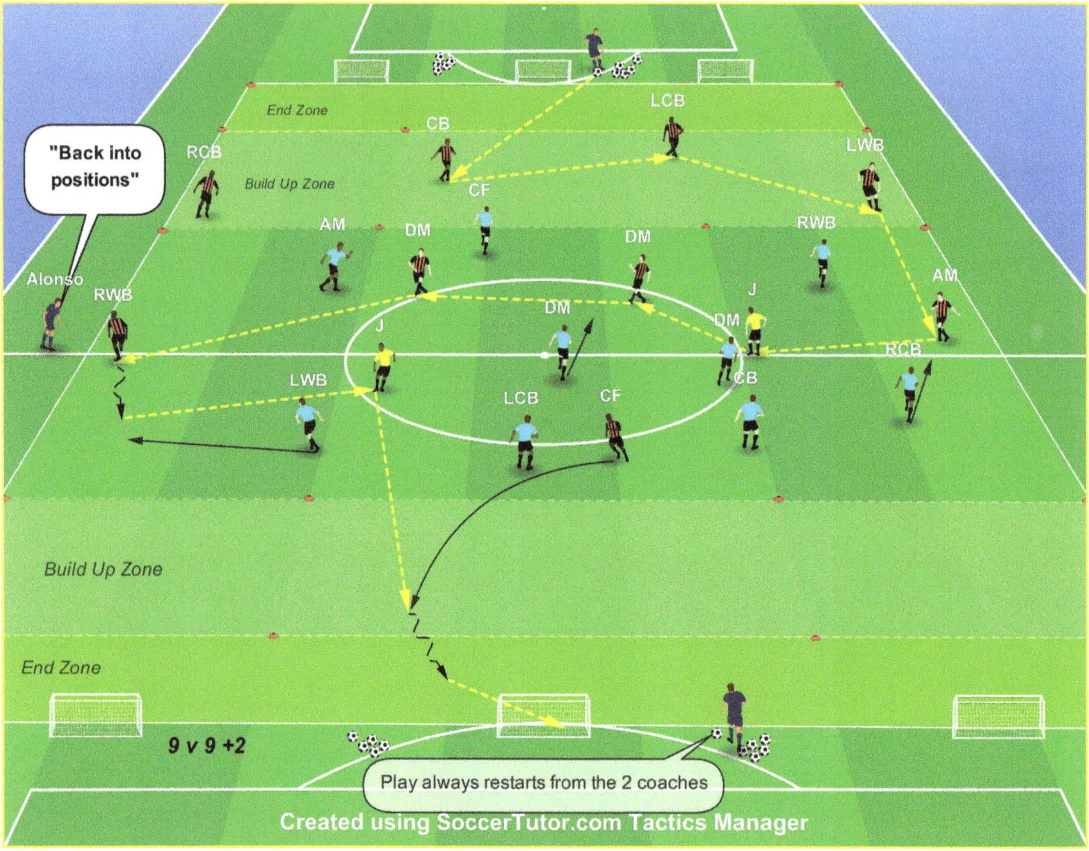

Practice Description

- In this 9v9 (+2 Jokers) game, the aim is to **break the lines of pressure and create space to score a goal** through effective combination play. The reds start with possession after the coach's pass.

- The **zones have rules which change so the players can work on different tactics**.

- To start, no defending team players are allowed in the *Build Up Zone*. Later, they are encouraged to high press in there.

- To start, players must score from within the *End Zone*. Later, they must score from outside the *End Zone*.

- **Alonso adjusts the team shapes during play**, starting with a 4-2-3 from Bayer's 4-2-4 build up shape *(see this diagram + pages 64-65)*. He is also seen changing the size of the *Build Up Zone*.

- If the blues win the ball, they try to score. If the ball goes out of play, a coach plays a new ball in immediately.

Source: Xabi Alonso's Bayer Leverkusen training session at Bayer 04 Leverkusen Training Ground - 2023

Xabi Alonso Practices: Positional Training Games

7. Build Up and Creating Opportunities to Score 9v9 (+1) +GKs Game with Changing Conditions

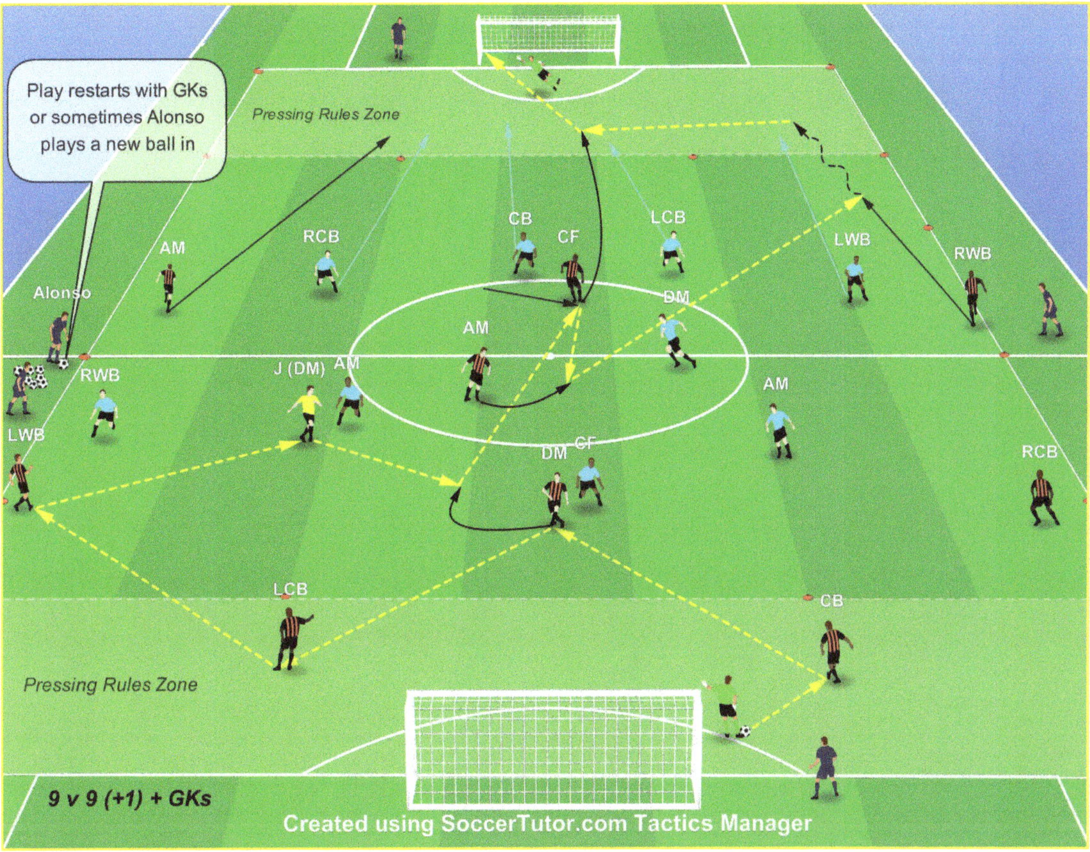

Practice Description

- In this 9v9 +1 Joker (+ GKs) game, the aim is to **break the lines of pressure and create space to score a goal** through effective combination play. The red team's GK starts with short distribution.

- The **Pressing Rules Zone rules change so the players can practice different game situations.**

- To start, no defending team players are allowed in the *Pressing Rules Zone*.

- This progresses through the practice with 1 player allowed to press, and then 2 players being allowed to press in there.

- If the blues win the ball, they try to score.

- Restarts are from the GK or sometimes from **Alonso** to the GK.

Positional Play

- Both teams are using Bayer's 3-4-2-1 formation. When in possession, they use the 4-2-4 build up *(see pages 64-65)*.

Source: Xabi Alonso's Bayer Leverkusen training session at Bayer 04 Leverkusen Training Ground - 2024

Attacking Set Plays

Direct from Xabi Alonso's Training Sessions

Xabi Alonso Practices: Attacking Set Plays

1. Coordinated Timing and Movement of Runs into Box and Finishing from Out-swinging Corners

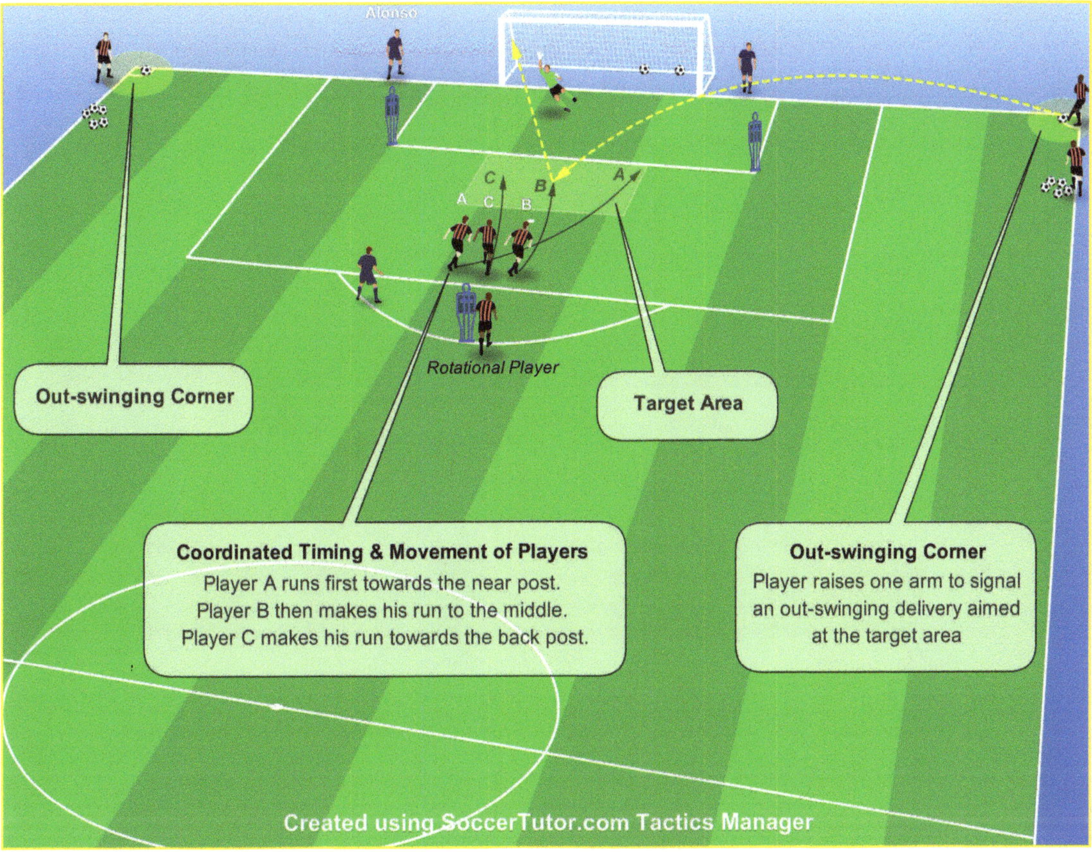

Practice Description

- There are 3 players delivering crosses from corner kicks.
- There are 4 players around the edge of the box, of which 3 participate at a time, with an extra rotational player.
- To start, the corner kick taker raises one arm to signal an out-swinging cross is to be delivered. The target area for the corner kick is highlighted.
- **Player A** makes his run first towards the near post.
- **Player B** then follows and makes his run towards the centre of the box.
- **Player C** runs towards the back post.
- In this example, the out-swinging cross is delivered into the centre of the box for **Player B** to score.
- The practice continues with a corner kick from the other side.

Source: Xabi Alonso's Bayer Leverkusen training session at Bayer 04 Leverkusen Training Ground - 2024

Xabi Alonso Practices: Attacking Set Plays

2. Coordinated Timing and Movement of Runs into Box and Finishing from Free Kicks Near Byline

Practice Description

- There are 3 players delivering crosses from wide free kicks near the by-line.
- There are 4 players around the edge of the box, of which 3 participate at a time, with an extra rotational player.
- To start, the free kick taker raises one arm to signal an out-swinging cross is to be delivered. The target area for the free kick is highlighted.
- **Player A** makes his run first towards the near post.
- **Player B** then follows and makes his run towards the centre of the box.
- **Player C** runs towards the back post.
- In this example, the out-swinging cross is delivered towards the near post for **Player A** to score.
- The practice continues with a free kick from the other side.

Source: Xabi Alonso's Bayer Leverkusen training session at Bayer 04 Leverkusen Training Ground - 2024

Xabi Alonso Practices: Attacking Set Plays

3. Coordinated Timing and Movement of Runs into Box and Finishing from Free Kicks (Level with Penalty Spot)

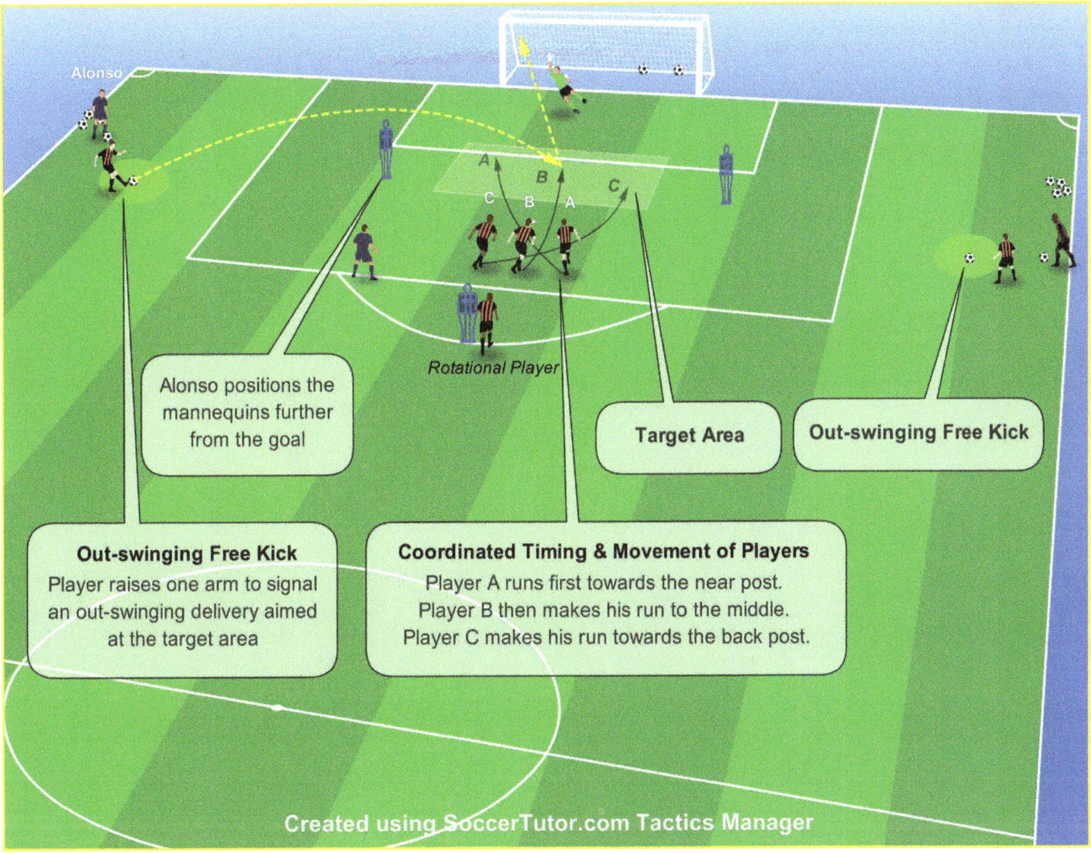

Alonso positions the mannequins further from the goal

Rotational Player

Target Area

Out-swinging Free Kick

Out-swinging Free Kick
Player raises one arm to signal an out-swinging delivery aimed at the target area

Coordinated Timing & Movement of Players
Player A runs first towards the near post.
Player B then makes his run to the middle.
Player C makes his run towards the back post.

Created using SoccerTutor.com Tactics Manager

Practice Description

- There are 3 players delivering crosses from wide free kicks level with the penalty spot. There are 4 players around the edge of the box, of which 3 participate at a time, with an extra rotational player.
- To start, the free kick taker raises one arm to signal an out-swinging cross is to be delivered. The target area for the free kick is highlighted.
- **Player A** makes his run first towards the near post.
- **Player B** then follows and makes his run towards the centre of the box.
- **Player C** runs towards the back post.
- In this example, the out-swinging cross is delivered into the centre of the box for **Player B** to score.
- The practice continues with a free kick from the other side.

Source: Xabi Alonso's Bayer Leverkusen training session at Bayer 04 Leverkusen Training Ground - 2024

Xabi Alonso Practices: Attacking Set Plays

4. Coordinated Timing and Movement of Runs into Box and Finishing from Free Kicks (Level with Edge of Box)

- Out-swinging Free Kick
- The Coach plays the role of a defender to block runs
- Target Area

Coordinated Timing & Movement of Players
Player A runs first towards the near post.
Player B then makes his run to the middle.
Player C & D make runs towards the back post.

Out-swinging Free Kick
Player raises one arm to signal an out-swinging delivery aimed at the target area

Practice Description

- There are 3 players delivering crosses from wide free kicks level with the penalty spot. There are 4 players around the edge of the box ready to make runs + 1 passive defender (a coach).
- To start, the free kick taker raises one arm to signal an out-swinging cross is to be delivered. The target area for the free kick is highlighted.
- **Player A** makes his run first towards the near post.
- **Player B** then follows and makes his run towards the centre of the box.
- **Players C & D** run towards the back post.
- In this example, the out-swinging cross is delivered into the centre of the box for **Player B** to score.
- The practice continues with a free kick from the other side.

Source: Xabi Alonso's Bayer Leverkusen training session at Bayer 04 Leverkusen Training Ground - 2024

Xabi Alonso Practices: Attacking Set Plays

5. Coordinated Timing and Movement of Runs into Box and Finishing from In-swinging Free Kick

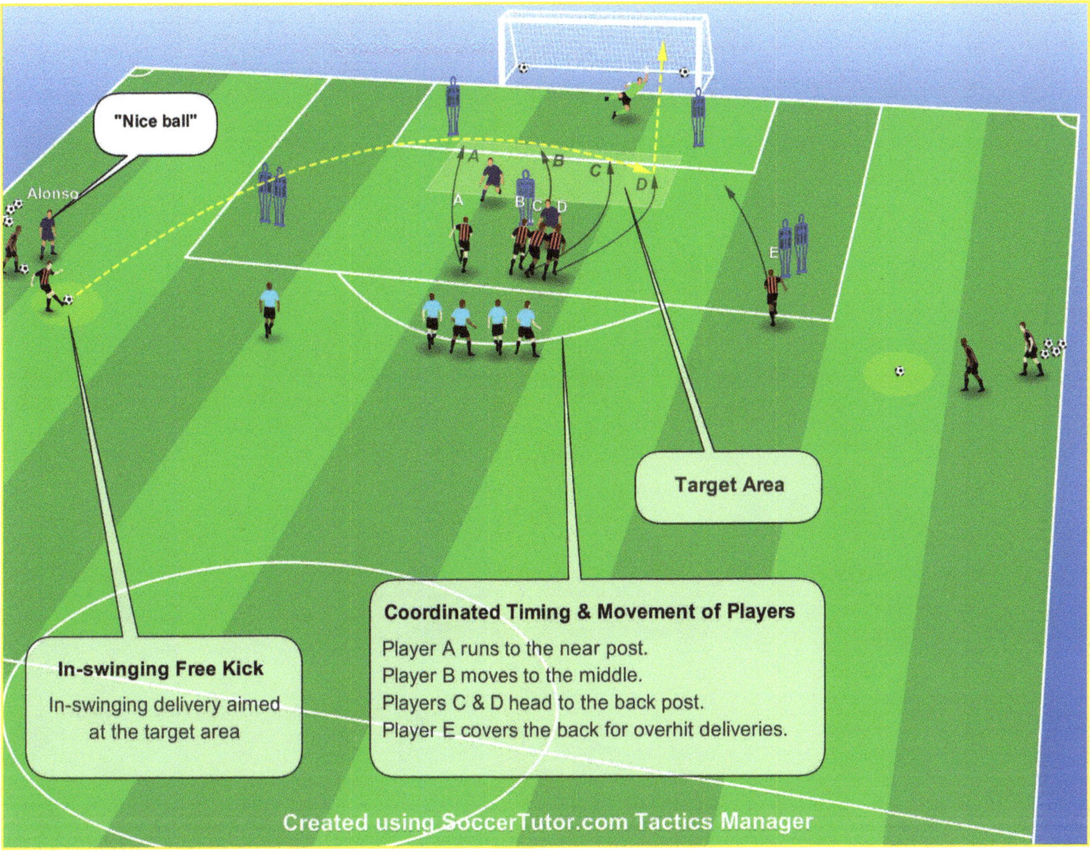

In-swinging Free Kick
In-swinging delivery aimed at the target area

Target Area

Coordinated Timing & Movement of Players
Player A runs to the near post.
Player B moves to the middle.
Players C & D head to the back post.
Player E covers the back for overhit deliveries.

Practice Description

- There are 4 players delivering crosses from wide free kicks in the positions shown. They practice in-swinging crosses and the target area is highlighted.
- There are 5 players around the edge of the box ready to make runs + 2 passive defenders (coaches).
- **Player A** runs towards the near post.
- **Player B** runs into the centre of the box.
- **Players C & D** run towards the back post.
- **Player E** covers the back post for any crosses which are over hit.
- In this example, the in-swinging cross is delivered for **Player D** to score at the back post.
- The practice continues with a free kick from the right side and the blue players making runs into the box to score.

Source: Xabi Alonso's Bayer Leverkusen preseason training session in Donaueschingen, Germany - 29th July 2024

Xabi Alonso Practices: Attacking Set Plays

6. Receiving a Throw-in Under Pressure, Turn and Cross + Timing and Movement of Runs into Box and Finishing

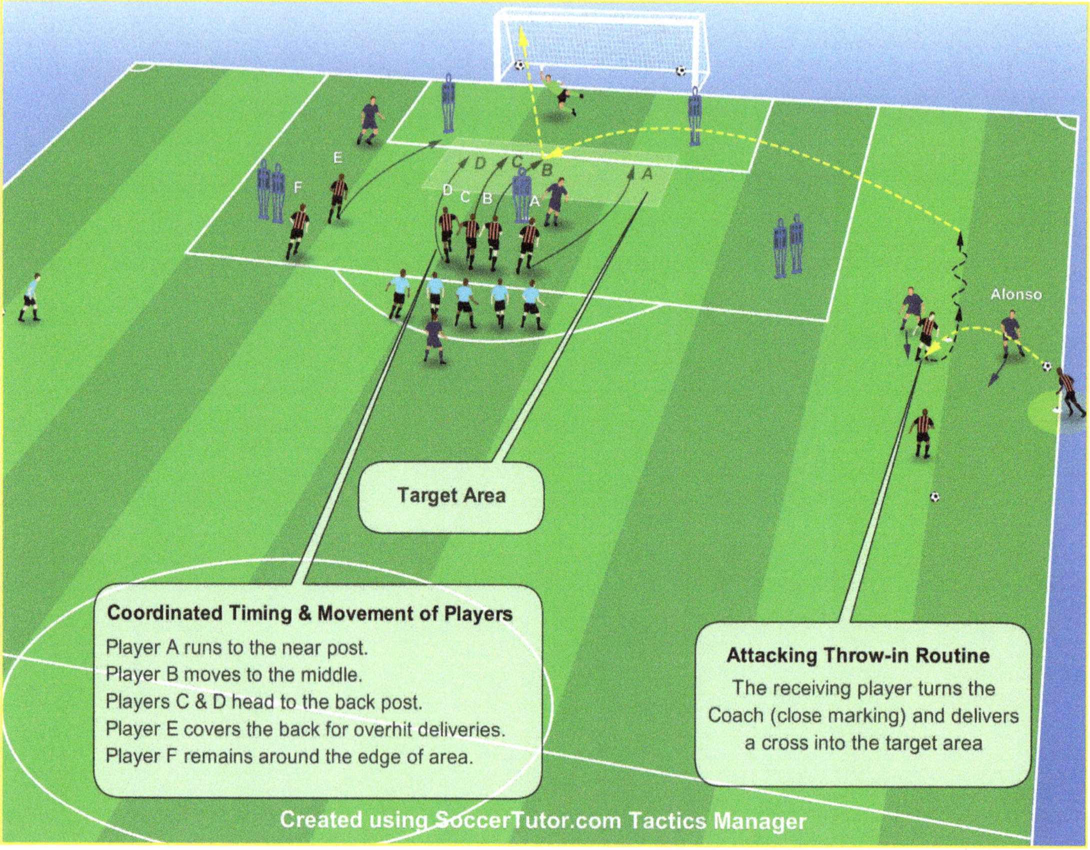

Coordinated Timing & Movement of Players
Player A runs to the near post.
Player B moves to the middle.
Players C & D head to the back post.
Player E covers the back for overhit deliveries.
Player F remains around the edge of area.

Attacking Throw-in Routine
The receiving player turns the Coach (close marking) and delivers a cross into the target area

Practice Description

- There are 3 red players out wide vs 2 coaches including **Alonso**. One player takes a throw-in to a teammate, who turns under passive pressure and delivers a cross into the highlighted target area.
- There are 6 players ready to make runs + 2 passive defenders (coaches).
- **Player A** runs towards the near post.
- **Player B** runs into the centre of the box.
- **Players C & D** run towards the back post.
- **Player E** covers the back post for any crosses which are over hit.
- **Player F** stays on the edge of the box.
- In this example, the cross is for **Player B** to score in the centre of the box.
- The practice continues with the next throw-in from the left and the blue players crossing and finishing.

Source: Xabi Alonso's Bayer Leverkusen preseason training session in Donaueschingen, Germany - 29th July 2024

Free Trial

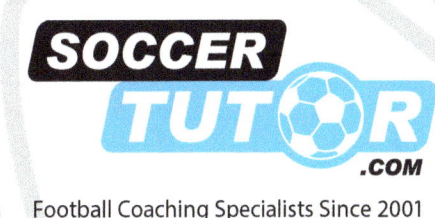

Football Coaching Specialists Since 2001

Tactics Manager
Create your own Practices, Tactics & Plan Sessions!

Tactics Manager App

SoccerTutor.com

Football Coaching Specialists Since 2001

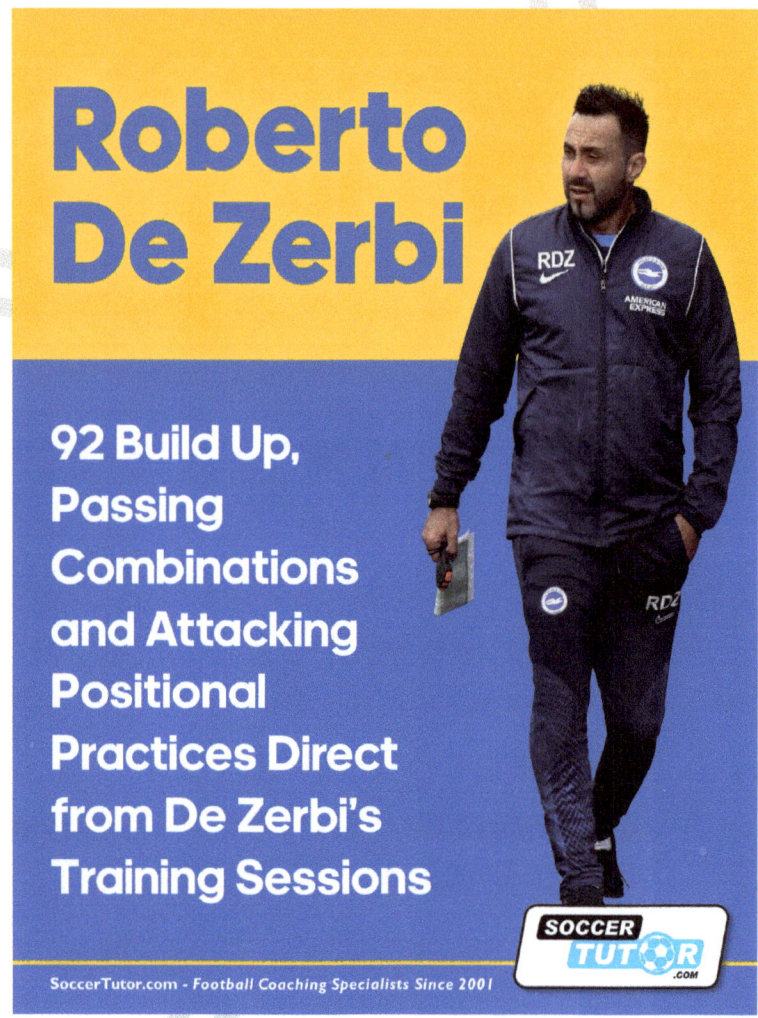

Coaching Books Available in Full Colour Print and eBook!
PC | Mac | iPhone | iPad | Android Phone / Tablet | Chromebook

FREE Coach Viewer **APP**

SoccerTutor.com

Football Coaching Specialists Since 2001

Jürgen Klopp
102 Passing, Counter-pressing Possession Games, Speed & Warm-ups Direct from Klopp's Training Sessions

Vol. 1

Jürgen Klopp
80 Attacking Combinations, Finishing, Positional Patterns of Play, Transition & SSGs Direct from Klopp's Training Sessions

Vol. 2

Coaching Books Available in Full Colour Print and eBook!
PC | Mac | iPhone | iPad | Android Phone / Tablet | Chromebook

 **FREE** Coach Viewer **APP**

SoccerTutor.com

Football Coaching Specialists Since 2001

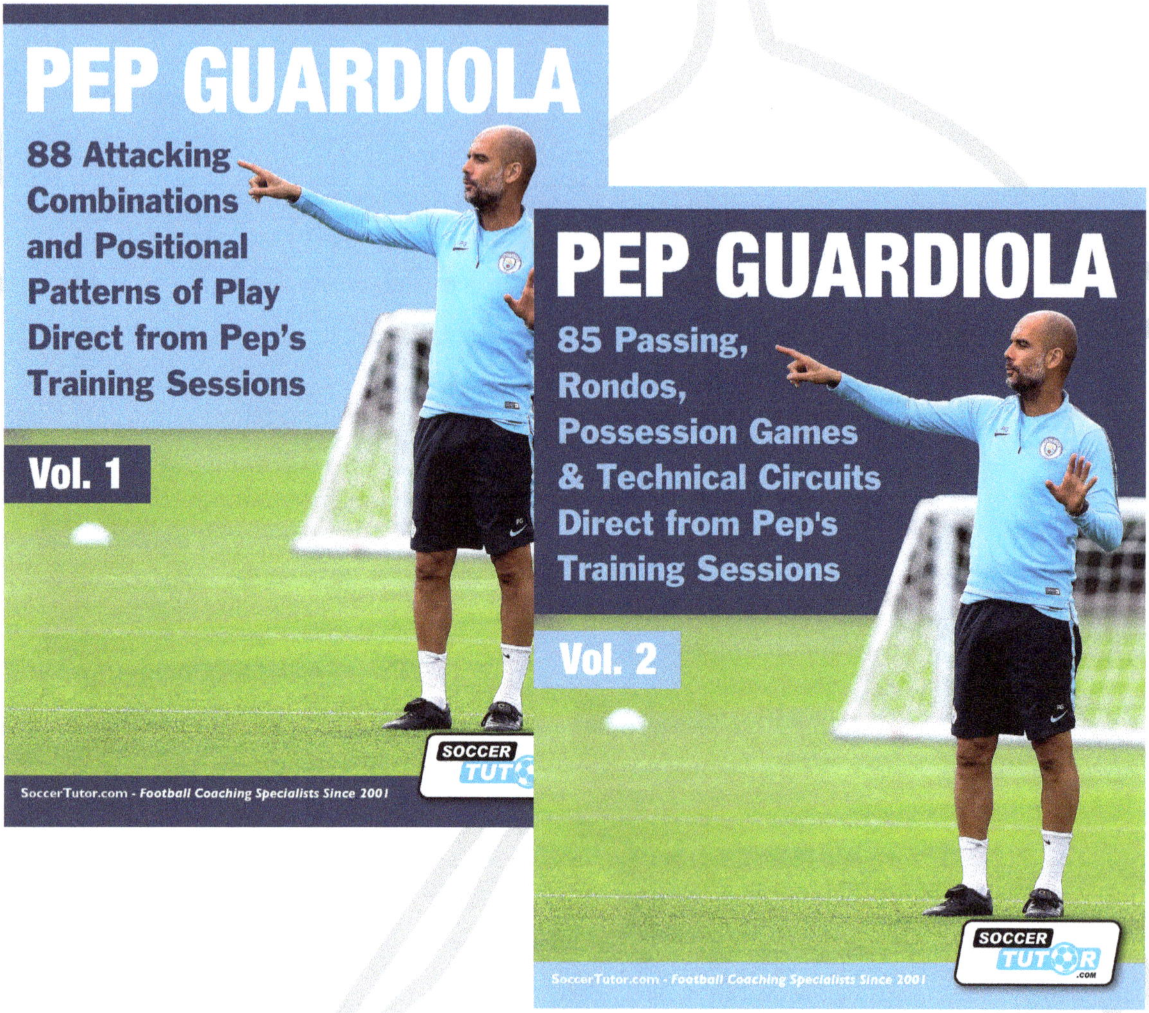

PEP GUARDIOLA
88 Attacking Combinations and Positional Patterns of Play Direct from Pep's Training Sessions
Vol. 1

PEP GUARDIOLA
85 Passing, Rondos, Possession Games & Technical Circuits Direct from Pep's Training Sessions
Vol. 2

Coaching Books Available in Full Colour Print and eBook!
PC | Mac | iPhone | iPad | Android Phone / Tablet | Chromebook

 **FREE** Coach Viewer **APP**

SoccerTutor.com

Football Coaching Specialists Since 2001

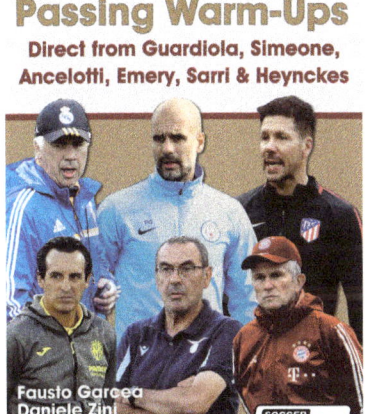
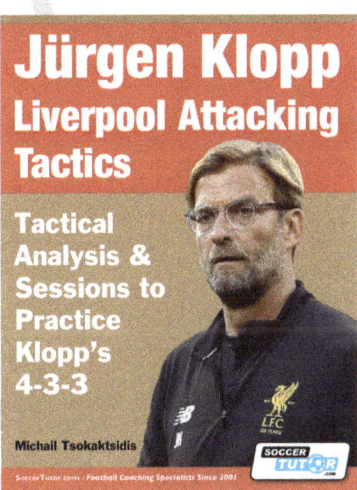

Coaching Books Available in Full Colour Print and eBook!
PC | Mac | iPhone | iPad | Android Phone / Tablet | Chromebook

 **FREE** Coach Viewer **APP**

SoccerTutor.com

www.ingramcontent.com/pod-product-compliance
Lightning Source LLC
Chambersburg PA
CBHW061208230426
43665CB00028B/2955